MW01634139

16 NOV 06

MARSHAL FERDINAND FOCH

AS THEY SAW US

AS THEY SAW US

FOCH, LUDENDORFF AND OTHER LEADERS WRITE OUR WAR HISTORY

EDITED BY

GEORGE SYLVESTER VIERECK

The Scholar's Bookshelf

AS THEY SAW US

First Published in 1929

This edition published 2005 by

The Scholar's Bookshelf

110 Melrich Road
Cranbury NJ USA 08512
www.scholarsbookshelf.com

ISBN: 0-945726-40-6

LC:2005923123

Printed in the United States of America

EDITOR'S NOTE

Superior figures in the text refer to "General Notes," Appendix III.

PREFACE

Here are parallel narratives by friend and foe of the deeds of the American soldier in the World War.

These narratives set forth and analyze in detail, from both the French point of view and the German, those decisive battles in which the American Expeditionary Forces fought on European soil. No memorial to those who fought and lived and to those who fought and died could be more fitting. The testimony of the two master strategists of the war, Foch and Ludendorff, is a monument in itself. That testimony is corroborated in detail by the opposing commanders in charge of those sectors where the Stars and Stripes intertwined with the Tricolour.

The idea of dealing with a great war in this fashion is distinctly an American contribution to the technique of historical research. Ordinarily, mankind must wait for centuries upon the historians. At last they dig out from dusty archives the conflicting testimony of the captains (great or otherwise) who faced each other in battle. Often one side only is articulate.

Cæsar wrote his Commentaries. But the leaders he vanquished were silent and their mouths stuffed with dust. Napoleon wrote memoirs on his rock in the sea. His analysis of his battles leave much to mystify. How grateful the world must now be had some contemporary proved sufficiently enterprising to secure parallel interpretations of the battle of Waterloo from Napoleon, Wellington, and Blücher!

It was the good fortune of the present writer to obtain the first parallel account of one of the great battles of the war from Marshal Joffre and the German Crown Prince. I refer to the First Battle of the Marne. Subsequently, at my suggestion, General Ludendorff and Marshal Foch analyzed the Second Battle of the Marne. Marshal Pétain and Crown Prince Wilhelm treated the historic siege of Verdun in a similar manner at my request.

The story of American participation in the World War remained to be told. I succeeded in procuring the coöperation of the leaders on both sides of the battle front. The result of this labour is this book. The present volume discusses from the French and German point of view those great battles of the World War in which America is most deeply concerned, the battles in which our own troops fought on the soil of France.

Marshal Foch and Quartermaster-General Erich Ludendorff lead the procession with their estimates of the American soldier. Both men recognize the magnitude of the American achievement. Neither condescends to flattery. Foch politely, Ludendorff more bluntly, voices criticism as well as praise. Their contributions are of vital significance to the American people because they speak with authority and with candour. Incidentally, both generals manifest the highest respect for each other. Ludendorff at various times frankly acknowledged the genius of Marshal Foch. When I asked Marshal Foch to name his greatest opponent the great soldier replied: "Incontestably, General Ludendorff. *Il sait son métier.*" He knows his business.

So did the Americans. The transport of two million American soldiers to Europe was in itself an achievement unique in human annals. The World War upset many precedents. It evoked extraordinary feats of ingenuity, prodigies of endurance, in every camp. But no marvel wrought by any nation among the twenty-seven engaged in the fratricidal conflict surpasses that which Foch himself describes as the miracle of American organization. The dexterity with which our army solved the problem of transporting such masses of men and munitions to a front three thousand miles away overthrew Ludendorff's calculations. The reader can find out for himself, from the testimony here adduced, whether or not American participation proved decisive in winning the war, in spite of our shortcomings. Blunders were made. Life was sacrificed, property wasted. We paid for our inexperience. The price was small compared with the immensity of the task.

Following the commanders-in-chief, the generals actually in command of sectors along the opposing fronts at Château-Thierry–Soissons, St. Mihiel–Metz, and in the Argonne and Meuse engagements, unfold for us the details of the struggle. The American doughboy was pushed hither and thither blindly by forces incomprehensible to him. The following account reveals to him for the first time in full the moves of the master players in the game in which he was a pawn.

General Reinhardt, General Savatier, General Hellé, General Berdoulat, General Ledebur, and General Gallwitz draw upon personal experience. Their recital is based on their own diaries and recollections, amplified by every possible aid from official sources. American generals and American correspondents are making valuable contributions to the theme of American participation in the volcanic struggle. Pershing is still to be heard from. But no story will be complete which ignores the accounts preserved in these pages.

Logically and chronologically, the struggle may be divided into three phases. The first phase embraces Ludendorff's onslaught for peace, or the *Friedenssturn*, started on the 21st of March, 1918. With a number of interruptions, this movement came to a standstill at Château-Thierry. It was finally checked by the Allied counter offensive launched on July 18th. The second phase consists in the elimination of the St. Mihiel salient. The third phase begins with the Allied push for the Rhine and ends with the Armistice.

Our material is exclusively of French and German origin. No attempt has been made to draw upon American sources, except in the preparation of the indexes. The freedom of expression granted to each contributor was unlimited. Nevertheless, no echo of the old rancour remains in this recital, except here and there, in verbatim reproduction of army orders, issued when the cauldron was boiling. Verily the war is over! The Germans yield ungrudging praise to their enemies. The French no less gallantly express their admiration of the soldierly qualities of their foes. Both unite in a tribute to America.

The possibility of such a symposium, couched in terms of mutual respect, hardly ten years after the war, is in itself a testimonial to the power of civilization. Civilized man refuses to remain the victim of war psychosis. Universal brotherhood may still be a distant vision, but the complete mental demobilization of the men who fought the war suggests that, after all, progress is not an illusion.

GEORGE SYLVESTER VIERECK.

New York,
Autumn of 1928.

CONTENTS

Part One:

Part Two:

Part Three:

LIST OF ILLUSTRATIONS

LIST OF MAPS

THE AMERICAN SOLDIER IN THE WORLD WAR AS SEEN BY A FRIEND

MARSHAL FERDINAND FOCH

IF EVER an immense problem was set a nation, it was that which the United States was called upon to solve in the spring of 1917. It was a problem immense in its scope. It consisted of nothing less than to put upon a war footing a nation of more than one hundred million inhabitants!

Everything had to be created.

The standing army, proportionate to the restricted needs of a time of peace, could furnish only the smallest equipment and aid in the mobilization of the great units which America had decided to organize.

As a matter of fact, the units had to be formed in their entirety, with their staffs, their officers, their rank and file, and the considerable material without which nothing can be undertaken in modern warfare. It was a new weapon which had to be forged.

And not only was it necessary to forge it on the vastest scale, but to forge it quickly. The war had lasted nearly three years. It was evident that its very amplitude and intensity would not permit it to last very much longer. To throw her weight into the final decision, it was necessary for America to hasten to Europe as rapidly as possible.

It is not to be denied that the Allies aided the United

States to the utmost of their ability. Nothing would have been possible without the masterly qualities of the American people. It is these qualities that assured the organization of the American forces during the war, an organization which, in spite of the defects or miscalculations inherent in all human performance, must be considered one of the most remarkable things done in recent years. Indeed, if, rightly or wrongly, the word miracle had been applied to the victory of the Allies at the Marne in the month of September, 1914, it can be applied equally to the miracle of American organization.

These same qualities which enabled the United States to forge with rapidity a mighty military weapon permitted the American army, after a very short preparation, to throw itself into the field of battle. There, it revealed itself at the initial onset as a force whose immediate worth the enemy had not at first suspected. It is to these qualities, having seen them at work in all ranks—command, staff, officers, and troops—that it is just to render homage here.

The American army threw itself into the struggle with the desire to come as speedily as possible to the aid of the Allies. In this it gave us the proofs of the *spirit of quick understanding* which animated it.

In the month of June, 1917, General Pershing landed in France. Immediately upon his arrival in Paris, which took place without delay, I received him in the office which I occupied at the Hôtel des Invalides. I was then Chief of the General Staff of the French army.

My first interview with General Pershing, the beginning of a collaboration which was to last two years, gave me at once, and left with me, the impression of a man of energy and of marked personality, conscious of the heavy burden which had just been placed on his broad shoulders. In the piercing look behind the lenses of his spectacles one discerned the perspicacity and penetration of the mind. In the large structure of the chin were seen the marks of decisiveness, sense of responsibility, the will and energy to succeed. These are precisely the first qualities that make great commanders. General Pershing was to furnish an immediate proof of this and at the same time to give evidence of that understanding that is clearly the basis of American activity.

After we had studied together the general foundations on which the organization of the Expeditionary Forces was to rest, the use to be made of them, the steps to be taken in order to carry the great enterprise to a successful issue, the General was not long in recognizing that he would not successfully direct the practical work of the organization from Paris. After a brief stay in our capital, he left for the zone of the armies, establishing himself in the neighbourhood of the fighting units and in particular of the French General Headquarters. There he would find all the necessary elements for the solution of the vast problems calling for his immediate attention—regulation of the ports of disembarkation, lines of communication, warehouses, etc.

The same spirit of quick understanding animated the staff and the detachments of specialists. These preceded the troops. They prepared without delay all that was necessary for the landing of the forces, and supervised their means of existence. It was the same spirit of quick understanding that permitted the first American division to reach the European continent eighty days after the declaration of war by the United States against

Germany; that, in eighteen months, made of a permanent force of 9,500 officers and 350,000 men an army of 180,000 officers and 3,500,000 men; that, in one year, permitted the transportation, without the slightest mishap, in spite of the dangers of a merciless submarine warfare, of more than 2,000,000 soldiers to French soil, grouped in 2 armies, 9 army corps, 41 divisions; that moved President Wilson to give me the assurance that, if hostilities were prolonged until the spring of 1919, there would be at that time (that is to say, two years after the entry into war of the United States) 100 American divisions in Europe. A spirit of quick understanding that manifested itself incessantly on the field of battle by the promptness of decision of the command and the vigour of execution of the troops; that led General Pershing and General Bliss to offer me, from the 28th of March, 1918, when the great German offensives began, the direct coöperation in the battle of all the available American divisions; that, two months later, launched the 1st Division into the victorious assault of Cantigny; that, the 15th of July, threw the 3rd and 42nd Divisions into an immediate and effective counter attack against the German columns debouching at the south of the Marne; that permitted the American First Army, after having, on the 12th of September, attacked on the right bank of the Meuse the salient of St. Mihiel, to enter an engagement on the 26th on the left bank in the Argonne region.

But in order to bear fruit, this spirit of quick understanding, which is surely one of the most marked characteristics of Americans, had to be complemented by military knowledge. And this military knowledge was rapidly acquired, thanks to the desire for instruction and training which we found developed to a high degree in all ranks, in the American army. Instructors qualified by experience were assigned, and in all the camps—in the United States as well as in France—military instruction was pushed forward with remarkable activity. Regular officers, to be kept constantly in touch at a distance with the struggle taking place in Europe, had no difficulty in adapting themselves to methods of combat in modern warfare and—remarkable fact!—reserve officers acquired with a surprising rapidity the technical knowledge which permitted them to face the trials of the battlefield under very favourable conditions.

Many of them, it is true, under the inspiration of men of foresight and caution, such as General Wood and President Roosevelt, one of whose sons was to fall gloriously in the service of France, had been trained long before America decided to enter the war. From 1915 they had completed, as volunteers, courses of instruction in American camps. There is no doubt that these preliminary stages contributed in large measure to facilitate and to hasten the constitution, when the moment came, of the American Expeditionary Forces.

One thing which equally hastened and facilitated this organization was the spirit which presided over the recruiting of the men, and particularly of the reserve officers whom it was necessary to find in such great numbers. In selecting them, attention was paid not only to the military capacity acquired during the course of instruction in the camps, but also to the ability that each man possessed as a result of his function and occupation in civil life.

This is a very interesting point as well as a lesson for

those who have the task of preparing the rapid organization of the forces of a nation. It is certain that the practice of business, with its demand for qualities of decision and method and its inculcation of the habit of command, gives an invaluable preparation for the conduct of troops in military operations. In civil life, as in the army, it is the same general qualities that make the leader. Let the captain of industry secure the technical knowledge which he lacks in the art of warfare and he becomes easily a military commander.

A spirit of quick understanding, a taste for study, such were the outstanding qualities which struck us from our first contact with the American army. But these were, in some measure, psychological qualities. Such traits certainly constituted an important basis of preparation for war, but they did not warrant any estimate of the resistance they would offer to the realities of the battlefield.

It remained to be ascertained how the temperament of the American soldier would react in actual warfare. We knew that his aptitude for sport, the practice he had had in it, would be important factors toward success. We thought this aptitude and this practice would serve (in much the way industry had served in the case of the newly appointed leaders) as an excellent preparation for war. But as long as the experiment had not been tried, nothing could be definitely affirmed.

Our experience was conclusive. It was demonstrated that sport is one of the best preparations for the career of arms. In the month of July, 1917, we saw the first organized American units march through Paris. They made an excellent impression. We were impressed in general by the height of the men, by their well-fitting uniforms, by their physical development and poise, by their splendid health and vigour. They presented a well-ordered and compact appearance. If their gait lacked something of suppleness, this defect was compensated by an accuracy and precision of movement altogether remarkable. I was in a position to verify anew these excellent qualities in manœuvring when, on the 10th of December, 1921, I had the pleasure of visiting the Military Academy at West Point and of being present at a review of the cadets.

It is one of Napoleon's precepts that "the success and well-being of the Army depend essentially upon order and discipline."

The discipline that we saw in force in the American army was of the strictest, and any infringement was severely reprimanded. The severity of the command was, moreover, easily explained by the fact that the majority of the men under its authority and direction had had no military training up to that time, since there is no compulsory service in the United States. From this point of view, everything was new for them. In order to turn them rapidly into an instrument of war, the employment of special methods, from which restraint was not excluded, was indispensable. It was also necessary to take into account, in this respect, the racial and temperamental diversities and the varying mentalities which the vast continent of America includes. All these had to be fused and melted into a solidly organized national army. This explained at the same time the severe discipline and also the important system of recruiting the staff and corps of officers that we found in the American army. Thanks to these two elements, a troop composed of very diverse elements was successfully and rapidly turned into a homogeneous entity. Its outward aspect was impressive and it presented on the battlefields solid units, perfectly under the control of their leaders.

But these very qualities, because they were developed to a high degree (as was necessary in a young army made up of all sorts and conditions), entailed the consequences which inevitably follow in similar instances.

The younger and consequently more inexperienced a troop is, the more one is inclined to keep it close in hand and to maintain it, in some sort, side by side. It is the easiest way in which to obtain rapidly the necessary cohesion. This cohesion, if it be too relentlessly imposed in battle, leads to rigid and crowded formations and, therefore, to losses which are often very severe. The precise and solid fire of modern battlefields demands, on the contrary, fighting formations of a limited number of men and guns. These reduce the losses to the lowest possible proportion, but they also call for intensive training of the man in the ranks. Such training can only result from long experience acquired especially during military service in times of peace, for lack of which it is gained on the battlefields and then costs very dear. This is the reason why the nations that do not have compulsory military service economize largely in money and forces; but when war comes, they pay for this economy by very considerable sacrifices in human lives. This is one of the prices of disarmament.

The American army was no exception to this rule. It can be stated that the percentage of its losses in relation to its effectives engaged and to the length of time it was in the field was found to be the highest of all the Allied armies in 1918.

The severe discipline which reigned in the American army found its explanation equally in the prevailing youthfulness of their forces. The American army was youthful from every point of view. It was its youth which brought new blood into the battlefields of France at the moment when it was most needed.

For three years the armies of the Entente had been fighting in the trenches. In the shelter of those trenches, new arms were forged and methods of warfare were augmented by them. In 1918 the weapon would be ready. It remained to be seen whether there would be enough men to make sure of it. For, during this monotonous, painful, depressing trench warfare, the Allied forces were worn out! Their human reservoir began to be drained and, by a cruel fate, Russia had just deserted! Through this desertion, Germany was in a position to concentrate all her forces toward France and Belgium. What must be the result of the terrible encounter impending?

The nations and governments remained in a state of uncertainty in expectation of the event and in anxiety for the future.

Just then an immense clamour arose from the other side of the Atlantic: America was coming to the relief of the Allies. Everything was saved. What matter if the assistance were delayed? One was sure it was coming and would know how to hold on until it came. A wonderful piece of news brought us by the sea breezes thus restored confidence at the approach of the storm! The breath of youth, from beyond the ocean, coming to give new life to ancient Europe in ruins, bringing triumph to the Allies and defeat to the enemy!

And behold the assistance arrives more magnificent

than one had dared to hope! With it is American youth full of its *enthusiasm*, its *faith in success*, its *confidence in itself*, admirable qualities which make great men and great nations! It is these qualities which bore the United States to the conquest of their independence, which in less than two centuries made them a power of prodigious energy and prosperity. It is these qualities which, in 1914, at the moment when war struck down Europe, brought, as the vanguard of an entire nation, the heroes of the Lafayette squadron, the volunteers, the men and women engaged in relief work, to the assistance of menaced Right and to the defense of violated Justice! It is these qualities which brought on the wing, in a solitary and sublime flight from New York to Paris, a Lindbergh!

It is these qualities which set the whole of America afire when, having decided to enter the World War, she threw herself in with all her force and all her soul!

Once again let homage be rendered to the magnificent spirit which brought the American phalanxes from the farthest points of the United States to all those places in France as yet unknown to the majority who were to fight and perhaps to die there: le Chemin des Dames, Château-Thierry, Belleau Wood, St. Mihiel, the Argonne . . . and led the starry banners of the great republic to the borders of the Rhine!

Enthusiasm, faith in success, confidence in oneself—we found them not only in the leaders of the American army, but also in each of its combatants. These are the sentiments which so powerfully aided in the rapid formation of the Expeditionary Forces and which manifested themselves under all circumstances through the medium of a rare enthusiasm of impulse.

Hardly had they landed before each man wanted to throw himself at once against the enemy. It is natural to youth to be bold at times, to think that audacity atones for everything, even for experience! But however legitimate the desire of the young Americans to be sent without delay into active service, it was necessary that they become progressively accustomed to the atmosphere of the battlefield. For this purpose, we decided that they should spend (after as short a passage as possible through the instruction camps of France) a certain time in the trenches, first in the quiet sectors and then in the more active ones.

The quiet sectors on the front were at that time in the east, in Lorraine and Alsace, where the French, like the Germans, had got the habit of sending for rest and reorganization those of their units which suffered most heavily in battle. Thus, there was established in this part of the front a relative calm. It was hardly ever troubled except by cannonades all the lighter because artillery munitions, of more use elsewhere, were allotted here with parsimony.

It was here then that, to begin with, the American divisions, as they arrived in France, were sent. They immediately demonstrated their willingness for action and their enterprising spirit. Incursions into the enemy trenches and surprise attacks on the enemy posts suddenly awakened these sectors of the front, peaceful for many months. The Germans did not fail to answer on their side. Bombardments of our lines became more frequent and heavier. They developed to such an extent that the French occupants—for the greater part, older men—could not help softly cursing the new arrivals and regretting the time when they were more tranquil in their corner. This proves once more that what pleases one does not always please another. In the present instance, it was of importance that the instruction of the young Americans be assured, since upon this instruction depended to a great extent the future of the operations and the effectiveness to be expected from them.

The spirit of the American troops did not suffer. In fact, from the moment of their passage into the trenches until the hour struck for engagements in the open, it was found not only intact, but even more eager to come to grips with the enemy, to measure itself against him in open combat. It was then the road to victory, from Cantigny (near Montdidier) by Château-Thierry, St. Mihiel, Montfaucon, and Grandpré, until the Meuse of Mézières! True, it was a road broken occasionally by long waits, sown with ambushes and difficulties. But American youth applied itself there whole-heartedly with a *bravery* and *audacity*, a *relish for danger* which led it, at times, through excess of temerity and also partly through inexperience, to tortuous and thrilling situations, but which finally overcame all obstacles and led it brilliantly to the goal.

The American soldier had the gaiety and carelessness of youth. His clear, frank laughter, his open friendly character bespoke his joy in life and created, wherever he passed, an atmosphere of easy, spontaneous cordiality. His conversation, touched with joviality, humour, and optimism, was the joy of his audience. Where is the man who cannot remember having heard certain stories, lacking neither savour nor point, mostly, it must be admitted, at the expense of the Negro? It was in this manner that the American soldier showed under all circumstances, in action as well as on leave, a *good humour* evincing the happiest balance of all his natural qualities and inspiring at once a sympathetic interest. Thanks to this, he always lived in perfect harmony among the populations he was quartered upon, showed a predilection for the children and a particular interest in them. He was not above playing with them and he loaded them with candy. Thanks to this disposition, he likewise always fought hand in hand with his French comrades in arms, sharing with them, if necessary, his munitions or his food, always ready to come to the aid of those who were more unfortunate and even to sacrifice himself for them. In such a fashion did he deport himself that, in spite of the difference of language, not only sympathy, but a close union, engendered by duties, trials, and dangers suffered in common, and a reciprocity of service for the same cause bound the American soldier and French soldier with indissoluble bonds. And this union, cemented upon the battlefields, is one of those that nothing can destroy. This is well understood by the American Legion, which has returned to France, there to celebrate at the same time as the memory of their dead also the brotherhood of the living.

After all, is not this fraternity of American soldiers and French ones still older? Did it not take root two centuries ago? The American soldier of 1918 took pains to bring us the proof by the *cult of remembrance* which he cherished for us. From generation to generation, across the ages, the idea was transmitted to the United States that America had contracted a debt toward France on the day when France came to help America win her liberty. When America felt that the hour had come to meet this obligation, she took pains to proclaim the fact aloud. In her turn, she sent her legions to the shores of France. As the grand interpreter of this mood, General Pershing, landing on our continent, visited a tomb in the cemetery of Picpus. Surrounded with wreaths symbolic of the gratitude of two nations, and bending toward the monumental stone, he pronounced those ever-memorable words: "Lafayette, we are here!" How many times have we found in the soul of the American combatant this admirable cult of remembrance!

This has been manifested to us as one of the traditions which America seems, with good reason, to cherish above all, and to comprise the very essence of her national soul.

We recognized this native soul in all ranks of the American army that we saw at work in France.

It was this spirit which filled General Pershing with the legitimate desire to see the Expeditionary Forces organized without delay under his orders into armies, army corps, divisions, enjoying a large autonomy. How could anybody blame him for it? None more than myself, in any case, was convinced of the truth that a troop never fights better than under the folds of its own flags. This is why we took pains to reduce to a minimum the preparatory period during which the American units, in order to become fully organized and on a regular war footing, needed a close collaboration with the different Allied armies. As soon as it was possible, the American army had complete autonomy. Its chief, like other generalissimos, received my orders for operations direct.

We found the consciousness of national sentiment, and of the greatness of the country, to be the same among the American combatants. This was revealed in the ambition always to do more and better, as also in the desire to distinguish oneself on all occasions.

The desire to establish a record which, in times of peace, is the object of so much solicitude in the United States, manifested itself here, on the field of battle, in the form of a persistent emulation. It was this, doubtless, which, from the first contact with French soil, prompted the American soldiers to go to reduce the famous "rupture of St. Mihiel," which they were astonished to find still in existence after three years of warfare. It was this, unquestionably, which upheld them, led them irresistibly into the struggle, which enabled them, despite a certain inevitable inexperience, to surmount the heavy trials they encountered, to overcome the difficulties besetting their path, and it was this, too, which, in the end, opened the way to victory.

Napoleon said: "A good general, good officers, good organization, good discipline, and good instruction, make good troops, regardless of the cause for which they fight."

The forces of the United States had everything they needed to become a good army. In addition, they fought for a cause which thoroughly harmonized with American idealism. It was this idealism which, in the final contingency, brought the United States into the war and hurled the sons of America into our battlefields.

They did not ask on which side stood Might—but where stood Justice. And when they saw that the hour was critical for those defending the sublime principles of the conscience of mankind, that Victory, uncertain, stood trembling in their camp—they came to rescue a civilization in peril, whatever the cost to themselves.

Just as the old Crusaders went off to war in the Holy

Land, to rescue there the tomb of the Christ from the hands of the Infidel, they—new Crusaders themselves—rushed from the remotest points of America to bring to close in triumph the Crusade of Right and Liberty, rallying all energies with their presence and their action, reviving all heroisms, setting everyone the example of the spirit of achievement, sustained by the desire to learn! Revealing what even a swiftly shaped national army can accomplish, when animated by youthful ardour and enthusiasm, by an unfailing confidence in itself and in success, by a spirit, a gaiety, a good humour proof against all trials, above all, when it has caught the finest national spirit and remains ever conscious of the grandeur and glory of its native land—such was the spectacle afforded us by the American army during the World War! It brought us not only the weight of its mass, but also, no less precious, the resources of its glorious moral qualities.

Seeing it at work, none could doubt that it was inspired by the noblest of causes, and that a great people was behind it.

PART TWO

THE AMERICAN SOLDIER IN THE WORLD WAR AS SEEN BY A FOE

GENERAL ERICH LUDENDORFF

THE AMERICAN SOLDIER IN THE WORLD WAR AS SEEN BY A FOE

GENERAL ERICH LUDENDORFF

SPEAKING of "soldier," I am employing the word in the widest meaning of what the term implies. To me, "soldier" does not only mean the combatant under fire, but also the officers in command, and those into whose hands the whole war organization is entrusted.

After the World War, in Germany as well as in foreign countries, I was reproached, time and again, for having misjudged, from a military point of view, the importance of America's entrance into the war. I was taken to task for having underestimated America's inherent capacity, not only in regard to the organization and the commissariat of a great army, but also with reference to military possibilities in general; that is, that I had underrated the opponent from every angle.

All this is incorrect!

As I have said freely before, soon after taking over the supreme command around the end of August, 1916, I came to the conclusion that the government of the United States would abandon its biassed attitude (which it had assumed from the beginning of hostilities) and actually enter the fray when military victory seemed within the grasp of the Central Powers. This conception, alone, forced me, as a means of preparation for the future, to study at an early date the American army and its possibilities for development into an efficient instrument of war. After America entered the struggle, I continued these studies painstakingly, on the basis of all obtainable informations, observations, and impressions. Data thus gained was compiled by the German General Staff, from time to time, in the form of memorials.

Even to-day, I still hold to the opinions and conclusions which were arrived at during the war. I find, in view of what I have read since then, that these convictions were absolutely correct. I intend here to portray the American soldier as I saw him during the World War, leaving it to the judgment of the reader to decide whether I saw rightly.

At the time of America's entrance into the World War, in the spring of 1917, the German General Staff estimated the strength of the regular United States army to be about a hundred and thirty thousand men, while the strength of the militia was held to be somewhat less in man power. Although the military strength of the National Guard was not considered formidable, we were under the impression that the complications with Mexico at that time were utilized as a veil behind which the regular army was made ready, as a nucleus for a big national army, along the lines of the Swiss military system.

We naturally expected a thorough reorganization and a considerable reënforcement of the American army. This would require quite some time. There was sufficient man power available in the United States, and even the question of equipment did not seem to present any great obstacles, inasmuch as the American war industry at that time was highly developed. The main difficulty I perceived to be the lack of training personnel, for which only the regular army could be drawn upon. Also formation and coöperation of greater military units (known to the American army in peace time only upon paper) would take time. I assumed that the formation of military units would be accomplished in American concentration camps before the soldiers embarked for Europe, while the actual war training would be undertaken in France behind the front and along quieter sectors of it. In general, this assumption of mine was correct. From America's official entrance into the war until American divisions actually took part in hostilities, fully fourteen months elapsed, despite the fact now known that preparations for war had already begun as early as 1915.

Our General Staff expected that for the formation, equipment, and training of bigger army units about ten months would be necessary. Therefore, we were of the opinion that until the winter of 1917–1918 no American units of any great number would put in their appearance on the European theatre of war, which we primarily considered to be France. To be sure, we realized the possibility that the government of the United States, as a tentative formation and for political reasons, might dispatch, as early as the summer of 1917, a weak expeditionary corps of about one or two divisions. We also expected that officers and special units would then arrive in France, as a sort of advance guard.

At the end of July, 1917, it became possible to draw more definite conclusions. The arrival of General Pershing in France, which had become known to us, seemed to point to the fact that, right from the start (as regarded formation, training, and equipment), close cooperation of the American army with the Supreme Commands of the Allies would be stressed. We also knew that, aside from the regular army and militia, a new national army was being assembled by draft. This was to be an army whose first units could not be ready before the beginning of 1918. Apparently, one division of the regular army had already arrived in France. Without real training, it was still in concentration camps, preparatory to assignment to quieter sectors of the front. The Entente did not seem to have received any promise of an especially strong and early support by fliers.

Around the end of 1917, we figured that the number of American soldiers shipped to France by that time amounted to 75,000 men. As we know to-day, actually 100,000 men or more had then arrived on the European continent. Until the spring of 1918 we expected that, at the most, fifteen American divisions would arrive—an estimate which proved too high when compared later with actual figures.

On the eve of the great battle in France, which commenced on March 21st, there were only seven American divisions on French soil. Of these, only the first could be counted upon as a combatant unit, while three others had entered the front lines for field instructions. The remainder were still in training behind the front. The gradual increase, from month to month, of American army transports was due to the imminent German successes in March. Thus, in the second half of July, ther ewere more than one million American soldiers on French soil, and at the time of the armistice, two million!

I admit that the German General Staff did not perceive, right from the start, the speed and full scope of this tremendous American achievement. The fact, to a certain extent, must be traced to an overrating of the effect of the intensified U-boat campaign. As far as the enemies' merchant marine was concerned, the submarine proved continually effective but, nevertheless, disappointing as an obstacle to transatlantic army transports. Of course, it was beyond my imagination to conceive what rigorous and unfair means would be resorted to by the Entente for the purpose of acquiring bottoms necessary for facilitating the increase of American troop transports.

I may point out here that the Entente—professing to fight for the rights of the small nations—violated the rights of neutral states, especially Holland.

I did not know to what extent American troops, after having arrived on the European continent, would be equipped by the Entente with war material. When such a procedure was resorted to, it became possible to transport a great many more men on each steamer. Toward the beginning of July, every doubt in reference to the rapidity of American transports had vanished from my mind.

America, with great skill and energy, surmounted the difficulties of the equipment and commissariat of an army of a million men. Let us not overlook the fact that French assistance proved of great value to the Americans. It should be mentioned here that a large number of factories in the United States, manufacturing war material, long before the entrance of America into the war, had moved their entire plants to Europe, continually supplying the Entente powers with their enormous output.

It seems to me that the lion's share of the praise, for the achievement of America's organization, does not belong so much to the pacifically inclined Secretary of War, Baker, as to Generals Pershing and March. I believe it to be to their credit, that in the spring of 1918 there was a decided change in the ratio of troop transports and that the all-important question of bottoms was effectively regulated. In this connection, the practical sense of the Americans in all matters of organization and their inherent technical capacity proved precious for them.

I must not omit to point out that the imposing figures I have mentioned are subject to essential reductions if a correct picture of their influence on the ultimate development of the European land campaign is to be arrived at. To ascertain the number of the effective troops, we will first have to deduct (in accordance with American figures) 40 per cent. of the men as noncombatants.

Marshal Foch, on July 1, 1918, estimated the number of American troops, within the Allied armies, to be 450,000 men. This is about one half of all the American troops that had arrived on the European continent up to that time. Other reductions to be made consist in the comparatively high field losses which, in the Meuse-Argonne battle alone, from September 26th to November 11th, amounted to 148,000 men. Losses due to influenza and dysentery also made great inroads in the ranks of the American army. The number of hospital casualties and missing amounted to some 75,000.

Doubtless, the best conception of the strength of the American combatant troops in European soil, toward the end of hostilities, may be derived from the number of divisions then in France: namely, 43 altogether. Of these, only two thirds, that is, 28 divisions, actually participated in battles along the front, or acted as reserves. Six additional divisions were still in the process of training along quieter sectors of the front. Another 6 divisions acted as depot troops. Three were apparently employed for special purposes in the rear. The total strength of the 43 American divisions amounted to 1,160,000 men, with 28 combatant divisions numbering 760,000 men. These facts must be borne in mind, inasmuch as on the strength of them greatly exaggerated figures—spread by propaganda—are reduced to their correct size.

The actual strength of the American Expeditionary Forces was entirely sufficient to supply Germany's enemies with formidable and ever-increasing reënforcements. Only on account of the timely assistance rendered by America to the Entente nations were the latter not only saved from utter defeat, but also enabled eventually to gain military ascendancy. This military superiority, however, in spite of what has been reiterated so often, did not prove the factor which ultimately forced Germany into unconditional surrender. Rather, it was the result of the collapse of the German home front.

The viewpoint of an English officer, as regards these conditions, presents itself in the following quotation which, incidentally, does not mention the influence of America on the ultimate outcome of the war at all. Says the English officer: "There is no other country in the world as generous as England in giving her gratitude practical expression. It would be undignified for the British people to forget how eagerly the socialist parties of Germany worked for them during the war. To be sure, we paid them at that time for services rendered, but that is insufficient. I propose that, at a suitable spot in Berlin, a monument shall be erected, bearing the following inscription: 'This monument has been erected by the British people as a token of their lasting thanks to the republican parties of the German Empire which, during the Great War, have served the cause of the Allies so well.'"

That the resistance of our field army had not been broken manifests itself in the unbiassed testimony of expert critics within the ranks of our one-time opponents. In addition, it was also seen that, at the conclusion of hostilities, the offensive strength of the armies allied against us had suffered greatly. Indeed the condition of their reserves and reënforcements was such that the execution of far-reaching operations would only have been possible after extensive periods of rest. Lack of space prevents me from going into details here.

The question now arises: How did I judge the inherent quality of the quantitatively enormous American instrument of war?

First, I will discuss the leadership.

General Pershing, their supreme commander, was almost completely unknown to us. We only knew of him that, in his youth, after returning from the Manchurian war, he had been promoted from captain to brigadier general and, as such, had played a leading part in the Mexico campaign. We did not doubt that he had followed military developments in the World War with intense interest and that, especially since his arrival at the European theatre of operations, he had endeavoured to put the finishing touch to his theoretical knowledge of modern warfare. Nevertheless, as far as the task of an army leader under conditions as they prevailed during the World War was concerned, General Pershing altogether lacked practical training.

The same holds true in regard to all the other American generals who held responsible command during the war, and also in respect to the American General Staff. In view of this state of affairs, I believed that I should not be obliged to cope with an American army operating independently until leadership, and the gross of the army as well, had gained extensive practical experience along quieter sectors of the front. This deduction proved correct. It is also known what difficulties General Pershing had to overcome before he induced the superior commands of the Entente to assent to the organization of his troops into one exclusively American army, to operate under his own command.

Not until September, 1918, did General Pershing give his measure as an army leader in the course of an independently executed offensive movement. It was directed against so tempting an object as that presented by the German salient position of St. Mihiel. With great discernment, a limited goal had been chosen for the task allotted to him. Demonstrating the sound ambition of a soldier (without which a military leader cannot be imagined) General Pershing very energetically insisted upon having this task allotted to him by the supreme commander of the Allied army. From an American point of view, he simply had to take such a course. I have tangible information upon which to base an assumption that the people of the United States and the army, for reasons of prestige, impatiently waited for

General Pershing to make his début as leader of an army.

I shall not withhold from General Pershing my recognition of the extensive preparations with which he very cleverly led up to the actual offensive. That pressure from the start was exerted almost exclusively on the wings of our far-flung wedge-like position. This was the result of simple and logical contemplation of the circumstances. It must not be overlooked at this point, that, in view of the fact that the Americans employed superior forces, their success was a foregone conclusion.

I had long since arrived at the opinion that it was simply impossible to defend our "unnatural" position —which had developed a few years before at the end of the mobile stage of the war—against an offensive supported by all the means of modern tactics. I had resolved, if necessary, to permit the troops employed at the salient to withdraw to the shorter line of the position in the Woëvre Plain. It had been fortified long before. General Pershing should consider it a stroke of good luck that the ultimate withdrawal of our troops from the salient, as ordered by me, was carried out too late, in spite of the fact that the offensive intention of the enemy had been recognized in time. Now that a defensive battle on the part of the weak German forces had become unavoidable, one of my divisions on the south front exposed to the main thrust of the Americans failed me. Inasmuch as the Americans succeeded in penetrating our position deeply at this spot, their whole enterprise developed into an unmistakable success. The amount of booty thus gained exerted great influence on the morale and leadership of the troops.

I venture the opinion here that it would have been

possible for the Americans to win a much greater and more decisive victory if their initial successes had been exploited with more decisiveness and firmness of intention. As a matter of fact, they did not succeed in preventing the German forces, on the heights of the Meuse, from withdrawing to the shorter line which had been prepared in advance for them. I am unable to decide whether this failure must be traced to the supreme command, or to the action of subordinate American officers.

As regards the achievements of General Pershing during the Battle of the Marne and in the Argonne, I offer my opinion with the strict reservation to-day, as well as during the war, that I do not know to what extent the American supreme commander depended in his decisions and actions upon orders from Marshal Foch. To my mind, even in view of the latest writings of Marshal Foch, the preliminaries have not been sufficiently cleared. It is not yet apparent to me whether the Marshal, with his general offensive (commencing about the end of September along the whole front, from the North Sea to the Meuse), aimed at a definite objective, or whether he merely intended to break up the German front by virtue of continual hammering. If, as frequently suggested, the Marshal's operations, as a whole, are considered from the point of view that it was his intention to encircle the Germans in the interior of Belgium, for the purpose of a great "Sedan," then it would have been the task of General Pershing and his army to deliver to both sides of the Meuse, along the outermost right wing of the gross of the German troops in northern France, the decisive blow against our left flank and our lines of communication at the rear. If this really was the intention, then it is necessary to record here that the American supreme command did not attain its goal. I believe, however, that General Pershing did not aim so much at achieving important objectives, but rather at smashing the German front opposing him. This I conclude from his army order of September 28th, in which he says:

> The Allied armies have now entered upon their biggest united movement along the whole Western Front. It is of utmost importance that the First Army advance with the greatest possible energy. Apparently, the enemy is retreating before us, and our success must be fully exploited. Pursuit operations must continue, in order to cause confusion and demoralization within the German line, thus preventing the enemy from reorganizing their wavering troops. I rely upon the splendid spirit and courage of our army to surmount all resistance. This is what our country expects of us.

But even this goal the Americans did not achieve. This remains true, despite their tactical successes in the Meuse–Argonne battle. They stand out sharply against the inferior results achieved by the French, attacking to the left of them from the region of the Champagne.

As far as details of American leadership are concerned, let me pay tribute to the cleverness with which they succeeded in camouflaging their extensive preparations for the great offensive between the Meuse and the Argonne—despite the fact that the date for the attack was advanced several days! True, the nature of the country, favourable lines of communication, and the weather, proved valuable allies. Only under these conditions was it possible to relieve divisions previously employed along this new line of attack, with shock troops transported mostly by motors, as late as during the night before the offensive actually started.

I would also characterize as an effective measure the fact that the Americans based their attack chiefly on the element of surprise.

After a nocturnal artillery preparation lasting only a few hours—quite contrary to the extensive firing indulged in by the French—they launched their infantry attacks from improvised positions, with thick fog screening their movements.

The first phase of the offensive, at the end of September, consisted of an attack by troops in close formation along a comparatively short front, with the main objective to be attained by the centre. It subsequently proved impossible to achieve the desired end entirely.

In the second phase of the offensive, beginning with October 4th, and lasting until about the middle of the month, the centre of gravity was shifted farther to the west along the Aire, and the attack eventually extended as far as the Argonne. Beginning with October 8th, the operations extended even to the east beyond the Meuse. There is still discussion as to whether such a procedure was warranted.

If, during the second phase, the attack had been limited, as it had been previously, to a short front in formation and in a strictly northerly direction, it might have been possible to remain upon the offensive a long time by repeated employment of fresh units. In case the Americans actually made decided progress in the Woëvre plain, the Germans must have abandoned their Argonne positions without offering any resistance.

It should not be overlooked that (primarily for tactical reasons) the defense had to desist from very effective flanking artillery fire from the eastern border of the Argonne, as well as from the other bank of the Meuse. As the pressure exerted in the Argonne sector necessitated the withdrawal of the right wing of the German Fifth Army behind the Aire, an additional strategical advantage developed for our opponents. The German Third Army, whose mass until now successfully withstood the French attacks in the Champagne, had to retreat behind the Aisne-Aire line during the nights of October 9th to 12th. Let me add here that, to my mind, the prolongation of the line of attack, beyond the Meuse to the east, appeared absolutely correct.

From my personal point of view (and this concerns especially the third phase of the offensive, which started at the end of October and lasted until the armistice), it seems that the American-French pressure against the eastern bank of the Meuse was far from being energetic enough or numerically strong enough. As far as the general scope of operations was concerned, the important task was to prevent the Germans from gaining a firm footing along their Antwerp–Meuse position. The most effective means to this end surely did not consist in exerting frontal pressure, but rather in the greatest possible intensification of pressure at the very spot where the other bank of the Meuse was already occupied, that is, to the north and northeast of Verdun. Tactical, as well as strategical, reasons would have prompted such a procedure. However, as I mentioned before, I am in no position to say whether that which I consider the inadequate pressure of an encircling movement at this spot is to be blamed on French or American leadership.

I now approach the question of the fighting value of the American soldier.

To prove that my opinion is in no way formed by what had became known after the war, I am basing my views exclusively upon the extensive material which came to me through reports from German commands and units, and through the interrogation of prisoners.

From the very beginning I clearly perceived that in the American soldier a fighter of physically splendid material presented himself. Young, well developed, enterprising by nature, and utterly lacking fear, trained for exertions and privations by sport, very well fed and equipped, his nervous energy untapped, the American soldier possessed precisely those qualifications which make a fighter.

In a memorial of the German supreme command drafted in the winter 1917–1918, I find:

> Replacement, armament, and equipment of the American troops are good. Their training is still insufficient. Notwithstanding this fact, the first American unit employed in the front line, against a German attack, behaved very well. It is to be expected that the American soldier, after additional training and war experience, will amount to a formidable opponent.

After the end of May, 1918, when American troops participated in battles to stem the German offensive tide, the judgment of the German supreme command, set forth at the beginning of July, was as follows:

> In general, the fighting value of the American divisions, considering their limited war experience and insufficient training, must be considered as good. When on the defensive, even the youngest troops gave a good account of themselves. The American soldier proves himself brave, strong, and skillful. Casualties do not daunt him. Nevertheless, leadership is still inferior.

The employment of Americans in bigger independent units for the time being will not be possible without French instruction and assistance. In judging the fighting value of the American soldier, it must be taken into consideration that, until now, only such units have been encountered as must be termed crack troops.

Of one of these crack units, the 2nd Division, it is said:

This division must be considered as a very good one, perhaps even as a shock unit. The material of the rank and file is very good indeed. They are healthy, physically well-developed men from eighteen to twenty-eight years of age. Their morale is inexhaustible, and they are imbued with a spirit of implicit confidence. Significant are the words of one prisoner: "Kill or get killed." All the attacks in Belleau Wood in July were executed briskly and without hesitation. Their nerves are still strong and they are well fed.

Whether this highly flattering opinion of the American soldier must be considered as generally applicable was beyond our knowledge at that time—summer, 1918. Another division, apparently employed prematurely, proved of "decidedly low morale and inferior spirit."

After the American First Army had put in an appearance in its first independent, tactical undertaking—the attack against the salient of St. Mihiel—it became possible for me to form a better idea of the fighting value of the American soldier. In opening the operations, the Americans displayed both strength and circumspection. There was an effective artillery preparation of four hours' duration. The batteries were very well sighted, not only in regard to our front trenches, but also as far as our lines of communication and dugouts in the rear were concerned. Whenever fire ceased, officers' reconnoitring parties, equipped with light machine guns, would advance along the whole line to ascertain the results obtained by the artillery.

Immediately behind the last heavy artillery volley infantry arrayed in great depths and in extraordinarily strong fighting units would charge with great speed. However, during the execution of the attack proper, lack of training and insufficient war experience manifested themselves clearly.

To corroborate this, I wish to quote verbally from a report which I received from the superior command of the Army Unit C, which opposed the Americans:

In their behaviour, the American infantry displayed insufficient military training. They advanced mechanically, demonstrating great awkwardness in the management of their consecutive skirmish formations in open country. Their shock troops were startled at the slightest resistance, giving the impression of clumsiness and helplessness. Officers, as well as privates, did not understand how to utilize advantages of the country. When encountering resistance, they did not take to cover, but endeavoured to make their way back in an upright position. To all appearances, the Americans do not know the art of advancing or retreating, by crawling along the ground, or by jumping up quickly. The American soldier first remains where he is, then tries to move on in an erect position. He is utterly uninitiated when it comes to fighting in shell craters; he does not know how to cling to the sides of the craters.

Exactly like the mass in formation, the individual soldier does not know how to behave during an attack. Undoubtedly he is brave, but he attacks very cautiously. Hand grenades usually put him to flight. When facing the prospect of being taken prisoner, he offers resistance until the last. He is skillful in the use of machine guns. In defense, he is stubborn, finding his best means of resistance in his numerous machine guns.

The artillery lived up to its task during the preparatory stage of the attack from initial positions. The manner of shooting is good, and the gunners quickly find the range. Apparently this is due to the great employment of technical devices, under the instruction of the French. In the shortest time, the Americans were able to achieve well-directed fire. Infantry and artillery cooperated faultlessly. As soon as infantry units met with machine-gun nests, they retreated for the time being, knowing that new preparatory artillery fire would soon be opened by coöperating batteries. Although the artillery is well trained technically, it lacked the skill and the dexterity necessary to mobile warfare.

The leadership was altogether clumsy. Evidently our opponent has many officers at his disposal. However, most of them do not possess the qualifications necessary to leadership. It was impossible to overlook the embarrassment displayed by the Americans as soon as their initial aims were achieved. They helplessly faced their new positions, unable to take any advantage of them. Frenchmen in such a situation are much more dangerous.

In pursuit, also, the Americans proved deficient in military skill. Favourable opportunities to overtake and to encircle us were allowed by them to go by. The high command did not quickly recognize and fully exploit new situations, even though it understood very well how to prepare the attack systematically. As soon as the infantry, charging straight ahead, had achieved its goal, leaders, as well as the rank and file, were nonplussed. They are insufficiently acquainted with the tactical maxims for the employment of division units to overpower the enemy. Thus, Army Unit C was able to shake off the opponent during the course of *one* night, and to arrange itself for a new battle in close proximity to the enemy.

To sum up: The American, as a soldier, is still too much of an amateur and, therefore, need not be feared in the event of a big attack. Our men, when encountering the enemy in reconnoitring enterprises, had found the Americans very proficient. The high opinion thus gained led them to expect great achievements from the Americans in the course of a big attack. In spite of local failures, in the battle of September 12th, when opposing the Americans, the confidence of our troops was enhanced.

In the course of the ensuing Meuse–Argonne battle, the opinion quoted above was generally confirmed. On October 13th, I received a report from Superior Army Command 3, in which the following observations and impressions were recorded:

The American method of attack consists in the employment of enormous masses. At the onset of the attacks, the infantry proved themselves to be strong of nerve, charging in close formation without preparatory artillery fire. However, as soon as the Americans encountered lively artillery and machine-gun fire, their charge came to a halt. Even poorly sighted volleys from our guns frequently served to force the American infantry to retreat in disorder.

The American infantry proved unable to exploit successes gained in the course of frontal thrusts by the employment of mass formation, supported by numerous tanks, and while under the cover of heavy fog. They also failed to take possession systematically of the trenches which they had taken.

The Americans display a distinct fear of being encircled. Even closely formed regiments or battalions, when their formation was penetrated, retreated to their main line of resistance as soon as they became aware of the fact that the mass of division was no longer close by. Frequently they failed even where, at first, they succeeded in executing a flanking thrust. When met by a counter attack, they would retreat, sometimes kilometers, rallying only when they reached their rear lines, and were once more under the cover of their machine guns. In the course of attacks, American units were quickly thrown into disorder. Their preparations for attack were often clearly recognized by our artillery, thus causing them to suffer severely from our fire.

Following September 26th, the next days, although enlivened with strong attacks, did not yield any essential results, inasmuch as the fighting merely consisted of partial onsets which were carried out independently of one another. On September 29th, statements by prisoners intimated that a pause in the battle had become necessary for the Americans, in order that they might reorganize their units, re-group their artillery, and regulate replacements. The prisoners complained that during the days of the attack no food had reached them. Also, ammunition had not been replenished, thus seriously interfering with the effectiveness of their artillery.

Attacks from the air, with machine guns and bombs, were received by the Americans with a remarkable display of coolness. They would immediately open fire with guns and machine guns against any flyers within range. According to the prisoners, this kind of fighting appeals to them primarily as sport.

Our men do not yet consider the Americans as full-fledged soldiers. However, our men are well aware of the enormous pressure exerted by American divisions in mass formation which, time and again, are recklessly thrown into the battle anew.

When on the defensive, the American, even in desperate situations, proves himself absolutely tenacious. For example, one American battalion, although surrounded and having suffered extreme losses from artillery, machine guns, and flame throwers, resisted for days. Eventually, when the German line was moved farther to the rear, a small number of the Americans succeeded in making their escape.

Losses suffered by the Americans are heavy. Most of the divisions which took part in the attacks cannot be judged altogether field-worthy for some time to come. It must nevertheless be taken in consideration that as regards replacement, the Americans are in a most favourable position. Undoubtedly, the severity of the last battles has made an impression upon them. The prisoners unanimously state that the battles in the Argonne and along the Meuse can in no way be compared with the results easily attained at St. Mihiel.

I shall add here two other brief reports, dealing with the behaviour of two American divisions said to have been especially well trained.

The 2nd Division, A. E. F., is considered a crack unit. This division has been twice cited in the Order of the Day. Its achievements, however, according to our German standard, do not entirely warrant the high opinion with which this unit is generally regarded.

During the attack between Orfeuil and St. Étienne, the infantry of this division charged briskly, utterly disregarding our artillery fire. However, as soon as the attackers met with resistance in the German trenches, in the form of infantry and machine-gun fire, their charge quickly ceased and they even faced about. These observations were made especially during German counter thrusts. According to information unanimously offered by all prisoners, American leadership failed altogether, units becoming confused and all communication and relay of orders ceasing. After the comparatively easy successes in the fighting near St. Mihiel, the rank and file seemed greatly surprised at meeting with such stubborn resistance on the part of the Germans.

In regard to the 26th Division, A. E. F., it is stated:

This division is known as a "raid division." The officer in command is General Edwards, a West Pointer who enjoys great popularity and high esteem. Lately, his division has been brought into action in all operations. Apparently, as a result of losses suffered since the end of July, the 26th Division does not seem to measure up fully to its old high standard. There are only a few of the original enlisted men left. Replacements are made up of very young men who are inferior to the old standard.

In general, these impressions were confirmed by additional observations and experience in engagements with American units up to the time of the armistice. Until the very end, the American infantry especially displayed faults due to hasty training. In war time, it is not sufficient simply to concentrate the inherent strength of a nation, mechanically equipping and arming it. Inasmuch as the Americans had to proceed along these lines, the tactical results achieved by them are so much the more praiseworthy. I do not hesitate to state that the American infantry, their strong nerves still intact, were more difficult to combat, during the fighting in the autumn of 1918, than, for example, the nerve-depleted infantry of the French. The latter advanced very guardedly, tackling us only when certain of success through their extensive artillery preparation or when covered by great numbers of tanks.

In judging the performances of the American Expeditionary Forces, the tremendous superabundance of their untapped nervous energy must be continually stressed. The Americans entered the World War at a time when the resistance of the German field forces, after a heroic four years' battle against a numerically superior enemy, gradually decreased and no new strength from home reached the front, but rather the enervating poison of a disintegrating pacifism. I am convinced that even in America there is nobody to-day who deludes himself in this respect, that is, if he is seriously trying to draw from the past lessons for an army of the future.

Even these remarks do not fully exhaust the problem with which this article deals. It is still necessary to analyze the psyche of the American soldier.

It is obvious enough that such an attempt is always difficult for the opponent. That is because he lacks direct and uninterrupted insight into the thoughts and feelings of the other party. However, even while the war was still on, I considered it an important duty to obtain for myself as clear and definite a conception as possible.

The most adequate facilities for this purpose were afforded through psychological analysis of whatever material came into our possession in the form of talks and contacts with prisoners as well as a thorough study of all letters that fell into our hands.

Of special value to me were such bits of information as could be deduced from reports received by our commands and units, in regard to the spirit that imbued the American soldier, and the effect which letters from home had upon him. Out of the mass of all these observations and impressions, it became possible finally to construct a true picture. To be sure, this picture, in more than one respect, greatly varies from that which to-day, in retrospective contemplation, Americans and their former allies are prone to outline. But I shall only record here what came to my knowledge during the war proper.

The sentiment of the American people in regard to Germany in consequence of a lively commerce was not, before the outbreak of the war, at all an unfriendly one.

As soon as the war had brought trade with Germany to a standstill, the needs of the Entente for agricultural products, and especially for war material, quickly filled the gap. Those American manufacturers who had to adapt their plants to the new state of affairs speedily succeeded in effecting the necessary changes. These proved highly profitable. Many who prior to the war suffered severely from a general economic stagnation were given a chance, not only for recuperation, but ultimately to reap profits never before dreamt of. The banks also thrived on account of the general war prosperity, and because of the financial assistance required by the Entente nations. Thus, two highly important economic factors—industry and finance—found themselves, through the European war, in a very favourable situation. As a matter of fact, their interests were closely bound up with a continuation of the World War.

England and France, two nations hitherto looked upon as the creditor nations of the world, faced the necessity of borrowing money in Wall Street. The United States, on account of the growing debt of France and England, was well on the way to wrest from London the position of the world's money centre.

The shaping of public opinion in the United States, especially through English propaganda, began early—with the assent of President Wilson. The longer the war lasted, the more intensive this propaganda became. The English press, in the possession of two transatlantic cables, supplied the American dailies with news from the start. Therefore, on the western side of the Atlantic Ocean, the opinion gradually and generally developed that Germany alone was to blame for the war. For the last forty years, it was pointed out, Germany had continually armed herself. She eventually decided upon 1914 as the most opportune moment to unsheathe her sword. In addition, cynical war lies about German atrocities in Belgium were spread far and wide in order to inflame public opinion.

At first the sinking of enemy ships by German submarines did not attract great attention in the United States. Even the sinking of neutral craft did not create any excitement so long as no Americans lost their lives. However, as soon as the torpedoing of American ships began, the American press, controlled by England and the Jewish people, easily succeeded in arousing the national pride of the American nation with "these German aggressions in defiance of international law."

Every explanation to the American people that Germany merely acted in self-defense against the English hunger blockade was systematically perverted. Now all those international and American interests which looked upon the continuation of the war with favour deliberately and purposefully joined the propaganda against Germany. Finally, soon after President Wilson was reëlected, a change of public opinion in America developed to such an extent that the United States government could declare war against Germany.

I quote the following from a report received on August 26, 1918, based on the unanimous statement of a number of American doughboys taken prisoner by us:

> The intensified submarine campaign and the destruction of additional American ships and lives merely provided welcome grounds for the declaration of war against Germany. The real reason, according to the statements of prisoners, is to be found in the war propaganda carried on by the big money interests, especially those banking houses which maintain close connections with England. In these circles, apprehension prevailed that one day England, and

especially France, would either refuse, or prove unable, to continue the war if the United States did not take a hand in it, thus inducing France and England to conclude an unfavourable peace. This, in turn, would endanger the huge sums of money borrowed from the United States. According to the opinion of prisoners, the imperilled interests of big industrialists, especially bankers and leaders of finance—who, in view of the political conditions prevailing in the United States, are in a position through united action to decide matters of state—afforded the real reasons underlying the entrance of America into the war against Germany.

Of course, the prisoners would not state the true nationality of the majority of these bankers.

It appears to me, that, at first, the great masses of the American people did not take the war very seriously. After all, the war was so far away in Europe! Only a few realized that eventually they might be called upon to fight and die. In general, the opinion prevailed that the moral weight alone of America's entrance into the war, the assistance of her fleet, and the increased quantities of war material, would serve to insure victory for the Entente. As to the extent to which, long before America's entrance into the war, the Entente nations had received American support, the broad masses of the people had only very hazy ideas.

When, at the first, for the purpose of reënforcing the army, volunteers were called to the colours, and later on, many others by way of the draft, the man in the street did not even then realize the imminent danger to his life. Apparently France was still farther removed from America than the horizon of the new world's contemplation extended. Moreover, the drafted men first had to be trained, and, finally, wasn't the soldier leading a very pleasant life, receiving good pay with no overabundance of work? Since time immemorial, armies had been the magnet attracting all those elements seeking to live comfortably, with as little work as possible.

Gradually, however, it dawned on the masses that war service was very difficult and serious. It could be successfully discharged only through hard work and intense application. The natural, inherent common sense of the American soon enough submitted to this unalterable fact with equanimity. Wherever opposition cropped up, it was stamped out ruthlessly and met with severe punishment.

Aside from the war propaganda aimed at the masses, an additional propaganda campaign was now launched, directed especially at the soldiers called to the colours. While in the training camps, the young men were systematically influenced by war agitators. Thus, on leaving America's shores, most of the soldiers were highly enthusiastic about the "crusade" upon which they were launched, and full of bitterness against the Germans. According to statements made by American prisoners of war, such sentiments were instilled into them by newspaper stories describing the cruel treatment prisoners were supposed to suffer at the hands of the Germans. Officers, too, were quoted as having told them that American soldiers, when taken prisoners, had nothing better to expect than to be maltreated, mutilated, or shot.

In one of the reports I received, it was said:

> It is always the same picture that presents itself from the statements of American prisoners. For about three hours, they tremble for fear that they will be killed. But soon they come to understand the true German nature. Relieved, they usually wind up with a curse on Wilson or Clemenceau.

Conversations overheard among prisoners of war confirmed this report.

> Back home they are telling 'em lies about the way the Germans treat us [prisoners would say to each other]. Nothing but lies, lies, lies . . . that they are poisoning us, cutting off our hands, maltreating and shooting us! Damn this crazy war!

Undeniable proof of the propaganda with which the people back home tried to influence the American soldier in the field was found in the study of innumerable letters that fell into our hands. These letters clearly showed the extreme bitterness into which the American people had been unscrupulously and systematically plunged by the daily press and in speeches, in the theatre, and in the movies. In these letters, the filthiest insults were heaped upon the German Emperor and the "Huns" in general. As a rule, women surpassed the men when it came to expressing themselves in a cruel and hysterical manner.

In contrast to this, letters written by the soldier in the field were, as a rule, free from such outbreaks; very often, as a matter of fact, our troops were praised for their valour.

Nevertheless, very strong hatred prevailed against us in the American army. A report of October 9, 1918, says:

> This extreme bitterness against the Germans (who, being "tried soldiers," should invite the sympathy of the sport-loving Americans) is obviously the result of a calculated propaganda that reaches right into the trenches. The American campaign paper, *The Stars and Stripes*, just like the propaganda press, actually revels in reports of German atrocities. Aside from this, much is made of sabotage committed by German spies in the United States, and so-called "torpedoing crimes," with the sinking of the *Lusitania* emphasized time and again.

Notwithstanding all this, I wish to stress the point that the innate good nature of the American soldier prevented him from indulging in unchivalrous treatment of his enemy. Our soldiers especially praised the Americans for never firing upon stretcher bearers when they had been recognized as such. To the American, the type of the French "nettoyeur" was utterly revolting.

An outstanding characteristic of the American soldier manifested itself in his naïve, unimpaired self-assurance and his absolute confidence in victory which, for the most part, was based upon America's daily growing superiority in men and materials. Although, even after the fighting in the autumn of 1918, a long campaign was still expected, the Americans consoled themselves with the hope that, by the summer of 1919, about four or five million American soldiers would have arrived on French soil, assuring an absolute victory then.

Despite a war psychosis, artfully infused by propaganda, there was precious little enthusiasm to be noticed among the soldiers at the front. Once in a while, prisoners with intelligible national pride would give expression to the thought that the United States was bringing world peace to war-tired peoples, at the same time liberating the enslaved Germans from the autocracy of the "Junker" caste. To the great majority of the doughboys—and in this respect they were absolutely correct—the war merely appeared to be of advantage to the governments and to the wirepullers of finance and commerce behind them. Unfortunately, they failed to discern in these wirepullers the international Jewish money-lending capitalists.

The question of what America was fighting for seemed

GENERAL ERICH LUDENDORFF

generally and correctly answered by the prisoners with: "I don't know." A great number insisted that they had only answered the call to the colours because they had to. Finally, a certain war-weariness manifested itself in many of them.

Discipline in the American Expeditionary Forces seemed good. This fact must be emphasized inasmuch as the free American citizen, not used to general conscription in peace time, naturally lacked the conception of strict subordination to the will of a superior. As far as the Negro regiments, which had been organized in two divisions, were concerned, we heard that in these units extremely strict discipline was maintained——even minor infractions men punished by death. When a captured Negro, in the course of interrogation, was asked to speak about the race question and the brutal treatment accorded to the coloured man by the white in America, the Negro pleaded to be excused from discussing the subject, maintaining that "these things were too horrible."

There appeared to be a decided percentage of foreign nationalities in the ranks of the A. E. F. These comprised Poles and Italians chiefly, mostly unnaturalized, who, as citizens of "free, sovereign" countries, had been unceremoniously pressed into American uniforms.

As far as the relations of the American soldier to his allies were concerned, there was a decided difference between the sentiments he harboured for the French and those he manifested for the English. The latter were not considered good "pals" and usually were not much liked. It was charged against them that they preferred to let others do their fighting. There were cases where American prisoners of war earnestly requested not to be sent to the same concentration camp as the English. "Right from the start, there will be fights! They are too obnoxious to us!"

On the other hand, the French were looked upon with sympathy, in spite of being criticized as "none too clean," and although the shopkeepers overcharged American doughboys outrageously. Inasmuch as the French greeted the sons of the new world with enthusiasm, as their saviour in time of need, friendly relations were quickly established. Frequently, the memory of General Lafayette was invoked.

To summarize the general impression which I gained in the World War in regard to the American soldier:

The formation and the commissariat of the American Expeditionary Forces, from the point of view of organization, were good. This was, however, made possible only by the fact that the World War had developed into trench warfare, which made for a protraction of operations.

In engagements during trench warfare, American generalship proved thorough and circumspect, in regard to their conception of, and preparation for, objectives; their endeavour to execute plans resolutely and recklessly never failed.

Nevertheless, they lacked keen discernment of tactical situations and the ability to exploit changing conditions by quick decisions. The absence of these indispensable qualities would have been ever more conspicuous in the course of mobile warfare, which is the true test of both leaders and rank and file.

The rank and file, until the very end of the war, displayed the deficiencies of a militia-like training. While both stubborn and skillful on the defensive, the Americans, when attacking in the course of position warfare, despite their inborn valour and good nerves, became exhausted comparatively quickly.

Whatever passion filled the soul of the American soldier had been engendered there artificially, breeding sentiments inherently foreign to him. In this war, forced upon him by Jews, initiated Freemasons, and Jesuits, he lacked the sweeping impetus of patriotic exaltation and a great national issue. How, after all, could it have been otherwise?

The World War did not serve to furnish any proof as to what performance may be expected of the American soldier in mobile warfare as distinguished from trench warfare. This is a question that still remains open; it is an issue which may be pondered on the basis of all that has been stated here.

PART THREE

AMERICAN BATTLES IN THE AISNE-MARNE TRIANGLE

AMERICAN BATTLES IN THE AISNE-MARNE TRIANGLE

1

INTRODUCTORY NOTE

THREE were the Triangles of Fate on whose battle-ploughed ground the American Expeditionary Forces, three thousand miles from their homeland, engaged in epic battles. The first triangle was wedged in between Soissons and Fismes, roughly following the course of the Vesle River, with its apex resting at Château-Thierry. This triangle was created by the German Peace Drive in the spring of 1918. The second triangle, pointing toward St. Mihiel and reaching in the north from the neighbourhood of Haudiomont to Pont-à-Mousson in the east, was a vestige of the German rush for Paris in 1914. The third triangle embraced the Meuse-Argonne section. From Sedan its base followed the upper course of the Meuse in a southeasterly direction toward Stenay and Samogneux.

In the following pages Generals Savatier, Hellé, and Berdoulat will describe American operations in the Aisne-Marne triangle as seen by the French, while General Reinhardt presents the parallel German account. American activities described in this chapter comprise operations from the spring to the beginning of August, 1918. At that time the German Peace Drive was launched and subsequently brought to a standstill by the Allied and associated armies. In the ensuing drives and counter drives American troops participated to a considerable extent.

The outstanding event in the opening phase of the last act of the Great War was the German thrust from the Chemin des Dames toward the Marne. In these battles Germany, bled white, was no longer able to muster replacements, while American reënforcements were new blood in the veins of France.

General Savatier was in charge of this sector on the Allied side, while General Reinhardt was in command of the German armies in the same region. Each general describes the state of the war, with special reference to his own sector. Both agree that the spring of 1918 was the turning point of the war.

The historical meeting at Doullens, which led to the unification of the Allied command and the designation of General Ferdinand Foch as commander-in-chief, took place on the 18th of March. The United States was not represented at this conference. However, two days later, General Pershing and General Bliss called on Foch at his headquarters and pledged to him their unstinted coöperation.

The number of Americans on French soil, according to the final report of General John J. Pershing, had reached at that time the formidable total of three hundred thousand, composed of four combat divisions (the 1st, 2nd, 26th, and 42nd), equivalent in strength to eight French or British divisions. The 1st and 2nd were at the fighting front. The 26th and 42nd had just been withdrawn after one month's training in trench warfare.

The Germans relied on picked "shock units" as a

compensation for their continually diminishing replacements. They planned a number of offensive operations with special stress on the newly developed tactic of "infiltration." Infiltration is a method of penetrating the enemy's lines with small picked units, to flank his movements.

Although the German supreme command included American reënforcements in their calculations, they did not expect that the Americans would exercise an immediate and decisive influence on the fortunes of war. Though convinced of the fighting value of the individual American soldier, the supreme command still doubted that the United States would be able to transport sufficient troops and war material across the U-boat infested ocean in time to save the day for the Entente.

The Allies, according to their own admission, were fighting with their backs against the wall. Aware of the desperate plight of their enemies and worried by the crumbling of the home front, the Germans hastened their preparations for the contemplated offensive.

General Ludendorff felt that the time for a last decisive stroke for peace must be delivered before American reënforcements, arriving in overwhelming numbers, rendered defeat inevitable. With the approach of spring the Germans feverishly completed their preparations for the Peace Drive, while the Allies anxiously scanned the ocean for American reënforcements.

American staff officers had arrived in France months ago. American units had made their appearance here and there, but the great host of oversea saviours were still overseas.

Psychologically the presence of American troops at

the fighting front outweighed in importance their numerical strength. Savatier, then in command of the French 34th Division, vividly describes the arrival of the 23rd Regiment, U. S. A., under command of Colonel, now Brigadier General, Paul Malone. With the assistance of material placed at his disposal by General Debeney and Captain Crochet of the French Liaison Service, Savatier analyzes the activities of the American forces. He begins with Cantigny on May 28th and concludes the first part of his narrative with a résumé of General Pershing's achievements since his arrival in France, drawing in bold strokes a picture of the gradual development of the entire organization of the A. E. F.

Reinhardt, as well as Savatier, gives a short outline of the events leading to the Peace Drive. He explains how the importance of the American reënforcements dawned upon the German army leaders after the abandonment of the so-called Blücher Offensive on June 4th. Cantigny on May 28th and Château-Thierry on June 3rd definitely established the measure of American influence.

The Americans were responsible to a large extent for the premature ending of the Gneisenau Offensive launched on June 9th between Mondidier and Noyon toward Reims. This in turn rendered abortive the Hagen Offensive planned against the English up north.

The full significance of the American participation in the war became glaringly evident to Reinhardt when the Seventh Army, of which he was Chief of the General Staff, was held back in the attempt to cross the Marne east and west of Château-Thierry. General Reinhardt renders a graphic account of the operations around the

Forest of Barbillon—that great charnel house on the Marne. Although his troops failed to obtain a firm hold on the opposite bank of the Marne, the German general regards the forcing of that bloody river as one of the greatest exploits of the entire war.

Beaten back, the Germans decided to retreat voluntarily behind the Marne on the 17th of July. Before they could attain this objective, the Franco-American counter offensive of July 18th, bursting upon them, prevented them from making an orderly retreat until July 23rd. Reinhardt's account leads up to the night of August 1st, when the Germans finally reached their hastily prepared defensive position.

General Hellé, whose account, following the narrative of General Reinhardt, concludes this record of the first phase of American participation in the World War and explains why the Germans encountered such terrific resistance along the Marne. Miracles of preparation and organization were frustrated by the superior intelligence service of the Entente. The French and American generals who faced Reinhardt's army knew in advance when the Germans would come down the sloped bank and where they planned to concentrate their efforts to force the river. Hellé traces the events leading to the American counter drive of July 18th and confirms the opinion of the cumulative effect of American man power.

II

THE AMERICAN DOUGHBOY GOES INTO ACTION

By General Eugène Savatier, former Assistant Chief of the General Staff and Commander of the 34th Division, French Army

How many times during the winter of 1917–1918 did not our thoughts turn to America?

We knew that from November, 1917—even before the disastrous treaty of Brest-Litovsk was signed—to March, 1918, the German General Staff had poured forty-two divisions, taken from Russia, the Balkans, and Italy, upon our front. We knew, too, that orders for an offensive in the Balkans and Italy had been given!

We who were exhausted in the face of this increasing menace often asked ourselves anxiously whether the American divisions would arrive in sufficient numbers and quickly enough to counterbalance this additional strength of the enemy, made possible for him by the Russian surrender.

Perhaps more than any other officer I had reason to be interested in the effort the Americans were making to come to our aid. I had many an occasion to study the subject deeply even before the declaration of war by the United States.

The very sympathetic and much regretted Karl Boyd, military attaché at Paris, often came to talk to me about it at the Ministry. This was toward the end of 1916, and in January, 1917, when I was Assistant Chief of the General Staff. For this reason, perhaps, I followed with the greatest interest the achievements of the American army from the time a few regiments were thrown into action in March–May, through the period of June–July (when several entire divisions took their places with our troops) until finally in September the American troops became an autonomous army with their own high command and general staff.

During the period of March–May, 1918, the situation of the German forces, as compared with their arrangement of the previous autumn, was as follows:

	On the Western Front			*On the Eastern Front*
	In Action	In Reserve	Total	
November 15, 1917	120	30	150	91
March 14, 1918	113	80	193	49

These figures show heavy displacements from east to west, and they indicate as well a reserve of the greatest possible number of divisions. All of these troops were trained in the tactics begun at Riga against the Russians and characterized by certain aspects of deportment. These included tactics of surprise caused by the shortness of preparation of the artillery (which used gas shells in great numbers), by throwing into action at the last moment the attacking units, the distribution of which had been made at night, and by the absolute secrecy of the preparation. There were also violent outbursts of mass formations, "staggered" in depth to produce the maximum amount of shock.

There was, likewise, depth of penetration. The attacking troops, profiting by their initial success, must march rapidly and penetrate deeply into the enemy positions. When they were far into the lines, they must consider turning to the right and to the left in order to widen the breach. Every division was trained in this kind of warfare.

Ludendorff considered on what point of our impoverished front it were best to apply the blows of this formidable ram. On the section of Ypres to Arras? The ground there was practicable only in April, and, moreover, the British were very strong there. On the sector of Verdun? The country was well guarded by the French and the ground hardly lent itself to a rapid advance movement. Therefore, he chose the Amiens sector, where he hoped to separate the English from the French, drive the former toward the sea, and throw back the latter toward the south.

He assembled three attacking armies, and placed them under the command of von Bülow, the victor of Caporetto; of von Hutier, the victor of Riga, and of von der Marwitz, who occupied the sector of attack. To add to the demoralizing terror he increased his air raids over Paris and trained the long-range guns (big Berthas hidden in the country around Laon and La Fère) on the capital.

The danger for the Allies was great. The attack had been foreseen, however, and General Pétain already, on February 28, 1918, issued the following notice:

HEADQUARTERS OF THE ARMIES OF THE NORTH AND NORTHEAST

Secret Note

The study of the last German operations, communicated to the great units (Battle of Riga; German counter offensive at Cambrai; German counter offensive in Galicia in 1917, and the manœuvres of German units at rest) have made us acquainted with the principles of the new doctrine of German offensive, and we know that we must expect a surprise attack, violent and brutal, with the extensive use of gas. The probable conditions of attack make it necessary for us to exert a continued vigilance and to maintain a deep formation of our troops in parallel divisions.

PÉTAIN.

The Allied forces were composed of the following units:

12 Belgian divisions along a front of 35 kilometres.

61 English divisions (including 2 Portuguese) along a front of 200 kilometres.

99 French divisions along a front of 530 kilometres.

The supreme command of the French army, though foreseeing an eventual offensive battle when the American arrived in sufficient numbers, gave directions in anticipation of a defensive battle, economizing in man power resources as far as possible. It was necessary that the French be prepared to bring in a great number of reserves, for modern strategy is characterized by the rapidity with which the physiognomy of battle may change at every point of the front. To-day calm may prevail where to-morrow the rumble of battle will be heard.

The reason for this is the powerful means of transportation, which allow the attacking power, as well as the defense, to vary rapidly the composition and the density of the forces. Hence, it is necessary to limit to a minimum those guarding the front in the course of a calm spell in order to be able to accomplish strong concentration at a given point at any time. It is indispensable to have many "pawns" to play such a game; that is to say, numerous "elementary units of battle" susceptible of being reënforced into powerful material forces. Those are the kind of divisions the supreme command constantly tried to have in large numbers.

The Allies could keep sixty-one divisions in reserve. At a given time, they must be grouped in army corps, armies and groups of armies, because the troops were of value only through the commander at the head of them, and the commander acts effectively upon his troops only through his general staff.

General Humbert was to command the Third Army. General Debeney, who was in the Woëvre, was to command the First Army. General Fayolle, back from Italy, momentarily without troops, had been put at the disposal of the commander-in-chief again; he was now at Verberie in command over the group of reserve armies (G. A. R.).

Means of transportation were prepared (railroads and autos) for rapid movement.

Finally, as we have seen, the plans were all prepared between the commanders of the French, English, and Belgian armies to assist each other reciprocally toward the accomplishment of a common aim.

Let us observe that General Foch was yet but the "President of the Interallied Military Committee." Under the pressure of danger as soon as it became evident (not before) he became the commander-in-chief of the Allies (26th of March, 1918).

Opposing 200 German divisions, of which 80 at least were held in reserve, the Allies have only 172 divisions, of which they put only 61 in reserve, the 111 others being indispensable on a front of such length.

Would the Americans be able to make up the difference? That was the question! They declared war on April 6, 1917, and in twelve months how many divisions did they send? Only four—and two of these for reserve and replacement!

I do not underestimate the value of the American effort, for which I have a deep admiration. I am eager to add at once that besides those four divisions, they sent us naval guns which, with General Buat, I saw disembarked at the camp of Mailly. ("Two American batteries of 32 Schneiders participated in the operations of Galoche in the Champagne and two batteries of 240 St. Chamond were put at the disposal of the First Army . . ." Hasty note of General Pétain on the 28th of February, 1918.)

We also received the escadrilles, whose praises need not be sung any longer, and some sanitary corps, who at Kemmel (April, 1918) went on the firing line to pick up my wounded. This was a considerable effort already and I will refer to it again later.

But to enumerate the help on the front line in March–May, 1918, I am obliged to take the simple figures and to count the divisions ready to help me.

One may say that on that date the material help was weak, that the powerful support on which we counted was only "potential," but at any rate, *the moral help was enormous.* On March 25th, General Pershing came to Compiègne to see General Pétain and said to him:

"You have asked me in your letter of the 23rd what America could do for the Allies in so desperate a situation. I immediately put all the American divisions at your disposal. Three of them can be placed on quiet parts of the front and thus relieve three French divisions, which may then go into battle; the 1st Division, which I judge to be sufficiently trained to represent the American army in current operations, can go immediately to any point you may indicate. Moreover, I put all the troops that land in France at your disposal. All these American units shall be incorporated, as soon as they land, into regiments and battalions."

Splendid words! They went to the heart of every Frenchman from the highest general to the lowliest drummer because they showed us that the Americans had entered into the struggle to the last man.

General Pershing deserves a great deal of credit for uttering those words, because he had come to France with the intention of organizing and training a great American army, formed in an autonomous manner, in a particular sector, under the orders of American generals. According to his plan, the units were only to be mixed with the French to perfect their instruction. After this instruction, they were to group themselves anew into American divisions and army corps. Because of the seriousness of the moment and the lack of better instructed units the American commander-in-chief temporarily abandoned his plan.

Let us pay our deepest respects to his spirit of abnegation, his heroic sacrifice!

We knew, of course, that a national army could not be improvised. We had seen the time it required for the English to raise a national army. We ourselves, in 1870, after the disaster of Sedan, had to reorganize, in the camps of the Loire, new armies with skeleton staffs and men who never served before. So, although wishing to see the American army come to our help rapidly, which was very natural considering our weariness, we clenched our teeth and steeled ourselves to bear the shock without them, hoping that we might in a few months apply that phrase which General von Moltke wrote from Versailles on the 14th of November, 1870, speaking of that same army of the Loire:

"One must do justice to the powerful resources of this country, and to the patriotism of the French. After having seen the entire regular army led into captivity, France has put a new army on foot, which deserves 'all our attention.'" The American divisions were also to "deserve attention" in the same way.

In March, the 2nd Division was at the front, in a sector of the Heights of the Meuse, the 26th (General Edwards) and the 42nd Divisions, made up of the National Guards, also entered the sector in the divisions of the 11th and 7th French Army Corps. The 369th American Negro regiment went from St. Nazaire to the zone of the 8th Army Corps; and three other Negro regiments arrived at the end of March.

In as far as the 1st Division is concerned, it is the subject of the following telegram of the French commander-in-chief on March 29th:

> Be prepared for movement as soon as possible and get in readiness for rail transit of the 1st Division; which will participate in the battle.
>
> Signed: DE BARESCUT.

It was soon to be in battle. At the time I commanded a division occupying a rather large sector in the region of Troyon, to the southeast of Verdun near Eparges which was very wooded. Personally, I was quartered with a resting battalion in the small, almost completely destroyed village of Rupt-en-Woëvre.

One fine morning, at the end of February, 1918, I heard my men, who were usually rather calm, shouting with joy and admiration. On the square, a regiment of American infantry, a regiment of artillery, and a regiment of engineers were drawn up. One of my poilus, giving his comrade a vigorous push, said: "Where is that confounded liar who bet that they would never come? Now we are saved. It is up to you, America, to hold them!"

"It all depends upon what they'll be able to do!" growled an older and more distrustful sergeant.

These phrases painted the two impressions which the arrival of those fine, well-equipped, well-trained men created on our very expansive soldiers. The first speaker saw the Americans come at last; he didn't want to count them, nor did he want to know how many divisions there were; for him (and he was right) it was the beginning of the end. The second man asked himself, "What are they worth?"

To the first I did not dare answer that only four divisions had arrived! I could have said (and I did say to him) that the pace of the transports would be speeded up and that soon there would be hundreds of thousands of doughboys on our soil, but that until then it was still up to him to "hold them back." Often the holding back would be hard!

The second one was to be answered by the Americans themselves, and forty-eight hours later the distrustful sergeant was reassured.

In fact, I had orders to complete their training by adding their batteries to my artillery, putting their engineers to work in the second line, and placing the regiment of infantry in a sector where I had to give them a "window." I let them rest for twenty-four hours, and every poilu admired the perfect order which prevailed in their units. The quality of their food especially attracted the attention of our men. They certainly looked well under their flat helmets or in the wide-brimmed hats. These lads breathed good health and the practice of sports, and in their eyes one read the wish to go into battle.

It was a regiment of the regular army, the 23rd, re-enforced by volunteers and under the command of Colonel Paul Malone, also a regular army officer. So I did not share the doubts of my sergeant. I knew that it was a real unit, well instructed and well trained.

I had minutely prepared its entry into the sector. Its front-line battalion was to relieve a battalion of the French 59th Regiment, an excellent regiment of mountaineers from Ariège. I ordered that the American officers should be in their positions twenty-four hours before their troops. For the purpose of familiarizing themselves with the ground they were to stay for a day and a night with the French units they relieved. All instructions were written in French and English and the ranking officers memorized them perfectly in twenty-four hours.

Finally, the French officers were to stay with their American comrades for twenty-four hours after the relief of their own troops. I took all these precautions not because of distrust, but as a matter of simple prudence, as is done with all troops entering a sector and also out of courtesy, because I was anxious to prevent our friends from falling victims at the start of a sally by the enemy.

But they were irrepressible! They did all they could to bring this very thing about! If the night relief took place without a hitch and in the deepest silence, as soon as the sun was high enough some of the doughboys, who had no place in the front line, wanted absolutely to "see the Boche" and "kill the Boche." They climbed, like cats, into the highest trees (the sector, as I have said before, was in the woods), and began to fire on the enemy sentries or on the platoons, which from the height of their observation post they could see running between the first and second line trenches.

All of the men of the 59th Regiment and even of other regiments in the line were furious! When one labours for four years in Artois, at Verdun, and other bad sectors, and one has had the good fortune to find a quiet and wooded spot, what bad luck to see some brainless men "excite the sector."

That was the general opinion. But bad examples are always followed! When one of the sharpshooters was tired, he soon had another successor in the treetop. Everybody wanted to look through this famous window. The enemy also found it extraordinary that the sector, usually calm, should become excited in such a manner.

They did, of course, what we had foreseen. When nightfall came, they sent a patrol of about twenty men to take a prisoner and learn the identity of this disturbing regiment. The American battalion, foreseeing this eventuality, had sent an officer and a few men between the lines and these soon came back to warn their comrades. The enemy was well received. Rifles began to fire, machine guns to pop, and even the munitions were replenished, though the number of shells used wasn't very great.

All those concerned had given the most wonderful example of calm and nerve under fire, so that the German batteries began to increase their barrage. In spite of this help, the enemy infantry, which had been so rudely received, began to beat a quick retreat back to their lines once more. But the few words they had heard, commands or warnings, pronounced with quite a different accent from that of the southern part of France, showed the men clearly what the German supreme command had carefully hidden from them—the beginning of the arrival of the Americans.

This news must have reacted on their morale as the arrival of our new allies had reacted upon our own two days before—only in quite a different manner. The affair had been all to the honour of the American battalion, and my men were delighted. One fact, however, saddened our hearts. A fragment of a shell killed one of the American soldiers. I quickly went with two of my officers to salute the remains of this first victim on the very spot where he had fallen, and placed the French Croix de Guerre on the breast of this brave fellow, whose heart after beating for us ceased beating far from his parents and his fatherland. I wanted to prove to him that in us he had found a new family, and we insisted on attending his funeral in great numbers.[1]

The entire 23rd Regiment of the 1st Division proved itself a perfect unit, well instructed and under the complete control of its commander. We were entirely reassured with regard to the value of their organization, their training, and their behaviour under fire. But what about their officers?

The three battalion commanders, including Major Edmond G. Waddill of the 1st Battalion, made at once a very good impression on me. But I especially wanted to gain an impression of the Colonel. I did not want to judge him solely by the fact that his regiment conducted this small scuffle well, although, of course, his influence was naturally foremost in perfecting their training. I later found other opportunities to appraise his military knowledge, as well as his aptitude for high command.

Every Wednesday I assembled the generals and colonels of my division around a table on which my pastry cook put all the samples of his art. Later we grouped ourselves around my desk, where we studied various hypothetical attacks both in our own sector and in the ground adjoining. These discussions, during which everyone freely expressed his way of looking at things and supported his opinion with logical arguments, were of particular interest. The studies took us away from the daily routine of the sector and allowed us to put into practice the teachings we had drawn from previous engagements.

I was careful not to forget in my invitations our new friend, Colonel Malone. It was in the course of these conversations that we became acquainted with him as a "great leader." Besides having been a professor at West Point, he was a soldier in heart and soul and had a well-developed tactical instinct. All of his observations were marked by good sense and the sound teachings the Foches and the Pétains taught us at the School of Tactics. I often said in all sincerity to the chief of my general staff: "I make no difference between Colonel Malone and the best of our graduated officers."

I do not say this out of flattery or from politeness to a foreign officer, but in perfect good faith. Moreover, I should like to add that later my opinion of other leaders was not the same. I was in the Woëvre district some time later (between St. Mihiel and Nancy). I had there as neighbour an American general who also held a sector with his whole division, without any French troops.

At first, we often exchanged courtesy calls, which became friendly ones later. Knowing that I had been chief of the cabinets of two generalissimi who preceded General Joffre in 1909 and 1910, and in that capacity had devoted a great deal of attention to problems in tactics and strategy, he was kind enough to ask my advice now and then. One of his first questions, which he repeated often to me, was the following: "How many men, cannons, and munitions do you think are necessary to take Metz?" By the way he looked at me, I saw he must be going to multiply by two or three the figures I might have been imprudent enough to give him! After this multiplication, he was confident of entering Metz with flags flying and drums beating upon the model of the old engravings of Joan of Arc with her banner entering Orléans or Mac Mahon planting his flag on "Mamelon Vert."

He was astonished when I finally told him that in the face of such a difficult task one acted with finesse. One masked the object by making it appear as if one were attacking right ahead, and that later one wheeled either to the north or to the south. It would be a mistake to waste our forces by taking the bull by the horns, and to double or triple the figures would give no solution either.

This sort of extravagance is all very well when buying property or purchasing a picture that one would like very much to possess. One pays out a big fat sum and the deal is made, but it doesn't work in war, especially with the rapid-fire arms of to-day. One doubles losses without getting results, and that is all. Despite the fact that I supported my theory with the example of the Germans in going around the forts of Haut-de-Meuse in August, 1914, and then breaking their teeth on Verdun, I am afraid that I did not succeed in convincing my neighbour. He did not have the knowledge of military science nor the mentality of Colonel Malone. At best, I probably succeeded in passing for a pusillanimous Frenchman, lacking nerve! Most likely, he tenaciously cherished the hope of realizing some day his glorious dreams, which would have been the subject of a very beautiful picture to leave to posterity.

To return to the 23rd U. S. I. R.,[2] it didn't take us eight days to find out the kind of help we might expect from them in future combats. When I received orders to leave the sector to go up to the northern regions, where my division was apparently headed for Amiens or even farther north, I asked immediately for an authorization from headquarters to take along this excellent regiment. We looked upon it as one of ours!

I emphasized all the arguments I could put forward, favourable to a division with four regiments instead of three. I showed the facilities of relief with the Americans, the fact that we already had very close tactical relations, and that a suggestion was enough for mutually understanding each other, and the like. But neither tactics nor sentiments prevailed. . . . General Pershing was in a hurry to form these regiments into divisions and the divisions later into army corps to constitute the American army.

This was quite intelligible, and we parted with regret. Moreover, as we were to see, the 23rd Regiment covered itself with glory some weeks later at Belleau

Wood. To my left a regiment of marines of the same division had been introduced into the 33rd Division sector under the command of General Buat. The impression of the latter and his entire division was the same as mine. And quickly the rumour spread over our front that the "Americans were amazing." Soon they furnished other proofs of this because events happened faster and faster.

On the 21st of March, at 4 A.M., the enemy started an intense preparatory fire on the British front. This stretched out between the Oise and the Sensée for miles, that is to say, from the neighbourhood of Arras to La Fère. At nine o'clock the German infantry began to attack. The length of the front of attack and the power of the mass of artillery in action left no doubt that the great battle, expected since January, had at last begun. The brunt of the battle was borne by the Third British Army (General Byng) and by the Fifth Army (General Gough). The main road from Cambrai to Péronne separated the two armies, the army of Gough linking up with the French Sixth Army at La Fère.

The Third Army lost little ground, but the Fifth was pushed back everywhere. Marshal Haig sent reserves along the whole front to reënforce it. At night, he asked the French command for help, he still hoped that the Fifth Army might be able to hold on at the Crozat canal. At twelve o'clock noon on the 22nd the French commander-in-chief sent General Pelle with three divisions of the Fifth Army Corps and three regiments of heavy artillery to establish himself in the triangle Noyon-Guis-Card-Chauny. There he was to put himself under the tactical orders of the British general in order to help him keep the line of the Crozat canal.

But events happened precipitately. The troops of General Pelle were not sufficient and the French general promptly decided that the commander of the Third Army, General Humbert, must take over the command of the zone at noon on the 23rd and defend the Crozat canal from Saint-Simon to Tergnier. His army consisted of the three divisions of General Pelle, five other French divisions, one British division, a cavalry corps, and the 1st Division of dismounted cavalry.

But these troops did not intervene immediately. Those of General Pelle had just been shipped, and the other units of General Humbert were only there by the 27th at noon. Would the British be able to hold out?

Marshal Haig had the presentiment of a stronger attack on Arras. He wanted to keep his reserves there and he accordingly asked the French to increase their front line up to Péronne.[3] The French general was himself afraid of another German offensive in the Champagne. The enemy had still a force of fifty-five divisions at his disposal! He asked himself how he was to lead enough effective forces in this region south of Amiens to stop the progress of the enemy, which promised to become appalling!

His decision was quickly made. He came to the rescue of the British commander in full force. It was no longer one army, but a group of armies for the battle between the Oise and Scarpe! General Fayolle was called and given command of the G. A. R.[4]

How laconic was the despatch announcing all this!

General Pétain hastened in the afternoon of the 23rd to Dury (a little bit to the south of Amiens) where the British headquarters were established. He explained to Marshal Haig how he looked at the situation and his measures to hold back the enemy who "will surely attempt to drive a wedge between the two armies."

The two commanders-in-chief, in absolute close contact, were to lead the battle in perfect agreement. The armies must not be separated! But the divisions engaged must allow time for orders to work themselves out, because even when the French came into their zone, they must not consider themselves relieved, but only reënforced.

Alas, on the 23rd events occurred rapidly!

The British Fifth Army failed to prevent the enemy from crossing the Somme to the south of Ham and the Crozat canal at Saint-Simon and Jusoy. General Gough had no more reserves to sustain his completely disorganized troops.

That same day, the 23rd, the French Fifth Army entered into line to the north of Chauny. The motor trucks got up as far as possible. Battalions were thrown into the firing line as soon as they arrived, without supply trains, sometimes without artillery, under precarious conditions regarding food and munitions. Danger justified the exceptional effort demanded of the troops. They answered unflinchingly the call of their leaders. They found the British and tried to delay the onrush of the enemy along a front of 20 kilometres.

But a breach was made farther north. Thereupon, the cavalry corps tried to establish a liaison toward Nesles with the British Third Army Corps.

On the 24th of March, the situation became even more critical. General Pelle held with difficulty the wooded region to the northeast of Noyon, called "little Switzerland." The other troops of the Third Army (Humbert) as soon as they arrived farther to the north tried hard to keep Nesles and to maintain in this region the liaison with the British, who retreated rapidly before the violence of the attack. The Germans passed the Somme at Bettencourt, the banks of which were henceforth lost to the Allies. The enemy advanced on Chaulnes and Roye. The British Third Army also sustained hard blows while retreating to the north of Péronne.

In the evening the French commander-in-chief saw quite well that the Third Army (Humbert) did not have sufficient men to stop the advance of the enemy. Still he did not want to throw into the furnace the divisions which he asked for in ever-increasing numbers. He wanted a concerted action and so gave instructions.

And General Debeney, come from Woëvre, also reached Maignelay, some kilometres to the south of Montdidier, where the command sent troops to him. Finally, the 133rd Division went on to Amiens, there to support the British right wing. General Robinet with the 2nd Cavalry Corps tried to keep up the liaison with the British right wing.

On the 25th of March, the enemy advanced in force on the right wing of Humbert, the 22nd Division lost Nesles, the British Third and Fifth Armies were in full retreat, and in the afternoon the enemy took Bapaume. Fayolle was able somewhat to strengthen Humbert's right wing, but he had no reserves to send to Nesles. Everybody asked: When will this retreat stop?

It was on the 25th, at night, as I have said, that General Pershing got to Compiègne to offer every one of his men to the Allies.

On the 26th of March the 2nd Cavalry Corps and the 22nd Division lost contact with the British to the left; the gap became deeper between the British and the

French, so much so that the British Fifth Army continued without stop to fold back toward the west. It became evident that only on the Avre would there now remain a chance to stop the enemy. General Debeney arranged for two divisions that had just arrived there (the 133rd and the 56th). General Fayolle gave him the 5th D. C.[5] in transit toward Roye and the 4th D. C. detraining at Moreuil. The commander-in-chief recommended on the 24th of March that the G. A. R. be not cut off from the rest of our forces. On the 26th, he doesn't want to be separated from the British either! He promised Marshal Haig to support him and he wrote on the 26th of March:

Personal and secret orders to
Commander General of the
Group of Reserve Armies.

HEADQUARTERS
No. 11 P. C.

The first mission of the G.A.R. is to close the road to Paris to the Germans and to cover Amiens.

The direction of Amiens shall be covered: To the north of the Somme by the British armies under the orders of Marshal Haig, who at all costs must hold the line Bray-sur-Somme—Albert. To the south of the Somme by the G.A.R. under your orders (British Fifth Army, French First and Third Armies) by maintaining the liaison with the troops of Marshal Haig at Bray and with the G.A.R. north on the Oise. This present order which aims at the same time at the keeping of Amiens and the continuity of the Allied front between the Somme and the Oise cancels all former instructions.

PÉTAIN.

Not until then was a new gap created between the French First and Third Armies. The 22nd and the 62nd Divisions were separated from each other and thrown back of the region of Roye. The two divisions of the

2nd C. C.[6] lost contact with the Fifth Army Corps on the right and with the First Army on the left.

Although the combatants in the field have always the impression that "things are going badly" the commander-in-chief upon information received already judged that the situation was improving appreciably. The threat of an attack on the Champagne front disappeared. Stronger reserves were asked for this sector, nearer to the battle.

Seven divisions and four regiments of A. L.[7] were taken from the G. A. N.[8]

All the aviation used in the offensive and kept until then behind the Champagne front was turned over to General Fayolle.

Our stream of troops conveyed by rail now began to reach Avre (in the night of the 26th–27th). On the 27th, sixteen French divisions were in battle and twenty-seven divisions on the way to participate.

We were now sure of holding Amiens (of such importance!) and the crisis we considered nearly over between the Oise and the Somme. The German command failed in its plan to separate the British from the French! As early as Ash Wednesday, General Fayolle (kept informed minutely regarding transportation) said to the Prefect of Amiens: "Never fear! On Easter Sunday we shall chant an Alleluia in your Cathedral!"

By the 27th of March, the combatants, as I mentioned, were not yet reassured. The British evacuated Rosières and Santerre, the 2nd Cavalry Corps was also obliged to fight a retreating battle. It fell back to the south and completely uncovered the right flank of the First Army. The right wing of this army (56th Division) lost Montdidier in the evening. Fortunately it began to receive reënforcements. The French general-in-chief, who, until now, to defend his main body of troops had to throw divisions into the furnace, organized for himself a large mobile mass. This comprised two armies: the Fifth (Maistre), withdrawn from the Champagne front, and the Tenth (Michcler), returned from Italy. The German move, through the stir it created, brought about the unified command, so long demanded, and on the 26th General Foch was summoned to exercise this function.

His first appeal on the 27th was to the energy and the bravery of the troops. Here are his words:

1. Not another meter of French soil can we afford to lose.
2. The enemy must be stopped where he is now; therefore, a defensive front must be organized rapidly.
3. Until then we must not consider relieving the troops now in action.
4. These must organize themselves to hold at all costs and hang on to their positions.

March 27, 1918. FOCH.

On his side, General Pétain wrote:

HEADQUARTERS — *General order No. 104*
No. 28277 T — March 27, 1918.

The enemy in a supreme effort has thrown himself upon us. He wants to separate us from the British to open up the road to Paris.

He must be stopped! Stick like leeches to your positions! Hold your front! Your comrades are coming! United you will throw yourselves upon the invader. It is the great battle. Soldiers of the Marne, of the Yser, and Verdun, I appeal to you! The fate of France is in your hands!

PÉTAIN.

And in fact on the 28th of March the enemy betrayed his exhaustion by the shrinking of the extent of his attack. The Allied troops at all points of the battlefield made vigorous counter attacks. The British Fifth Army began a return offensive on its left. The greatest German effort was still directed against the region of Montdidier and in the direction of Amiens. The 29th showed an even more distinct improvement in the outlook of the battles. The offensives attempted by the enemy were hurled back. If the attacks, especially on our right, still continued on the 30th and 31st of March, one might still say that the front was now secure, and that it must become stable in the first days of April.

But the commotion among the Allies had been great. In a few days, the Germans had penetrated 60 kilometres into our lines and at a particularly vulnerable spot, threatening Paris as well as Amiens. Moreover, the supreme command did not consider the battle over; it might flare up again either more to the north or at the same place. That is why the constitution of these armies continued actively. The German offensive struck against Bailleul on April 9th and later it proved even more formidable at Kemmel. The reënforcements arrived more rapidly upon the battlefield and limited the German advance that evening.

The German armies might want to resume the battle for Amiens! The commander-in-chief of the Allies ordered a new front to be fortified. He even began a series of limited offensives, to facilitate the great offensive foreseen when the Americans were in sufficient numbers. During one of these improvements of the front line, the 1st Division A. E. F. was used. It had the honour of being the first to unfold the star-spangled banner.

The commander-in-chief put the American 1st Division at the disposal of General Debeney. It was commanded by General Bullard and had been a unit in the training of the American Second Army Corps in the Neufchâteau region. It arrived on the 18th of April in the country northeast of Beauvais. On the next day, it reached the grouping zone of Roissy; on the 20th the men got ready to enter into line. Their vanguard reached the front (Gannes–la Herelle–Chepoix). The headquarters were fixed at Froissy. In twenty-four hours more it came under the orders of the Sixth Army Corps and entered the sector between the 2nd and the 162nd Divisions. It kept one brigade in line and one in reserve.

The aim of the projected operation was to obtain the western part of the plateau of Cantigny and thus improve our local situation in this region (especially from the point of view of observation), besides taking away from the enemy the corresponding advantages.

General Bullard decided that the attack should be conducted by the 28th R. I. supported by two companies of machine guns of the 2nd Brigade and if necessary by the 18th R. I. This last filled the place of the 28th, and thus relieved the 22nd, which on the 24th of May withdrew slightly to the rear. After this training, it entered the front line on the nights of the 26th–27th (Battalion B) and the 27th–28th (Battalions A and C). The battalions of the 2nd Brigade, relieved by the fresh regiment, established themselves as supports in the region of Bois Saint-Eloi, Villers, Tournelle, and Cantigny Woods.

General Bullard had ready the planned attack on the 22nd of May.

The plan was executed in a perfect manner; one recognizes in General Bullard a leader completely master of his profession, understanding the conditions of modern warfare admirably.

His orders were very complete; everyone knew his neighbours thoroughly; infantry, artillery, and tanks saw their action minutely coördinated and directed toward a common aim.

As soon as the attack had succeeded the French generals commanding the neighbouring divisions came to Mesnil-Saint-Firmin to congratulate General Bullard. Also came the commanders of the army corps and General Debeney, commander of the First Army who in his orders extolled the 28th R. I. U. S. in the following terms:

> Regiment animated by a magnificent offensive spirit.
>
> On May 28, 1918, under the orders of Colonel H. E. Ely, darted forth with irresistible impetus to attack a strongly fortified village. Attained all its objectives and held the conquered ground despite repeated counter attacks.

General Pershing also hastened to congratulate the first of his forces to bear against the enemy the star-spangled banner.

During the battle (as Captain Crochet and the report of the First Army tell us) the divisional general was at his post of command, connected by telephone with his attacking battalions. He knew what was going on. He gave orders to his active artillery, based upon what he knew. He handled his reserves himself. In one word, he directed the battle—the great difficulty for the command in the middle of No Man's Land.

Moreover, he had the intense satisfaction of knowing that he had gained a desired objective with a minimum of losses. In the present case, the losses were only considerable in the course of the German bombardments against the conquered positions, and there unfortunately the leader's skill is powerless. Only the counter batteries are able to silence the enemy's guns.

If these young troops showed great bravery in the attack, as well as later on in the defense, they also gave proof of a nervousness natural in the units unfamiliar with war, which made the execution of the orders quite difficult. For forty-eight hours the situation was exceedingly tense, so an eye-witness told me. At the time, the 28th Regiment realized that its position was critical, and it even signalled more or less imaginary counter attacks with tanks (which existed only in the imagination of some observer) and caused barrages and counter preparations which were quite useless.

These troops, whose bravery was incontestable, showed how nervous and impressionable they had become in undergoing a prolonged bombardment, a fault principally due to the lack of experience in war, and perhaps also due to the American temperament, which is much less phlegmatic than the French usually imagine it to be.

The 1st Division did not gain from this success all the glory that it deserved, for on the eve of Cantigny the Germans started their offensive at Chemin des Dames[9] which diverted public notice. After Cantigny, the 1st Division still stayed for over a month in the sector, taking greater advantage of the enemy each day through the activity of its artillery and especially through repeated hand-to-hand engagements.

One fine afternoon, a sergeant of the 18th Regiment, feeling bored in the trenches, went crawling through the wheat fields which covered the plain in front of the Park of Grivesnes and captured a German observer who dozed in a shellhole. On another morning, Major Theodore Roosevelt of the 26th Regiment, son of President Roosevelt, captured the whole garrison of a German trench (about sixty men) with the loss of only one man, a brave officer.

This fine division only left the sector of Cantigny on the 9th of July; it had lost more than four thousand men in dead and wounded, but it could boast of having given the Germans their hands full, and these two months of continuous struggle had made it considerably more fit for war.

A beautiful page was certainly written at Cantigny[10] by the 1st Division, the first page of a golden book of which the Americans might well be proud. We French must be grateful because it was written on our soil.

The effort already produced was enormous, and we must trace it out in order to understand exactly how the divisions, starting in July, began to multiply so rapidly.

To raise millions of men, a veritable national army, the United States first had to make an immense effort to call, instruct, and fit these young men, who knew nothing about war, into their places. But they also needed a particular organization in France where at every step General Pershing found and overcame continual obstacles.

Having arrived in Paris in September, 1917, General Pershing there organized his general staff and began the reorganization of his army. He had two fixed aims from which he never departed. One was to make an autonomous, completely American army, and the other was to give the Allies the maximum of help. As soon as he had determined the way in which he could perfect the training of his army, through conversations with the British and French leaders, he established his headquarters at Chaumont behind the sector of the battlefield which most probably was to be his. At Tours he left the second echelon of his general staff especially charged with provisions, transports, and medical supplies. At Chaumont, the armament and instruction drew more particularly his attention.

The armament of the infantry (portable arms and munitions) was furnished by the American factories, which promptly reached production figures that were until then unknown. (The production per day was 320 machine guns, 8,000 rifles, 1,800 revolvers, 15,000 grenades, 11,000,000 cartridges.) But until the United States could manufacture, in great numbers, machine-gun rifles and cannon of the admittedly excellent Browning model, they utilized the French machine-gun rifle, the .37 cannon, the French .240 mortar, the V.B. Grenade and the English Stokes mortar. This was the reason for the delay in the training in specialized weapons.

It was the same way with the artillery, and that was a much more serious situation. American industry had laid out a great programme for furnishing the army with .75's and big-calibre guns, but to execute it much time was needed. From the battlefields came the stories of the superiority of the French .75's, and finally the French government furnished the material for the artillery at the rate of five .75's a day from September, 1917, on, and two .155 shorts a day from October on.

The French furnished the American divisions with their entire supply of .155 shorts even before the French divisions had been entirely equipped with this modern material. But it follows that American troops had to familiarize themselves with these types of weapons, and as soon as they landed in France, they went to various camps to perfect themselves in firing. This was one of the principal reasons for the delays in forming active divisions ready to go into battle.

The same holds true for aviation. The Americans had adopted the Liberty motor and the Haviland plane, but it was only in 1918 that they began to produce the imposing figures of 5,000 a month. The result of these delays was that American aviators went into battle in 1918 in French machines, without being able to use the maximum of the excellent and numerous personnel which had been formed in the United States and Europe. General Pershing desired—and with reason—that the training of the troops and especially that of the command should take into account the lessons of the war; but these teachings modified themselves and would even become more deeply modified by the new conception formulated by General Foch. "The offensive alone brings results" is an aphorism admitted by everybody. As soon as Foch saw that the American effective forces would allow him to begin the offensive, he advised them all to prepare for it. But the French officers sent to America as instructors spoke especially of their experience in trench warfare. It was only in France and in the course of 1918 that the American divisions could catch a glimpse of these new tactics. In short, one may say that in March the individual instruction of the combatants, given in America, was finished; but that the training of the divisions in the use of special weapons (more difficult and slower) could only be given in France. Moreover, the American division is cumbersome.

The landing of American troops took place at the ports of Brest, Saint-Nazaire, Nantes, La Pallice and Bordeaux. But these five harbours offered, at the beginning, facilities for disembarking only ten thousand tons a day. Important improvements had to be made to bring this figure to sixty thousand tons to answer the needs of an army of a million men. The American general staff undertook these enlargements without delay. La Pallice and La Rochelle were enlarged and railroad tracks and stations built. At Lassens, near Bordeaux, a new harbour was created with kilometres of railroad tracks. Near every port enormous camps were erected with plumbing, electrical current, railroad tracks—in short, real cities. From these ports or maritime bases two lines of communications ran to the Zone of the Armies.

France was short of rails, rolling stock, and personnel. We had to increase the tracks back of the front to constitute the "clusters" (*épis*) intended for the artillery which moved on rails. In the south, with infinite sadness, we tore up rail that had cost very dear to lay out and that it would be very expensive to lay again. We had to ship them to the army zone. I remember the happiness of Colonel Gassouin, in charge of the railroads in the interior, when he came one morning into my office at the War Department to tell me the good news:

"The Americans are bringing us a thousand kilometres of rail."

"But we haven't the vessels necessary to ship them."

"They are seeing to that themselves."

The American railroad battalions (created immediately after the declaration of war) were the first to be sent, and soon they sent locomotives and cars. (At the end of the war, there were in France 1,200 American locomotives and 17,000 railroad cars.) The French, lacking workmen, could not repair the worn-out rolling stock which had been put in the "scrap yards." To make them useful again, the Americans repaired 1,500 locomotives and 48,000 cars!

The most serious mistake was in not having the American effectives shipped earlier. A plan for transportation had been laid out, but it was difficult to have it executed by America alone, the tonnage being employed for foodstuffs and the raw materials the Allies were clamouring for loudly. The Allies themselves did not pay sufficient attention to this important problem. They should have used their shipping facilities in common, in order to speed up the arrival of the reenforcements, and the British tonnage should have given more assistance earlier.

In March, 1918, Germany doubled her onslaught and got nearer to Paris and Amiens in gigantic strides. It seemed as though American help had failed! Having promised millions of fighting men, there were only three hundred thousand troops and those still needed four to five months' instruction.

What excitement prevailed at the British and French headquarters! The embarrassment of General Pershing and the emotions of the American people and of the Allied nations at such a situation are intelligible. But we were to see the transports increase, and were to witness how in the face of such a precarious situation the freshly arrived American troops were thrown into battle with such sacrifice and with incomplete and sometimes only rudimentary training.

As I mentioned before, the moral effect caused by the arrival of the American troops was enormous. At the ports of debarkation and in cities adjoining the camps the people who despaired of seeing the end of the war now shouted: "A new force! Victory approaches!"

III

THE A. E. F. HALTS THE GERMAN MARNE OFFENSIVE

By General Walther Reinhardt, Former Chief of the General Staff, German Seventh Army

IT WAS in the beginning of spring, 1918, that America's entrance into the World War made itself felt with intensifying emphasis. In spite of strenuous training, during forty years of uninterrupted peace, Germany's standing army deteriorated into a national militia. Conditions on our side in spring, 1918, were such that only superhuman exertions could break the iron ring forged by the Allies around the Central Powers before the American Expeditionary Forces decided the war against us.

In the course of the war, American assistance on the side of our adversaries became more and more noticeable. At first, American-made ammunition served to lend greater strength to the resistance of the Allies. Then, after the United States had officially entered the war, French railroads were greatly improved. France, as well as Great Britain, was efficiently supported by money and material. Even more important was the moral support which the Allies gained through America's entrance into the war. Without the stimulation of this moral factor, the French army would doubtless have collapsed during our *Friedenssturm*—our rush into the fray for the sake of forcing peace.

The first American division set foot on French soil in June, 1917. It was followed, in turn, by five additional divisions, by the spring of 1918. Americans belonging to the 1st Division, A. E. F., were taken prisoners by us to the east of Nancy as early as November 1, 1917.

Our supreme command inferred that by the spring of 1918 the United States would be unable to land more than four hundred and fifty thousand men on European soil. Moreover, these troops would not be sufficiently trained to take part in the battles fought along the west front. Nevertheless, they would have to be considered, inasmuch as American divisions would serve to relieve the worn-out divisions of the French and British. Subsequent developments proved that we were right. American units could not be immediately employed for offensive purposes. We learned in due time also that the Americans, when they were sufficiently trained, proved formidable foes.

The situation on the west front in spring, 1918, was such that Germany's *Friedenssturm*—our last supreme effort to force the Allies to conclude peace—seemed entirely feasible, and likely to succeed. No doubt, the *Friedenssturm*, as intimated before, must have compelled the peace we longed for but for the fact that the Allies by this time were assured of America's unstinted assistance. When, near the end of May, 1918, the entire front of the Allies was in danger of crumbling, the premiers of England, France, and Italy appealed on June 2nd to the President of the United States for immediate succour. The premiers not only expressed their own fears, but also quoted General Foch's apprehensions thus:

General Foch has presented to us a statement of the utmost gravity which points out that . . . *there is a great danger of the war being lost unless* the numerical inferiority of the Allies can be remedied as rapidly as possible by the *advent of American troops.*

He . . . urges with the utmost insistence that the maximum possible number of infantry and machine gunners . . . should continue to be shipped from America in the months of June and July *to avert the immediate danger of an Allied defeat* in the present campaign owing to the Allied reserves being exhausted before those of the enemy. . . .

He [General Foch] represents that it is *impossible to foresee ultimate victory* in the war unless America is able to provide such an army as will enable the Allies ultimately to establish numerical superiority. *He places the total American force required for this at no less than 100 divisions* . . . [to be established] at as early a date as this can be possibly done.

We are satisfied that General Foch . . . is not overestimating the needs of the case. . . .

This call of utter distress, coming from the highest political and military authorities on the side of the Allies, not only meant: "We are unable to win the war without one hundred American divisions!" but rather: "*We shall lose the war in case American assistance is not available very soon!*"

As far as we Germans were concerned, the foregoing meant even more. It meant that in four years of war we had not only succeeded in preventing the enemy from invading the soil of our Fatherland, but at the beginning of the fifth year we were forcing the foremost leaders of the Allies to admit defeat; to confess that they were unable to hold their own unless one hundred American divisions, all fresh and well equipped, each twice as strong in man power as our own divisions, were sped across the ocean as quickly as was humanly possible! Moreover, it must not be overlooked that the Allied nations, thus severely pressed for assistance, had access to the open sea and were free to communicate with the rest of the world. We Germans, on the other hand, were surrounded by enemies, numerically and economically stronger. We were ourselves deprived of all the resources available to our opponents. We had neither veritable squadrons of tanks at our disposal nor still inexhaustible allies rushing to our assistance across the Atlantic.

Our men, even in the front lines, were undernourished, our home front actually starving. The international money market, and especially America's enormous financial assets, were hopelessly inaccessible to us.

The first contingent of the American Expeditionary Forces landed in France on June 26, 1917. Approximately by the beginning of the winter these troops were employed in actual warfare without, however, taking part in vital engagements. Later, in April and May, 1918, smaller enterprises, at Seicheprey[11] and Cantigny (the first inaugurated by our own troops, the second by American-French forces) led to some fighting. Toward the end of May, we judged that seventeen American divisions were in Europe, most of them, of course, still in need of final training and definite organization.

It was then that the German "Blücher Offensive" started. French and English divisions, torn to shreds, rolled back before our men. We were well on our march to Paris! Then and there the 2nd and 3rd Divisions, A. E. F., were rushed to the threatened front. While the 3rd Division, east of Château-Thierry,[12] remained behind the Marne, the 2nd Division spread out to both sides of the road leading from Château-Thierry to Paris by way of La Fèrté-sous-Jouarre. Eventually, vanguard skirmishes developed between us and units of both these American divisions. However, no decisive battles were fought with the A. E. F. at that time, inasmuch as we abandoned our "Blücher Offensive" on June 4th.

The actual part American troops played in these developments seemed far less important than the effect created by their participation upon the morale of the Allied troops. An American division, fresh and well equipped, imbued with the conviction of its strength, had successfully blocked the advance of the much-feared opponent at Château-Thierry—just where we had come nearest to the French capital! The report of the American general staff quite correctly states in this connection:

> The entrance of a fresh American division into a decisive battle, at such a vital point, was dramatic.

The German supreme command clearly perceived that, with the Allies continually reënforced by new American contingents, our task was growing more difficult from day to day. This state of affairs became especially evident in June. Things grew quite lively opposite the German Seventh Army. I had the honour of being the chief of its general staff. In the ensuing engagements, the 2nd Division and the 7th Regiment of the 3rd Division, A. E. F., played a conspicuous part. From the beginning of June until July 7th tenacious fighting went on for the possession of Belleau Wood[13] and the villages of Bouresches, Belleau, and Vaux. Then, about July 9th, the 26th Division, A. E. F., arrived there.

In the course of the fighting around Belleau Wood, Bouresches, and Vaux, the brunt of the American attacks bore directly against the Army Group of General von Conta. At the onset of these engagements, he reported that the Americans, renewing their first unsuccessful onslaught, had succeeded in gaining a foothold at Bouresches. According to General von Conta's reports, the impetus of the American attacks attained a great effectiveness owing to their artillery fire. Day after day, the Americans attacked Conta's Army Group until on June 12th the hard-fought Belleau Wood was definitely abandoned by our troops. However, in the course of the next day, we succeeded in blocking the Americans from advancing beyond Belleau Wood.

The American artillery, supported by gas, seemed especially intent upon preventing our reserves from reaching the fighting front. This we felt all the more keenly since there were very limited reserves only at our disposal. This state of affairs manifested itself particularly on June 18th, when our 45th Division of Reserves became the target of incessant attacks by the Americans very efficiently supported by their tanks and artillery. The American onslaughts during this day, against our front between Ambléný and Château-Thierry, served to consume the strength of our troops. All divisions held in reserve by us proved insufficient for replacement. The American assaults here were only a part of a whole series of attacks launched against our front with the obvious intention of undermining the entire west front of the Seventh Army. The situation appeared all the more serious to me at that particular moment, as I was informed that I must not count on reënforcements by reserve units then held behind our front at the disposal of the supreme command.

Before describing the fighting in July, 1918 (frequently, but I believe, erroneously, considered the turning point of the whole war), I wish to sum up the situation at about the end of June, 1918.

At that time the majority of the German people were still resolved to break the iron ring with which the Allies were trying to strangle us into submission. The German supreme command made ready to venture everything to relieve us from the deadly embrace of the Allied and associated powers. All realized that our situation had grown from bad to worse in more than one respect. At last, our Austro-Hungarian allies had been induced to embark upon a major offensive along the Italian battle front without, however, achieving results decisive enough to influence the situation along our own fronts. In July, two Austro-Hungarian divisions reached the west front but it took a number of weeks to put them into shape before we could employ them effectively. Not until the end of August did two more Austro-Hungarian divisions reach the western theatre of war to support our exhausted armies.

As far as replacement from home was concerned, we could not figure on more than sixty thousand men a month, most of them just released from hospitals. In both quantity and quality the replacements proved insufficient to fill the ever-widening gaps in our ranks. Inasmuch as the supreme command did not relish the idea of calling out the contingent of 1900, young men of seventeen and eighteen years of age, there was nothing left for us to do but to dissolve one company in each battalion, thus reducing the actual head strength of our units. In addition, the grippe took its fearful toll. For example, on July 7th, each and every division of the entire German Seventh Army counted not less than from three hundred to two thousand men stricken with grippe in hospitals—most of them front soldiers and officers!

Moreover, conditions at home were such that the replacements sent out to us clearly showed our people tottering under the agonizing pressure of four years of war and unnerving starvation. For the time being, the splendid spirit still animating the actual front sufficed to "digest" the defeatist propaganda brought out to the battlefield by the men arriving from home. Also, our industry still produced ammunition in sufficient quantities, although we were unable to construct enough of those important new weapons—tanks.

However, all these adverse conditions did not serve to undermine the aggressive spirit of the German supreme command, still intent upon working out plans from new offensives. The supreme command did not even now stand ready to surrender the initiative to the enemy, not in the very face of the growing number of American troops.

As I mentioned before, the actual participation of the Americans in active warfare still remained limited, although their mere presence on French soil formed a great moral asset to our opponents. There was no doubt in my mind as to the personal military ability of the American doughboy. On our side, leaders as well as the rank and file admitted this unhesitatingly. Right from the first encounter with American soldiers we came to appreciate their physical strength, their manly prowess, their splendid equipment, and the very important fact that they were well fed. We did not doubt for one moment that the American soldier must inevitably make himself a vital factor in the ensuing development of the situation as a whole, and that his inherent fighting qualities made up for his lack of tactical dexterity and experience. At the same time, we estimated the fighting value of our old, battle-hardened regiments as superior to that of our new opponents, provided our men got some semblance of rest. We expected the Americans, on account of their inexperience, to suffer heavy losses. As a matter of fact, I heard that the 2nd Division, A. E. F., until replaced by the 26th Division on July 7th, lost not less than 10,000 men. But then, unlike ourselves, the Americans had available all the man power necessary for replacements!

When the captured captain of a battalion of French Zouaves learned of one or the other of our successes, he quickly rallied and said: "What does it matter? Just wait until the Americans get into the fray!"

On June 9th, the German Eighteenth Army launched, between Montdidier and Noyon, the so-called "Gneisenau Offensive." Although this enterprise, aside from the ground it won for us, netted about fifteen thousand prisoners and a hundred and fifty guns, we did not attain all our objectives. It was now our intention to smash the French front on both sides at Reims and, by encircling parts of the enemy front, open as wide a gap as possible. In turn, such a breach through the French lines would force the enemy to transfer the gross of his troops to the south. Then the time would have been ripe to launch the long-planned "Hagen Offensive" against the English, farther up to the north.

Not only the supreme command, but also the rank and file of our armies, believed it possible to accomplish this task successfully. To be sure, beginning with March 21st, the day our first major offensive opened, the greater part of the German division fought one battle after another. When retired from the front for replacements, these exhausted troops always resumed their fighting after utterly insufficient rest and reorganization. And now we faced an especially difficult task! The right wing of our Seventh Army, right at the onset of the offensive, must force the Marne—a river from ten to fifteen feet deep—along a front of not less than seventy kilometres! To this end we made detailed preparations which had to remain secret, since the success of our enterprise rested upon the necessity of keeping the enemy completely in the dark.

One of the difficulties consisted in the fact that we had only a few tanks at our disposal, most of which we took from the English and French and later rebuilt. Thus we were in no position to protect our advancing infantry. Our men were not preceded, or accompanied, by the fire of machine guns and light field pieces mounted on motor-driven vehicles. Thus we lacked almost completely the valuable moral impulse that this weapon lends to infantry charges. These tanks had another advantage, inasmuch as they could be employed unexpectedly and with hardly any preparations whatever.

In addition, our contemplated attack was rendered yet more difficult for us. In contrast with previous attacks, launched from old established lines, our present onset must be made through positions only recently captured. Moreover, rail connections in this area did not meet the necessity of our situation. The lines were also continually harassed by enemy fliers besides being dangerously close to the front at Soissons.[14]

Our supreme command knew very well that around Soissons great difficulties faced us. However, at that stage of the game, mere apprehensions could not influence decisions. It had simply become imperative to take a chance if we meant to win, after all the sacrifices and deprivations of our people during four long dreary years.

For the time being, and right up to the day of attack, nothing indicated that our opponents had the slightest inkling of our intentions. It seemed absolutely out of question to us that the enemy had embarked upon any preparations whatever to head off our offensive.

At this period—July, 1918—we estimated the number of American troops on French soil at approximately one million two hundred thousand men. We did not venture to judge what percentage of these troops were fit to be employed at the front proper. However, we figured that, altogether, our opponents had at their disposal (although not actually engaged in fighting at that time) about thirty to thirty-four French divisions, twenty-seven English divisions, and thirteen American divisions. The majority of these divisions were apparently concentrated to the west and north, behind the actual front. We surmised that of these divisions, those nearest to the front to be attacked by our Seventh Army were stationed in the neighbourhood of Villers-Cotterets. Behind the exact spot to be overrun by us no reserves of appreciable strength seemed then assembled.

The organization of the German assault divisions (eighteen of the Seventh Army, eleven of the First Army, and ten of the Third Army, with ten more divisions farther behind, together with 2,010 batteries in all) proceeded according to plan. Enormous amounts of building material for bridges, etc., together with the necessary companies of engineers, had been moved close to the

Marne. Also, a number of rebuilt and newly constructed tanks were held in preparation for the forthcoming attack. *To all appearances, one of the greatest achievements, in regard to organization, seemed to approach successful consummation.*

In the dead of the night of July 14th to 15th our artillery opened up wide! Orders had been issued that at 7 A. M. the engineers, together with building material, were to rush toward the Marne. However, just ten minutes before this time, the enemy inundated the northern slope of the valley with an artillery barrage of terrifying intensity, proving to us, in this way, that he must already know the details of our planned offensive!

Nevertheless, we launched pontoons and units of our infantry crossed the river. Despite the withering machine-gun fire that greeted them on the opposite bank, we succeeded, at first, in pushing back the enemy. Additional infantry followed, while our engineers worked feverishly, ferrying them across or building temporary bridges and footplanks.

When daylight came, things became still more difficult. Aside from the effective artillery fire with which the enemy covered the Marne valley, squadrons of his combat flyers now entered the fight. Nevertheless, our engineers succeeded in either building temporary bridges, or, wherever this proved impossible, ferrying our troops across the river. *To me there is no doubt that the forcing of the Marne in July, 1918, constituted one of the greatest achievements of the German army, and will forever remain a monument of glory to our valiant engineers.*

This crossing of the Marne was undoubtedly the most difficult part of our whole task! But, in spite of this, right here on the Marne—and almost only here!—we well-nigh reached the objectives prescribed for our shock divisions for July 15th and 16th. Especially all divisions of the Seventh Army achieved brilliant initial successes, with the exception of the one division on our right wing. This encountered American units! Here only did the Seventh Army, in the course of the first day of the offensive, confront serious difficulties. It met with the unexpectedly stubborn and active resistance of fresh American troops. While the rest of the divisions of the Seventh Army succeeded in gaining ground and tremendous booty, it proved impossible for us to move the right apex of our line, to the south of the Marne, into a position advantageous for the development of the ensuing fight. The check we thus received was one result of the stupendous fighting between our 10th Division of infantry and American troops, which I shall describe in detail presently.

The army group of General von Kathen, with the 10th and 36th divisions in their most advance positions, got ready to force the Marne, according to orders at the westernmost point of our attacking front. The most difficult part of the job fell to our 10th Division. This division did not find it so hard to gain the approach to the river proper, between Mont St. Père[15] and Chartèves,[16] but the opposite bank of the Marne afforded no cover. It consisted mostly of open country exposed to the wooded slopes near Blesmes and Crézancy.[17] The height to the south of Courtemont commanded an especially good view over the ground we had to cross.

If, on that day, we had followed the commander of this particular division to his observation point at which he—as far as this is still possible nowadays—intended

MAP OF THE AISNE-MARNE TRIANGLE

From the Archives of the former German Great General Staff (GROSSER GENERALSTAB). *For explanation see back of this page.*

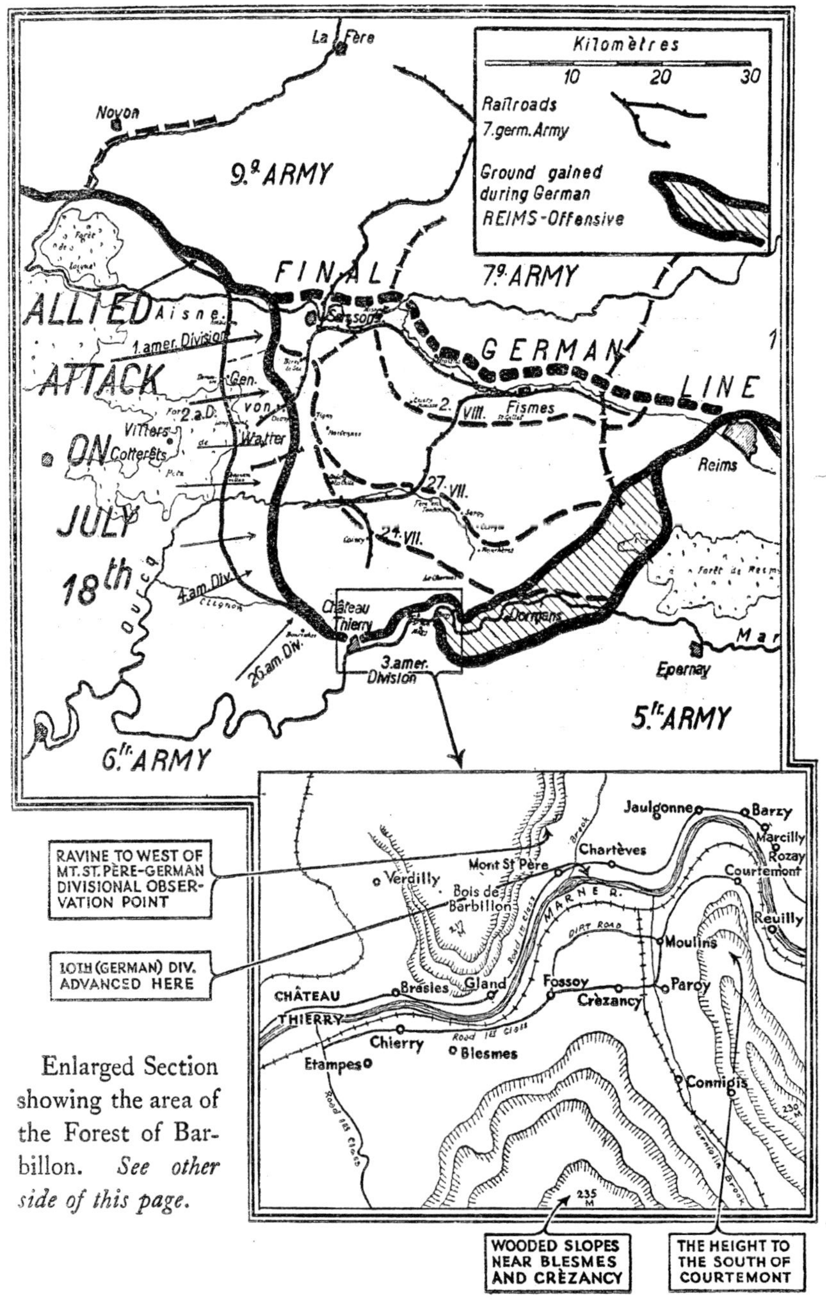

Enlarged Section showing the area of the Forest of Barbillon. *See other side of this page.*

MAP OF THE AISNE-MARNE TRIANGLE

The maps on the other side of this page are self-explanatory.

The larger map, prepared especially for this book from official German material, shows the different stages of the German retreat from the Marne, the thin broken lines denoting the German positions on July 24th, July 27th, and August 2nd.

The nationalities of the different armies engaged are indicated by "amer.," "fr." and "g.," spelled without capital letters in conformity with German style.

Details of the enlarged map of the Barbillon area are explained in General Reinhardt's narrative on p. 103ff, and in General Hellé's article on p. 146ff.

to direct his troops, we should have noticed that all telephone connections terminated there; we should have seen also the installation of heliograph and wireless apparatus. Mounted orderlies, wicker baskets with carrier pigeons, and runners were also available, together with a whole array of motorcycles and motorcars. The latter, however, in so advanced a position, could be utilized only to a very limited extent, inasmuch as all streets were usually covered by enemy artillery, and roads in general were in such a condition as to render fast travel impossible.

In the afternoon of July 14th, the divisional commander arrived at the observation point together with his staff. There, to the west of Mont St. Père, a ravine creeps up to the forest near Barbillon.[18] Camouflaged behind bushes and trees, a telescope permitted a good view through the deeply indented Marne valley over the positions of the enemy, hiding under cover. We failed to see the enemy proper, inasmuch as his troops hid behind fallen walls and in the underbush of the woods. This prospect grew darker and darker, as night spread its shadows. Now and then, opposite, as well as behind us, something whizzed over our heads, with the angry growling of a thunderclap, and a hissing noise not unlike the fiery breath of a dragon, assailed our ears. Whether close by or in the dim distance, this source of awe made all the ground echo with a demoniacal scream, spreading death and destruction.

But all this was not yet the battle proper. The battle itself presented an entirely different picture. Just now, everything was comparatively quiet, but in a few hours, the real thing would break loose!

Thus night fell. Troops moved into positions, nearer

the very area where daylight must usher in the bloody contest.

Shortly after midnight, we discovered that the enemy had destroyed our telephone connections. We immediately restored them as well as darkness and lack of time permitted. Meanwhile, individual regiments moved into their assigned positions. They reported to the divisional commander in what condition—whether without losses or not—they reached their jumping-off line.

At 2 A. M., we informed the divisional headquarters that the infantry stood ready. Once more the telephone wires were blown to bits, and once more they were hastily rebuilt.

One more hour of anxious waiting, and then dawn!

The engineers down along the river signalled their readiness to launch their pontoons. Some of the regimental staffs successfully ferried across the river. Some battalions followed. Others, dispersed by the enemy's artillery, heard him meanwhile open up. About 4:50 A. M., I heard that we now apparently faced American troops, and that the first of the pontoon bridges would be ready within twenty minutes' time.

The one battalion, dispersed before by enemy artillery, meantime reformed and crossed the river. Additional battalions gained the opposite bank of the Marne, encountering resistance which they quickly overcame. At this time, several reports reached the divisional commander. He now learned details of importance. Our troops met with strong counter attacks, from the direction south of Crézancy. A few prisoners were brought in. These men stated that details of our offensive reached the enemy fully eight days before. He was prepared to meet us!

At 6:30 A. M., more definite information! We actually faced American units. These attacked our infantry Regiment No. 398, bringing our own assault to a standstill. Inasmuch as this regiment lost connection with adjacent units to its own left and right, the divisional commanders ordered that Regiment No. 47 be inserted between regiments No. 6 and 398, to attack the flank of the Americans in the direction of Grèves-Ferme.

Meanwhile, Chartèves and the terrain to the south of it felt the American artillery so effectively that it proved impossible to force the Marne at that point. We failed in our effort to build a second pontoon bridge, and our attempts to ferry across the river led likewise to frustration.

Reports received by carrier pigeons informed us of fresh disaster. The enemy blocked our attack along the railroad on the opposite bank of the Marne with heavy losses. Shortly thereafter we heard that Regiment No. 6 was being encircled. A few minutes later, this regiment was either being cut up, or captured. Fragments of it regained our side of the river, with the enemy in close pursuit.

Terrific fighting took place all during the day for the possession of the railroad embankment on the south bank of the Marne. Temporary bridges no sooner spanned the river than the enemy blew them to bits. At 5:30 P. M., we detected signs of the enemy's preparation for an extensive counter thrust, in the woods east of Fossoy[19] and the Bretonnerie-Ferme.[20] I learned, too, that Regiment No. 398 had suffered severe losses, especially among the officers.

Thus, the afternoon passed and evening came. There could be no doubt any more that we had not a ghost of a chance to force the river successfully at this particular point. Accordingly, General von Kathen ordered the 10th Division to retire behind the Marne as soon as darkness facilitated their withdrawal. Although the enemy disturbed the retreat by keeping up a lively artillery fire, the south bank of the Marne had been abandoned by morning. Regiments of the 10th Division, starting out with fifteen hundred to two thousand men, soon paid a terribly heavy toll. Of Regiment No. 6 not more than a hundred and fifty men survived or returned; of Regiment No. 47, about four hundred; and approximately the same number of Regiment No. 398. In the course of the next few days, these figures improved somewhat when missing men made their way back to their units.

During the following night, the 10th Division was relieved. However, these depleted regiments dared not rest and reorganize. On July 18th, and until the 21st, this division met fresh demands for participation in heavy defensive actions south of Soissons.[21] By then, the number of men in the individual battalions had been reduced even more. *Then and there, the truth came home to us! We simply faced a task beyond our strength!*

To protect the flank of the attacking army group, on the evening of July 15th, the 10th Division retired to make room for the 36th Division. This division managed to cover the flank of our assault group. Hence, the success achieved by the Americans, in throwing the 10th Division across the Marne, for the time being, lost somewhat in tactical importance. *However, the American achievement greatly helped to bolster up the morale of the French.*

Ensuing developments influenced the supreme command to desist from further attacks to the south of the Marne. Nevertheless, we continued the onslaught to the north of the river, to flatten out the enemy salient projecting toward Reims.

The offensive opened up with such great expectations, with three of our armies—the First, Third, and Seventh—thus proved abortive! True, we took more than eighteen thousand prisoners. The enemy did indeed suffer terrible losses. But so did we. And we did not open a breach in the enemy's front, thus failing to attain our objective!

The supreme command did not hesitate to draw the necessary conclusions. Preparations were hastened for the "Hagen Offensive" against the British, and for this purpose units from the Champagne front went at top speed to Flanders. By now, we all saw that it would be impossible to hold the position of the Seventh Army to the south of the Marne, although the supreme command longed to keep the enemy busy there while launching the "Hagen Offensive" farther up in the north.

However, at the insistence of the staffs of the Seventh Army and of the Army Group under the German Crown Prince, the supreme command permitted our brave shock divisions to retire (in accordance to plan) behind the Marne. On the evening of July 17th, the Seventh Army embarked upon this retreat.

Looking back now to those hectic days of July, 1918, I surmise that at this stage of the Great War the Allies reasoned as follows:

The Germans, since the end of May, through their attacks between the Aisne and the Marne, have succeeded in taking considerable ground from us. On the other hand, they now find themselves in a very difficult position. They occupy a salient projecting far into our lines. To escape the danger inherent in such a position, they will presently crowd still more troops into this salient. That must make things even more difficult for them, especially as the salient has insufficient railroad connections. It is now up to the Allied armies to push forward from the west toward Soissons and—even more important—beyond Soissons! The farther this thrust extends in the direction of Reims—maybe even as far as Fismes!—the more difficult will it prove for the Germans to extricate themselves from their present position. It may even prove impossible for them to save their troops, between the Aisne and Marne, from utter annihilation.

Preparations for such a thrust by the Allies could best be conducted under cover of the Forest of Villers-Cotterets. The best effectives to serve as a spearhead for such an undertaking would undoubtedly be fresh American divisions, aided by countless tanks, the element of surprise, combat flyers, and the like.

On our side, matters meanwhile became still more critical. The Austrian-Hungarian troops went down before the Italians! None of our Allies were in a position to render us effective assistance. Germany now stood alone! As to actual strength in terms of man power, our units grew smaller all the time. In regard to the danger threatening us from the direction of Villers-Cotterets by way of Soissons, we were but insufficiently informed. By and large, our supreme command relied primarily on the spirit that still imbued our troops, and on the strategy and tactics of our leaders.

Perils loomed from the direction of Villers-Cotterets. We actually faced developments there blindfolded. The preparations of the enemy were effectively screened by the Forest of Retz. However, ever since the second week of July, we noticed that the enemy apparently arranged his artillery in some sort of defensive formation. His batteries moved back as far as feasible which, in turn, induced us to move our batteries closer to the actual front. As a matter of fact, not before the night of July 16th did the enemy advance his batteries, hardly forty-eight hours before the great onslaught began.

Our units stationed to the southwest of Soissons consisted throughout of exhausted divisions, badly in need of rest and replacement. Depleted units were further reduced by the grippe, which filled our hospitals even beyond emergency capacity. In addition, our troops went hungry on account of a lack of potatoes and sugar. What food we set before them was so unpalatable that the men could barely gulp it down! There were battalions in some of the divisions with one solitary lieutenant to lead them while some companies numbered as few as seventeen rifles!

All during the day of July 17th, things remained quiet to the southwest of Soissons. Not the slightest intimation reached us beforehand of the counter thrust that was unleashed against our lines only a few hours later! Our units, at this part of the front, consisted of the Ninth Army, inserted between the Eighteenth and Seventh Armies. The 42nd Division, the 14th Division of Reserves, and the 115th Division, as part of General Theodor von Watter's Army Group, occupied the most advanced positions between Dommiers[22] and north of

Ancienville. To the east of Villers-Cotterets, at the most important part of their line, the enemy had stationed the 1st and 2nd American Divisions with the 1st (French) Moroccan Division inserted between them. I may state here that the enemy, in the course of the ensuing fighting, only at this very spot succeeded in obtaining results worth while. To the north and south of this region, other Allied effectives took up their position.

Shortly after 5 A. M. on July 18th, hell broke loose along this sector. A terrifying artillery fire extended as far as the adjacent subsectors. Only one hour later, all our telephone wires west of the line Berzy[23]–Villemontoire–Hartennes collapsed. Air reconnoitring soon convinced us that the enemy meant to execute his major offensive here. Not until before another valuable hour passed—it was 7 A. M. meanwhile—were we able to discern that the enemy had succeeded in breaking through our positions near Longpont,[24] having already occupied Vauxcastille[25] and Moulin de Villers Helon.

Units of the 2nd Division, A. E. F., reached Vauxcastille early in the morning, but our troops resisted the attack until noon. The whole region here, partly consisting of a ravine hard to traverse, had been fortified by us with rifle pits and machine-gun nests. Tumbled-down walls and such fragments of houses as were still standing enabled our men to resist the onslaught, and the Americans gained ground here only after the most stubborn fighting.

We did not yet know the worst. Only after we got reports that strong forces of the opponent had already reached Vierzy[26] did we clearly perceive that our infantry was overrun almost along the entire length of the sector, and that a great part of our artillery must be in the hands of the enemy!

Everything now depended upon preventing the enemy from driving a deep wedge into our front. For this purpose, we lined up our divisions from Chaudun[27] to Vierzy and west of Blanzy, at the same time moving in new artillery units. We finally succeeded in arranging our artillery in effective defensive positions. When night fell, we experienced, nevertheless, new difficulties in moving in the necessary ammunition. The enemy continued his attacks.

Severe fighting during all the day proved to us that our exhausted infantry, although repulsing one attack after another, was no match for a numerically much stronger enemy supported by whole fleets of tanks. Darkness put an end temporarily to thc fighting. The enemy had reached a line running roughly from east of Mauloy Wood. Farther to the south we had blocked the advance of the enemy somewhat earlier, although there, too, we were forced to retire some miles.

On the morning of July 19th, the two American divisions once again tenaciously continued their onslaughts. The 1st Division, pushing toward Berzy-le-Sec, and the 2nd Division, aiming at Tigny,[28] succeeded to such an extent that, in the afternoon, our situation assumed a decidedly critical aspect. The waves of the American infantry assault reached the Hartennes-Soissons highway. We evacuated Vierzy, Parcy, and Villemontoire. Finally, the newly moved-in 20th Division of our Seventh Army brought the advance of the Americans to a standstill in this region and the next day—July 20th—seemed to promise a change in the situation. Although the 1st Division, A. E. F., still held on to Berzy-le-Sec, after this village had changed hands time and again, our front, once more grown stronger, withstood all assaults. That afternoon, at about four o'clock, southeast of Charantigny, began an especially furious attack, supported by many tanks. Our 20th Division fired point-blank at the attacking forces and beat them back.

Subsequent enemy attacks on July 21st did not yield any important results. For the time being, our front seemed firmly reëstablished.

The American-Franco counter attack, beginning on July 18th, was fraught with dire consequences for the Germans, although we successfully blocked the thrust. It gained just a few square miles of area for the enemy. There can be no doubt that our opponents employed for the spearhead of this enterprise the very flower of all the effectives at their disposal: two American divisions and one Moroccan. A great number of tanks supported these troops, thus apparently assuring the success of the undertaking from the start.

The two American divisions employed in this adventure justified all expectations, no doubt. Time and again, with a great display of tenacity, these units attacked. On July 19th, it seemed quite doubtful to us whether we would be able to stem the American tide at all. However, war experience and thorough training, especially as far as leadership is concerned, cannot be replaced by even the most exemplary bravery, or the most inexhaustible stamina, nor yet by the very best equipment imaginable. *War experience and training are indispensable essentials!* Did we not ourselves pay the price for confounding patriotic fervour and indomitable enthusiasm with assiduous training and actual experience when, in October, 1914, we hurled newly organized corps of volunteers, consisting of the very flower of our youth, against the English positions in Flanders, only to have them annihilated almost to the very last man?

More than one report I received, in connection with our encounters with the Americans, mentioned that their infantry, closely following their tanks in deep and densely arranged formations, broke down under our defensive fire the moment our men overcame what we learned to call "tank shyness." Of course, the French supreme command had the right idea in trying to hit at the flank of our troops assembled in the "Blücher Salient," between the Aisne and the Marne. That this attempt was rendered abortive by us is owing to the lack of generalship in the crack units employed. Americans, as well as French, made it possible for us effectively to disperse tactical formations utterly unsuited for that kind of fighting.

On July 21st, the fury of the American attacks abated somewhat. We could clearly see that no more immediate danger threatened the Seventh Army. Nevertheless, we believed it inadvisable for the Seventh Army to retain its present front line. The German Crown Prince, therefore, recommended to the supreme command that the strategical retreat to the Vesle and Aisne, suggested by Lieutenant Colonel von Boehn, commander-in-chief of the Seventh Army, be approved. The supreme command finally permitted this move after considerable hesitation.

Once before the supreme command had ordered an analogous retreat in the late fall of 1916, when part of our west front withdrew to the Hindenburg Line. At that time, the retreat proceeded strictly according to schedule, with the result that the enemy untiringly shelled and furiously attacked those advanced positions which we had already abandoned. Our strategical retreat at that time afforded us the additional advantage of giving the enemy no end of trouble in moving his lines forward, in order to reëstablish contact with us.

Now, in July, 1918, the general situation along the front of the Seventh Army was identical with those developments which led to the withdrawal to the shortened and well-fortified Hindenburg Line. Once more we sought to keep the enemy out of a position suitable for his counter attacks. These, no doubt, would have involved great parts of our armies in actual fighting along an unfavourable front line. Again we aimed at shortening our line and at reëstablishing ourselves in carefully chosen new positions. These the enemy could not undertake to attack without first embarking upon long-drawn-out preparations. However, there was a difference between the contemplated strategical withdrawal of the Seventh Army and the retreat to the Hindenburg Line some nine months before. We had now to evacuate ground gained only a few weeks previously in the course of our *Friedenssturm* offensive. No doubt a retreat, so soon after a victorious advance, would create a deep impression not only on the army, but also at home. Under no circumstances could we expect this impression to be a favourable one.

Such a retreat now seemed feasible. This was due to one fact. We blocked the enemy's advance toward Soissons! In this way, we had gained a breathing spell during which the necessary preparations for such a strategical retreat could be carried out. Our situation was so very grave, however, that if our supreme command had delayed matters for even a few hours we must have lost this one chance of stemming the enemy's tide west of Soissons. *To my mind, there is no doubt that the events of July 18th on the American-French front could have resulted in a speedy decision of the war had our opponent actually succeeded in reaching Soissons at that time.* Fortunately Soissons remained securely in our possession until we were ready to evacuate it according to plan.

During the developments which led up to our retreat behind Aisne and Vesle, the French armies proved that they had greatly lost in stamina and impetus. Their leadership still remained such as to make strategical successes possible for them. It sheds light on the war situation as a whole, that Frenchmen, taken prisoners during the Marne fighting, after expressing their surprise that the Germans actually succeeded in forcing the river, time and again stressed two facts. They regarded these as an assurance of ultimate victory for themselves—America's ever-increasing assistance and the ever-growing German food shortage.

In the contemplated strategical retreat of the Seventh Army the utmost care seemed imperative to prevent the pushing-in of the right and the left wings of our front. While we had barely succeeded in checking the American onrush to the southwest of Soissons during the fighting of July 20th and 21st, no such anxious moments worried us when we faced Italian divisions at Reims. As regards the pressure on our line by American troops

(3rd, 4th, 26th, 32nd, and 42nd Divisions, A. E. F.) just approaching, this could result only in pushing us farther back in the very direction we chose to take. Perhaps things would have taken a different course at this stage of the war had the French agreed to the formation of a strictly American army earlier than they actually did. In that case this American army could have been employed very effectively in the neighbourhood of Soissons.

The only attacks of any importance directed against us, between the Ourcq and the Marne, on July 22nd, were those executed by American troops. The impetus of these attacks came apparently from the 26th Division, A. E. F. They were directed against the German positions, to the north and northeast of Château-Thierry. They did not yield any results for the enemy inasmuch as our troops succeeded in balancing most of these attacks by counter attacks. On the other hand, it proved impossible for us to prevent the forcing of the Marne near Barzy—a feat due solely to the participation of units of the 3rd Division, A. E. F.

On the evening of July 22nd, the gravity of our situation became ominous indeed. The supreme command issued orders for us to embark upon the prepared strategical retreat during the night of July 23rd. Specific orders to be strictly adhered to were given for the individual units. The first and second stages of the retreat were to be performed during the nights of July 24th and 27th, beginning in the centre and gradually spreading toward the left wing. The right wing was to remain at Soissons for the time being. Then, after a pause, during which stocks of war material must be removed to the rear, the third and fourth stages of the retreat were to be undertaken. These consisted in a retirement of the wings of our army to their new positions. It is quite gratifying to me to state here that our retreat was actually conducted, in accordance with these plans, with hardly any changes.

Once again, on July 23rd, the enemy tried to break through the west front of the "Blücher Salient." However, as parts of the 1st Division, A. E. F., retired the day before, the brunt of the attack was more easily borne by our men.

In regard to the fighting of July 23rd, my diary states:

> The major attack predicted by prisoners to occur yesterday, actually broke loose to-day with unmitigated fury. After preparatory artillery fire of severe intensity, white and coloured Americans, as well as Frenchmen, pushed forward, between the Aisne and the Marne, along the entire west and south front of the Seventh Army. Accompanied by numerous fleets of tanks, assault troops, arranged in continuous deep and dense assault waves, time and again advanced against our men, who bravely defended their positions. While the attacks on the two preceding days gave the impression of merely impromptu exploitations of results obtained on July 18th, attacks launched on July 23rd seemed more carefully planned. However, we had meanwhile made thorough defense preparations. In the evening not less than 43 destroyed tanks were lying in front of our lines.
>
> Determined resistance, such as our brave men displayed, proved impossible to overcome because the enemy's infantry charges lacked sufficient shock. Wherever enemy infantry lay unprotected by their artillery, or where we succeeded in blowing up their tanks, it appeared impossible to induce the rank and file to advance farther. Enemy infantry retreated even in the face of counter thrusts launched by our numerically inferior units. On account of being in deep formation, for the sake of imbuing them with a feeling of strength, the losses of the enemy forces were heavy wherever they happened to come under the fire of our artillery.
>
> Thus the plans of the able leaders of the enemy came to naught since their rank and file lacked inherent strength.

The enemy having suffered such a severe defeat, we were able to embark upon the first stage of our retreat, according to schedule.

There was lively fighting from July 24th to 26th, but we did not lose any essential parts of our front. Then, in the night of July 26th, we embarked upon the second stage of the retreat, again undisturbed by the enemy. We succeeded in removing all stocks of war material from these sectors. The third stage of the retreat was to be accomplished during the night of August 1st.

Perceiving our intentions, the enemy once more attacked us on July 28th. However, the west front of the Seventh Army stood like an iron wall! Only at the south front did the enemy succeed in making slight indentations.

My official diary, under date of July 28th, shows that the greater part of the enemy's pressure was directed against the army group of General Wichura. As late as the afternoon, Americans belonging to the 28th Division occupied the outskirts of the village of Cierges[29] for a short time, making strenuous efforts to advance in the general direction of Seringes[30] and Sergy.[31] Apparently, these were units of the newly moved-in 42nd Division, A. E. F., which, at the very same spot on the following day, attempted a new and more forceful assault. However, the first attack resulted in heavy losses for the Americans. Only in the course of the evening did they definitely succeed in gaining a foothold in Seringes and Sergy.

The Americans appeared inexhaustible. On July 30th, together with French units, they once more aimed powerful assaults against the whole length of General Wichura's army group. All of these proved abortive and costly for the enemy. In the course of the evening, they succeeded in again driving forward into Cierges. During the day, units of the 28th and 32nd Divisions, A. E. F., had occupied the Bois de Grimpettes[32] after bitter fighting at close quarters, with plenty of cold steel employed.

Hardly any change occurred in the general situation on the following day. However, on August 1st, the enemy, as if informed of our retreat, scheduled for that very night, once again hammered our position with all his might, in the region of Fère-en-Tardenois and to the west of it. Small, localized successes, achieved here by the enemy, did not amount to anything. In spite of hecatombs recklessly sacrificed, the opponent did not gain his objectives here.

Thus, during the night, we completed the third stage of our strategical retreat. Under cover of darkness, we succeeded in shaking off the enemy without any friction. On the morning of August 2nd, the enemy still busily inundated our evacuated positions with a hail of shells, subsequently launching attacks against the deserted positions. As we had so well succeeded in camouflaging our retreat, the enemy suffered a great loss of time. Our pursuers were unable to reëstablish contact with us in the course of the same day.

After we evacuated the country south of the Vesle during the following night, our strategical retreat was successfully accomplished. Nevertheless, even as late as August 4th, the 32nd Division, A. E. F., wrested from us Fismes,[33] situated in the valley on the south bank of the Vesle.

At any rate, the time we gained by conducting our retreat, step by step, according to schedule, sufficed to remove all valuable stocks of war material. The enemy had not been able to interfere with the execution of our "Blücher Movement," to give this operation its official name. The American-French counter attack, launched on July 18th and continued for days and days, attained no objectives, although the enemy's casualties in connection with it were reported to be simply staggering. On the other hand, we, too, lost important gains.

As I see it to-day, it is incorrect to insist that military successes, achieved by the Allied and associated powers during the last two weeks of July, 1918, subsequently accounted for the decided change of the strategical situation as a whole. I admit, however, that these developments contributed to this end. The remarkable endurance displayed by the German people, after four long years of war, could be sustained by them only were victory seemingly within their grasp. If victory were denied us now, the natural reaction could not be avoided. This realization dawned upon us shortly after our retreat behind the Aisne and Vesle. And only in this sense were the developments in the second half of July, 1918, of historical and far-reaching importance.

Just how far did the American Expeditionary Forces contribute to these developments?

In my foregoing recital I have more than once directed attention to the fact that the moral effect of the participation of American troops exerted a tremendous influence on the exhausted French, and most probably also on the no less war-weary British. The mere fact that six hundred thousand Americans had arrived in France, to be followed by additional hundreds of thousands, stiffened the backbone of the British and French in March, 1918, to such an extent that they accepted our offensive. The same fact put sufficient courage into the British and French to continue the war even after German troops, after the first big, victorious battles of the *Friedenssturm*, had advanced as far as Château-Thierry and Amiens.

However, mere expectations of military achievements do not translate themselves into accomplished facts through the simple presence of uniformed masses. Actual results in battle are necessary to this end!

The question now arises: Did the Americans, in the course of the battles of spring, 1918, fulfill all the hopes that centred on them?

This question can be answered with an unconditional: YES!

There is no doubt that the American Expeditionary Forces lacked training; that their leaders lacked generalship and actual war experience. These facts led to casualties heavier than were necessary and probably accounted for their limited tactical success of July 18th.

However, the American troops brought with them across the ocean something much more important than training and experience, something that cannot be taught, but must be inborn: The will to attack, the firm resolve "to kill or get killed"—warlike qualities which brave men never hesitate to praise even in the enemy!

Through the entrance of America into the war, the French leaders once more obtained what they had already lost: troops who could be relied upon to expend unstintingly every atom of strength they possessed for the sake of ultimate victory.

My opinion of the American soldier may be summed up by quoting King Frederick the Great. Some two hundred years ago, the potentate of a neighbouring country criticized Frederick's troops before he had seen them in action. Prussia's great monarch remarked: "They may not look so good—but hell, how they can fight!"

IV

THE A. E. F. IN THEIR FIRST GREAT OFFENSIVE

By General Joseph Hellé, former Chief of Staff of the late General Charles Mangin, with the collaboration of General Pierre Émile Berdoulat

WHAT of the Americans? The outcome of the Great War, the very fate of the world depended on them in the early summer of 1918.

And then came the answer! In quick succession, heroic feats were performed by our deliverers from across the ocean. There was Belleau Wood, now officially known as Bois de la Brigade de Marine, in honour of its capture by the Marine Brigade of the 2nd Division, A. E. F. There was Torcy,[34] where the 26th Division, A. E. F., fought; Epieds,[35] unforgotten for the valiant deeds of the same division, and the 56th Brigade of the 28th Division. There was Le Charmel,[36] the Ourcq, Seringes-et-Nesle, Sergy, the Vesle,[37] and Fismes shining examples of the incomparable bravery of the 3rd, 32nd, and 42nd Divisions, A. E. F.

Verily, our new allies from across the seas had arrived! Breathlessly, we followed up the advance of the Americans. For hours at a stretch I would pore over my maps in the headquarters of General Mangin, whose chief of staff I had the good fortune to be at the very time the Americans performed those astounding feats. It was only a few weeks later that, in behalf of my chief,

I issued the following general order in praise of the American units, who had fought side by side with us:

Officers, non-commissioned officers, and soldiers of the Third U. S. A. C.

Shoulder to shoulder with your French comrades, you have thrown yourselves into the counter offensive, which began on July 18th.

You rushed to this battle as to a party!

Your splendid attack has routed the enemy. Your indomitable tenacity prevented the enemy from using their fresh divisions in counter thrusts.

You have proved yourselves worthy sons of your great country, thereby gaining the admiration of your brothers in arms.

Not less than 91 cannon, 7,200 prisoners, enormous booty and 10 kilometres of conquered ground—that is your own share in the trophies of this victory.

Moreover, you have come fully to realize your superiority over the barbarous enemy of all mankind, against whom the children of liberty are fighting.

For you, to attack means to vanquish the enemy!

American comrades, I am indeed grateful to you for the blood you so generously shed on the soil of my country. I am proud to have had you under my command during these days of battle and to have fought together with you for the deliverance of the world.

MANGIN.

Countersigned,
HELLÉ
Chief of Staff

Three important developments illuminated the situation of the Allies in the early summer of 1918: the selection of Marshal Ferdinand Foch as commander-in-chief; the application of General Pétain's tactics and the improving morale of the Allied troops as a whole, due to the arrival of the American contingents.

It was at the time when the German advance toward Amiens and Montdidier assumed threatening proportion that the Allies finally agreed at Doullens to entrust the general conduct of the war to a single commander-in-chief. The question had been brought up several times. For those who had studied the fatal results of the dual command in all wars, it was purely a matter of common sense.

The British, until then, had been against it. The Americans, on the contrary, were always in favour of it. It was advocated by General Pershing since his arrival in France, by Colonel House in the course of his investigating tour of the continent, and by General Tasker M. Bliss at the Committee of Versailles. Finally, President Wilson telegraphed: "Such a measure is the happiest omen of definite success."

The choice of General Foch was singularly felicitous. Through his writings, his teachings, his expert knowledge, and his optimism, Foch had made a deep impression on everyone. He was perhaps the only French general from whom the British were willing to take orders.

Ludendorff and his staff had kept track of the lack of coöperation between the British and the French. It seemed impossible to reconcile these differences sufficiently for the purpose of a sole command.

The actual appointments of Marshal Foch to his post of supreme responsibility impressed the enemy as a purely official fact, corresponding to no reality in the military situation. I thought at the time—I have seen no reason to change my view since—that the Germans failed to grasp the significance of his appointment.

The newly appointed commander-in-chief had absolute confidence in General Pershing, General Pétain, and Marshal Haig. He was determined to take the offensive. Under no circumstances must Ludendorff be permitted to take any initiative.

Once the initiative passed to the Germans, all that we had staked in the game about to open might be lost before night.

The initiative!

Ludendorff and the general staff at German headquarters meant to seize it, to retain it. That was the warning of their shells.

If the Americans did not fail in the emergency, we might foil Ludendorff. He must have taken the measure of the Americans. He must be well aware that on this July morning Foch could dispose of nine American divisions only. It is true that ten more American divisions were under instruction—some of these, indeed, actually holding sectors between the French and the British. In fact, there were no less than seven American divisions besides those I have mentioned. But we could not yet deem them effectives for the purposes of the battles just ahead. They had only lately arrived from their camps at home. We dared not risk them in their condition. All Europe was awaiting, with a natural curiosity, the outcome of the American experiment. It would have been madness to make the experiment under conditions more favourable to Ludendorff than to ourselves.

I had seen reports by our experts on the subject of the Americans. There were two theories, I gathered. Some thought our new allies—they had declared war a year before—too inexperienced to be important. Others said they were reckless in action. All agreed that they required training, training, training. Obviously! But, despite what we were told by our British friends, a soldier cannot be made in a year.

All these considerations ran riot in my head on that day in July, 1918, as I listened to the motors setting our own cars and lorries and guns and tanks into an activity that indicated the execution of a critical manœuvre on our side.

My impression was confirmed by a bulletin announceing the entry of no less than two hundred and forty-five thousand Americans into the movement. Through this force, Marshal Foch meant to seize and retain the initiative.

Long before the Americans actually moved up to the front lines, everybody seemed to know that they were coming over in great numbers. During their furloughs, our soldiers saw the countryside covered with American camps and schools and everyone repeated what General Savatier's poilu had said in April, when Colonel Malone arrived with his 23rd Regiment: "It is the beginning of the end."

There was even danger that the poilu would figure too much on being replaced by the doughboy, and would not want to sacrifice himself as before! This danger was recognized by the commander-in-chief in a letter of June 19th to the Minister of War in which he said: "Not by a long shot is the American army powerful enough to throw the balance in our favour at the moment. The country must not think that we may limit our efforts and become mere spectators."

I know now (although I merely suspected it then) that Ludendorff and the men in Berlin set great store by the weariness of the Allies.

We had been told again and again that the Americans would not come.

The ministry at Paris knew better. Again and again

the defeatist propaganda at home had said that the Americans would not come.

American bluff! That was the German reply to every official assertion at Paris that France had in the Americans allies who would "come."

"We have allies," Clemenceau shouted in the chamber, "who are coming!"

Everything depended upon how they would come—like giants or like pygmies? Effectually or ineffectually?

Ludendorff, now the dominant mind in the councils of the enemy, was taking no chances.

He would not wait until we had taught our new allies whatever they could learn from ourselves.

Ludendorff's hope of breaking through our front, of piercing a vital point, of thus ending the struggle, was not unreasonable.

His opinion was shared by the great Berlin general staff.

I am well aware that in the Allied countries at this time there prevailed an impression that Ludendorff was in fact the war lord of Germany. He was assumed to have eclipsed the great Hindenburg. As for the Kaiser, he had sunk to insignificance at home.

The truth I take to be that Ludendorff was at all times under the influence of the general staff in the German capital.

The best military minds in Germany had worked out a calculation based, as we were later to learn, upon a fairly accurate estimate of the strategical situation.

Ludendorff, Hindenburg, and the rest of them relied upon the advantage they derived from the rectangular line of the front. Behind this line, they had the use of railways built with special reference to strategical considerations and for the purpose of a war on two fronts.

With reference to ourselves they enjoyed the enormous advantage of interior lines. It was a simple matter to Ludendorff to concentrate the masses of his troops within his lines at either angle and then direct them speedily to right or to left, toward the Lys, the Somme, Noyon, or La Champagne. In making these calculations Ludendorff could depend likewise upon a numerical superiority at the points of contact with ourselves. We on our side, with the Americans, might outnumber him, but he was in a position, for the moment, to outnumber us wherever we were most likely to collide with him.

Ludendorff had given his commanders—and in this he carried the great weight of the name of Hindenburg with him—detailed orders regarding his offensive. It was to be thorough. It was to be violent. It was to embrace the element of surprise.

I had seen what the Germans were capable of in the way of an offensive when they rushed upon Amiens in the previous March. The situation had been saved for us then through a bold use of the French reserves. They leaped into the void left when the Germans overwhelmed the exhausted and scattered British. There was a dark day, indeed, when General Debeney, who then commanded our First Army, had with only a few members of his staff held quite a stretch of an abandoned front. Not until the next day could his forces, arriving in their trucks, reach and support their commander!

Ludendorff got no news of this heroic feat until it was too late to be of use to him. But it impressed him and his staff. They meant now to repeat what they had accomplished in the spring, and I felt certain that no episodes like that of which General Debeney was the hero would find the foe asleep.

But the Americans would have to do the rushing into any voids that Ludendorff might effect in this month of July!

He did not, I am certain, overlook that consideration. But he failed to take it with sufficient seriousness.

Marshal Foch lost no time in attaining that unity of purpose among the Allies which was to be the effect of the unity of command. He used his authority to issue a strict order to General Pétain. That gifted strategist was to prepare a plan of campaign for the days ahead—a plan permitting the closest coöperation of all the Allied armies: British, French, American, Belgian, in the attainment of an ultimate offensive.

Pétain's strategy, by which I mean his plan of campaign as a whole, never lost touch with his tactics—that is, his operations on the field of battle. Pétain was not one of those commanders who win brilliant but useless victories. He emerged from that severest of all tests of a great captain: the conduct of a retreat. He could lead an army into battle but he could likewise lead it out, this last being usually the most difficult task of all.

His manner was cold and reserved. Beneath that somewhat frigid exterior beat a heart that loved the man in the ranks. And the man in the ranks was quick to discern this feeling and return it.

General Pétain's appearance at this difficult moment in the capacity of master strategist—and that, too, at the behest of Foch—confirmed the impression formed of him by the Americans. Those among the Americans who held high command felt sure that Pétain did not relish the stationary, reposeful, inert sort of war now prevalent. Pétain had shown as much in the collisions with the foe that began in the spring. Not that he was reckless in his application of the idea.

"We must," I heard him say among a group of us, "take the offensive when we can seize it, but for the moment we must practise the defensive."

This was what is known in military textbooks as an "offensive-defensive." Pétain had a marvellous gift for lucid exposition. He had displayed it years before, when I was among his pupils at the War School.

"He spoke only four minutes," I heard one of my classmates say to another at the time, "but he has given us the fruits of as many hours of meditation."

The gift that served him so well then shone brightly now. He made obvious to British and to Americans, as well as to ourselves, the reasons which prompted him to open our impending campaign with a few coördinated movements. His logic was irresistible, his initiative exquisite. His plan enabled every member of the high command to grasp his own part in it.

In all that he said and did, General Pétain was sustained by Marshal Foch who, in turn, was supported by General Pershing. We, on our side, were determined to permit no useless sacrifice of American lives by any premature advance. Whether the Germans understood our dilemma at that moment I do not know.

General Pétain brought us inspiring news of the progress of the Americans in their camps and schools. We heard that, in the zone of operations, they were prone to forward rushes, disinclined to stay in trenches. But this was a good sign.

We were still further encouraged by what we learned from the enemy. On one occasion some deserters explained to me that German troops brought to the western front from Russia had been bolshevized by contact with Soviet troops. They seemed to develop a revolutionary mood, with which their commanders found it more and more difficult to cope.

I do not mean that this mood affected the enemy's morale sufficiently to influence the operations of Ludendorff in front of us. General Pétain agreed with me that the Germans were showing determination. Their attacks were at times all but annihilating.

They would begin their morning's work with a bombardment. When the shells had prepared a path for them, they advanced several lines of infantry. We could not always see them through the smoke screen. They covered the advance of their infantry with a rain of shells, usually followed by the shrieking projectiles from their *Minenwerfer*.

I had whole companies wiped out one week.

Our men were no longer fighting shoulder to shoulder. The gaps in our lines were discovered by the enemy. His penetrations were stealthy yet incessant. I had to order counter attacks, at the risk of compromising our defensive attitude.

I became certain that Ludendorff was bent upon forcing us into a premature offensive. The trump card in his hands was a forward movement of our forces, before the Americans were in a position to sustain it with us.

General Pétain felt that, at all hazards, the enemy must not gain his object. The American divisions were indispensable to our victory. The seas were heavy with transports. How eagerly I heard Pétain go over the figures of arriving Americans! The 64,000 men, who came to our aid in March, were precious. In April,

93,000 landed on our soil. May brought 244,000. In June came 278,000 more. The July figures were received with a cheer—308,000 men!

No wonder Ludendorff was forcing the pace! Only a few weeks previously General Pershing had gone over with Marshal Foch the possibility that in the year to come we might make even greater demands than these upon our American allies. Perhaps, the Marshal said, we might want a hundred American divisions more—all by the summer of 1919. "Why," General Pershing retorted, "limit us to a hundred divisions?" The question had echoed on the other side of the Atlantic. The Congress in Washington had passed the necessary laws. There was no doubt of the American will to victory now, General Pétain said. I recalled the words of one of my own troops when he saw the Americans come into our camp for the first time in the previous April:

"It is the beginning of the end!"

The fury of the German attacks upon us now served to convince me more and more that Ludendorff must be telling himself the same thing.

But we French were not wholly free from a new sort of dread altogether. Perhaps Marshal Foch himself put it best.

"If and when," he said to the Minister of War, "the American army becomes strong enough to decide the balance in our favour, we must never let ourselves be misled into playing the passive part of spectators."

"Attack!"

Marshal Foch used the word of command to General Pétain during the first week of July—the third, to be exact. There had indeed been attacks in the previous weeks. Americans had taken part in them. But I have in mind now the great general offensive. Just before the fateful order was issued, General Pétain put a question to our chief.

"Why not," he asked, "wait until the enemy has involved himself in his own advance? That will facilitate our offensive, seeing that we have now the advantage of superior numbers."

The idea was tempting. Foch conceded it. He was determined, none the less, to adapt no more Allied movements to those of the enemy. There had been, in the opinion of the Americans, too much of that already.

It would be difficult to convey an idea of the relief with which the announcement was received by the commanders of the American Expeditionary Forces. General Pershing and his division commanders made no concealment of their delight. They had become persuaded that Ludendorff planned a dash to Paris. He had been pent up for some weeks within the salient that lives forever in military history under the name of Château-Thierry. Foch, I suspect, might have been persuaded by Pétain to delay his assumption of the offensive, but for the psychological effect upon our allies from over the ocean. The Americans were now weary of waiting.

The eagerness of the Americans for a rush against the enemy was all the more amazing to me because they were by no means fully prepared. Their lack of artillery was so decided that I received orders to make it good as far as possible from the French machine guns. The Americans were aware also that we had been severely handled in the attacks of Ludendorff. They were in an excellent position to form an opinion of their own.

This they did. I am betraying no secret when I say that their best experts feared for the safety of the French forces. Americans had been with us (though not in great force) when the Germans made their dash at Amiens.[38] The Americans gained some experience later on, as all the world knows, when the enemy had to be faced at Château-Thierry. I shall not dwell upon the participation of the Americans in the actions along the Marne. General Harbord, a seasoned soldier, General Bullard, a daring leader, General Lewis, cool, bold, a master of tactics, to say nothing of the others whom I learned to remember with admiration, had got their impressions of our plight by sharing the perils of our spring skirmishes and our early summer drives. These men seemed to feel that French and British alike were letting the whole war drag.

We were now on the eve of the great struggle for Soissons. Never before since the World War began had there been such a whirl of movement. It seemed for a few days as if every American then on the soil of France was on the go. For the Americans, we must remember, were convinced of our dire need of them. They did not conceal their impression that Paris was within measurable distance of capture. And believing this, they were willing to risk everything upon a single action involving the whole Allied line!

Apparently, they had made a convert of Marshal Foch.

"I am certain," I ventured to tell him, "that the German Crown Prince will attack before many hours."

Marshal Foch did not dispute the accuracy of my information. "Our plan," he said simply, "will go through."

"A general offensive?"

He bent his head gravely. "We take the offensive south of Soissons." I glanced at the map. "We shall be on the defensive in Champagne."

"Who will lead?" I asked the question, expecting that two commanders had been named.

"General Pétain will conduct both battles."

I went back to my headquarters with all the details of the attack at Soissons in my head. The affair might be preceded by a tremendous action in the Champagne and there, too, the Americans were now in force.

If the Germans failed rightly to estimate Foch as supreme commander, some Americans, it appeared to me, were not prepared to interpret him from the French point of view.

Foch stood for what may be called the Napoleonic theories of strategy and tactics.

It seemed important, then, to dwell upon this detail to the Americans. Many of them fancied that all previous experiences of the art of war had been discredited by what we had gone through since July, 1914.

Foch, as an authority on the art and science of strategy, always insisted that in the event of a war with Germany we French must act upon the Napoleonic idea.

His campaigns, the campaigns of Joffre, the principles we were exemplifying—all were Napoleonic.

Foch, as a preceptor at the military schools, long before the World War began, had indoctrinated his pupils with this view of his.

Any departure from the maxims he had derived from the lessons of Napoleonic warfare would have demoralized us. We French must have felt that the fate of the struggle was in the wrong hands. The Germans, true to Napoleonic concepts if we were not, would have turned our flank again and again. The slaughter of Americans would have been terrific.

Fortunately, General Pershing, trained at West Point, saw the situation from Foch's point of view. His influence, together with that of President Wilson and the American staff, was with Foch. The effect upon our own morale was prodigious. We felt that our American allies understood us.

Pershing's influence confirmed us in what we had been doing from the very first day of the struggle—waging a series of Napoleonic campaigns until the enemy was beaten to his knees.

The doom of the German army was sealed, accordingly, upon the day the Americans threw their influence in favour of a single command, with Foch as the directing mind. The outcome of the campaign we were then absorbed in proved a vindication of the Napoleonic art of war.

Before definitely assuming the offensive, the Allies had been put to a severe test when, on the 27th of May, a surprise attack was made by the Germans in the salient of Château-Thierry. At one o'clock in the morning, an intense bombardment of four thousand guns smashed our whole front line from Reims to Soissons. Thirty batteries of guns per kilometre of front line. Never in the history of war had there been such density!

The Germans attacked with thirty-five divisions, sweeping everything before them. The bridges of the Aisne were taken at nine o'clock in the morning, and the Vesle crossed at some places.

In vain did the divisions of the second line attempt to check the German torrent. They were not numerous enough to form a dam. For four days, the enemy, who had broken our line over a stretch of sixty kilometres, continued his onward march, pursuing the remnants of the Sixth Army closely, making prisoners by the thousands, and picking up an enormous amount of materials and supplies. They took Soissons to the west, passed southward Fère-en-Tardenois, Ville-en-Tardenois, dug a salient of great depth, reached Château-Thierry, and followed the Marne from Château-Thierry to Dormans.

While the salient formed, neither Foch nor Pétain remained inactive. They concentrated their efforts on the two pillars, Reims and Soissons, which limited the width of the breach. They estimated, after the personal investigation of Pétain in the midst of the combatants in the Tardenois, that the Marne alone could limit its depth.

The nucleus was the two French armies that were in the region of Beauvais. These were called upon, one to the south of Reims, the other in front of the woods of Villers-Cotterets. Around these two armies, thirty French, British, and American divisions, brought there hastily, but with marvellous precision, constituted again the Fifth Army to the east, and to the west the Tenth Army. From the 31st of May, the two armies thus formed made their action felt on the two flanks of the enemy. They were forced to slow up their forward march. After three days of fighting, the enemy stopped definitely, without being able to cross the Marne.

The 3rd U. S. Division (General Dickman) conducted itself remarkably well. "We were in the camp of Châteauvillain," a liaison officer reported to me, "where we were just finishing our instruction. Instead of going into a quiet sector in the Woëvre, as has been announced, we were thrown in the midst of the battle without our regiments of engineers, and without our artillery. The motorized machine-gun battalion (No. 7) entered first into line and pushed on to Château-Thierry where, in the evening of the 31st of May and the first of June, mixed with the colonial troops of the Division Marchand, it fought foot by foot with the Germans for the suburbs of Château-Thierry and covered itself with incomparable glory."

The 2nd U. S. Division was also to distinguish itself at that date—a fact that did not surprise those who, like myself, had seen it enter the sector. General Harbord, former chief of staff of General Pershing, commanded the famous 4th Marine Brigade, the flower of the corps. The 3rd Brigade (General Lewis) and the 23rd Regiment (Colonel Leroy Upton and Colonel Malone) were anxious to outdo the Marines. The artillery brigade, especially well equipped and trained, was commanded by General Chamberlaine, future chief of the reserve of American artillery of big calibre.

This division proceeded by stages toward the French First Army, when its chief, General Bundy, received orders during the night of the 29th–30th of May to proceed to Lizy-sur-Ourcq, with the infantry on trucks, and the artillery by rail. As soon as they reached their destination, the troops directed themselves in remarkably orderly formation to the enemy lines. It was the true war of movements. The 2nd Division there reaped the fruits of the training in offensive previously ordered by General Pershing and Colonel Malone. On the 1st of June, they supported the French 43rd Division, and on the 2nd of June they went through it and effected immediate contact with the enemy along a front of twelve kilometres.

From the third to the seventh of June, the infantrymen of General Bundy, attacking with fire and with bayonet, began to gain the upper hand over the Germans, forcing them to retreat and taking Bouresches. General Bundy intensified his attacks, and on the moring of the 10th, the brigade of General Harbord at the left attacked Belleau Wood, which is partly full-grown forest, partly copses or glades, including natural caves. These make shell-proof shelters to say nothing of rocks which, fortified with machine guns, form veritable strongholds. The artillery of General Chamberlaine, strengthened by two regiments of .75's and a group of .155 shorts already in place, supported the Marines with forty thousand shells, of which twelve thousand were of big calibre.

An important portion of the woods was taken on the 10th, and on the next day the central part followed, with four hundred prisoners and thirty-seven machine guns. In spite of all the German counter attacks which followed, and in spite of a failure on the 21st, the wood was completely taken on the 25th.

Marshal Foch now definitely formulated his plans for the offensive he contemplated. Already in his instructions of the 26th to the 30th of March, in organizing the defensive, he had sown the seed of the idea. Every one of our divisions, in changing sectors, conducted a war of movements, with the object of taking again the initiative in operations.

When, on the 11th of June, in answer to the attack

of Hindenburg on the salient of Compiègne (an attack which was to spend itself in the swamps of the Aronde), my late chief, General Mangin, went over to the counter offensive along a front of eight kilometres at the head of five divisions, preceded by tanks, it was the beginning of the offensive! Foch felt that the Germans had exhausted themselves in their violent attacks, and though they still had many divisions in reserve, they were morally worn out, from lack of victory. He also considered the Americans to be bringing him enough resources.

On the 14th and 16th of June, he ordered the preparations of an offensive on Soissons, and General Pétain immediately conformed himself to these instructions. He executed the preliminary moves, having as an aim the improvement of the position at the point of departure, as shown by the attacks of the 28th of June on St. Pierre l'Aigle, the 3rd of July on Autreches, and the 8th of July on the farm of Chavigny. There was no question here of a counter offensive, but of an offensive programme prepared long ahead. This was to be inaugurated by the Sixth and the Tenth Armies after they were reënforced.

From the 1st of July, moreover, the intentions of the enemy were known. An officer of the 24th Battalion of Sappers had been made a prisoner and, through him, we learned that a crossing of the river was in preparation at Dormans and the material therefor gathered in the woods.[39] It was the western extremity of the next German attack—the "*Friedenssturm*," the attack to assure peace! The German Crown Prince was to direct it from Jaulgonne[40] to the outskirts of Massiges.

"Why, then," said General Pétain, "shouldn't we wait

until the enemy has already launched his attack, to start our offensive? There are only advantages to be gained."

The idea was tempting, but Foch, who felt himself master of the operations, did not want to subordinate his attitude to that of German headquarters. He ordered us to attack, no matter what happened. He grouped our reserves in such a way as to enable them to engage in both battles—one at our initiative to take the offensive, south of Soissons; the other to take the defensive in the Champagne, awaiting the move of the army.

On the 13th of July, it became evident (because our ways and methods of investigation improved) that the troops under the Crown Prince would attack within forty-eight hours; and Pétain, as soon as he heard of this decision, telegraphed to General Fayolle, Commander of the G. A. R. (Group of Reserve Armies), that the attacks by Mangin and Degoutte must open on the morning of the 18th of July.

The French supreme command was master of the hour. If the Allies were not attacked in the Champagne, the reserves, grouped to ward off this offensive, were to be used to help with the offensive at Soissons.

Three times in the spring of 1918 the Allies were surprised: on the 21st of March (German attack on Amiens); May 27th (attack on Château-Thierry); and to a less degree, in the attack on the Hills of Flanders on April 9th. By "surprise" I mean that the high command did not know definitely, until two or three days before the attack, the exact part of the front against which it would be directed. By then it was too late to take the necessary precautions to limit *quickly* the progress of the attack.

It was not like that on the 15th of July. Command and staff did their very best to fathom the game of the adversary. A betterment in the procedure, an improvement in the processes of plotting by sound, the scientific regulation of the waves of the radio, better exploitation in the field of photographic apparatus, indications given by the films, the bringing up to date of the procedure of ground and aërial observation, were all among the many means by which the intentions of the enemy could he brought to light. The slightest oscillations of the network of their command and their massed reserves could be calculated with almost mathematical precision.

In spite of the fact that Ludendorff again put the measures for camouflage and secrecy under Draconic laws, the quest of information exemplified sufficient skill to prevail this time over the refinements of the enemy.

The information obtained from prisoners was added each day to that gathered from other sources. It became more and more apparent that the enemy burned with eagerness now to launch an extended attack against our lines. In view of these developments, at the command of my chief, General Mangin, I issued the following Army Order on July 14th, in connection with the employment of the 1st and 2nd Divisions, A. E. F.

Order No. 232

The objective of the army, when assuming the offensive, is to break through the enemy's front between the Aisne and the Ourcq, pressing forward continuously in the direction of Fère-en-Tardenois in coöperation with the Sixth Army. Ultimate objectives will be fixed in accordance with results achieved.

The forces employed along the attacking front consist of four army corps, each comprising three or four divisions. The 1st and 2nd Divisions, A.E.F., are to form part of the 20th Army Corps.

The latter, synchronizing its operations with those of the 30th Army Corps, will overrun, from the north and south, the northeastern border of the Forest of Retz, taking Chaudun and Vierzy. Their ultimate objective is the plains to the northeast of Hartennes, to gain a firm hold south of the Ravin of Crise.

MANGIN.

Countersigned,
HELLÉ, *Chief of Staff.*

On July 14th, the truly ant-like activity of the enemy infantry and the surprise attack of the 366th Infantry Regiment at 8 P.M. taught us that the preparation by the enemy artillery would start on the 15th at one minute after midnight and would last from three to four hours. We knew the length of the front upon which they would attack, and the troops which the German Crown Prince had at his disposal.

Between 11:00 and 11:40 P.M. the French artillery, following the information gathered, surprised the German batteries by opening fire on them, also destroying the enemy infantry in their first-line trenches.

Consequently, when at 4:15 the Germans left to attack, their ranks had already been thinned; they were received by an intense barrage, following which they were scattered by small posts, composed of specially picked detachments, which remained in their places and informed our artillery. Their first line needed four hours to cover two or three kilometres, which separated them from the lines of resistance. They got there worn out and exhausted. Nowhere had the line been seriously broken. From the first day, General Gouraud had the distinct impression that the battle was won between Reims and Massiges. The Germans would not pass.

The American 42nd Division (General T. Menoher)

took part in this offensive. This was the "Rainbow Division" made up of the contingents of the National Guard of all the States. It included the 165th and the 166th (83rd Brigade) and the 167th and the 168th Regiments (84th Brigade). It was one of the first four divisions to arrive in France. General Menoher had already led it at the front in the region of Vaucouleurs, then at Rolampont. They distinguished themselves by daring raids, and by a splendid resistance of the 168th near Badonvillers. A few days after their splendid conduct there, they received the visit and congratulations of General Pershing and Secretary Baker.

Having arrived on the 5th of July in the region of Suippes, the division was installed by brigades along the height of the second position; the 83rd (General Lenihan) to the right behind the French 170th Division; the 84th (General Brown) to the left behind the French 13th Division. It had three battalions in front of the so-called intermediary position.

Toward seven o'clock, the enemy infantry engaged this position, and the three American battalions broke all attacks. A battalion of the 166th threw back as many as seven successive attacks. A little later, as the two centres of resistance fell into the enemy's hands, two companies of the 167th American, united to two French companies, counter attacked, recaptured these small redoubts, and threw the enemy back along the whole front.

The artillery of the American 42nd Division was specially singled out by the Germans. "They incurred rather serious losses," it was reported to me, "but their attitude under fire was splendid. They had, moreover, superb targets and they fired for hours direct shots on sight at infantry and artillery columns, which were very effective and vigorously executed."

The American 3rd Division (General Dickman) whose machine-gun battalion had distinguished itself at Château-Thierry a fortnight before, was operating with the Thirty-eighth Army Corps under General Mondesir who reported as follows, on the conduct of these excellent troops:

In vain the enemy tried to cross the Marne in masses. The infantry of General Dickman *fire as if on the butts* and throw back with the bayonets all fractions which have been able to penetrate the front line.

The questioning of prisoners confirms our belief. The substance of reports from prisoners of the opposing German forces was as follows: "On the 15th of July, at ten minutes past midnight, before the bombardment of the German artillery began, the French-American barrage was directed on the northern border of the Barbillon woods; it was the exact spot where the German battalions were to emerge to go down to the Marne. The Germans lost heavily and were broken up in disorder in the woods. When the American artillery fire shortened its range a bit toward the Marne, the men were brought together again by sections and half sections and at last crossed the river in small groups, which included men of all companies. One battalion thus gained the lower bank, where advance was very difficult. Isolated Americans, lying flat in the field, caused us very heavy losses."

The commander of the 9th Company of German 6th Grenadiers reported thus, when questioned: "The operation should have been executed with great ease. We were very much impressed by the conduct of the American troops, who showed great bravery and a great deal of skill in the use of the terrain."

From another prisoner of the 6th Grenadiers: "The fire of the American machine guns prevented the advance of our infantry at the very outset. The 5th and 6th companies had hidden themselves in the ditches where they were surprised from the rear by the Americans and either captured or annihilated."

The Commander of the French Thirty-eighth Army Corps summed up the operations by saying:

If we succeeded in keeping our front line intact and repelling all attacks, we owe it to the very effective fire of the Franco-American artillery and to the magnificent resistance of the infantry of General Dickman.

In short, as far as the Sixth Army was concerned, the enemy scored a complete victory on our extreme right, which had to retreat five or six kilometres, but the Thirty-eighth Army Corps, which included some of the best American troops, remained immovable.

I consider it a great privilege to speak here for my late respected chief, General Mangin, in connection with those all-important days of July, 1918. What I record is based mostly on my own personal knowledge, as chief of staff of General Mangin, and on reports received from ordnance and liaison officers.

The U. S. 1st Division had just gone through two very hard months at Cantigny, reported Captain Crochet, when we received orders to proceed to Dommartin-en-Goele; we thought we would join the U. S. 2nd Division toward Château-Thierry to constitute together the First Army Corps. But in the evening of the 14th of July, a general staff officer brought to General Summerall, commander of the division (replacing General Bullard called to command the Third Army Corps), the first indications concerning the operations of the 18th of July. The U. S. 1st Division was to join the Twentieth Army Corps toward Mortefontaine, north of the forest of Villers-Cotterets, where just prior to deploying the 1st Division, A. E. F., for the attack of July 18th, the headquarters of this division had been established.

As far as the infantry was concerned, there was no

difficulty in shipping them by trucks. However, the problem of transportation seemed well-nigh insoluble to the artillery and the quartermaster's corps, whose horses were in a sorry state indeed. For various reasons, the horses always were a weak point in the American army. On the 14th of July, those of the U. S. 1st Division were exhausted through the preceding marches and certain columns arrived considerably late.

Happily, the U. S. 1st Division was commanded by an energetic man, animated by a spirit of discipline and absolute duty, General Summerall, to whom I am glad to pay my respects.

On the morning of the 15th, the order came "to postpone all movements." Then toward noon another order, to "execute foreseen movements." There were, as is inevitable at such a moment, orders and counter orders which created some difficulties in transportation, but these matters were finally straightened out. Reports from our artillery, however, were extremely disquieting.

To throw an interesting side light on the activities of the 1. C. A. U. S and some brigades of the 4th D. I. U. S, I wish to quote here from an order dated July 16th, issued by my respected colleague, General Degoutte, commanding the Sixth Army.

Personal and secret
No. 3509

In order to threaten the enemy's rear, during operations between Château-Thierry and Reims, the Tenth Army is to take for its first objective the line Saconin-Breuil, Chaudin, Villers-Helon. Results achieved are to be exploited in the general direction toward the plains to the north of Fère-en-Tardenois.

The attack of the 2. A. C. is to be extended to the right by attacks of the 7. A. C. and the 1. C. A. U. S. Minimum objectives to be reached are as follows:

For the 7. A.C., consisting of the 164. D. I. and one U. S. A. brigade:—Chevillon and Saint Gengoulph, with Cointicourt, Hill 172 and Hautevesnes as possible ultimate objectives.

For the 1. C. A. U. S, the small woods to the southeast of Hautevesnes and Torcy-Belleau.

It is to be understood that, while the 2.A.C. is to take advantage of any progress the Tenth Army may be able to make, the 7.A.C. and the 1. C. A. U. S. are expected to follow up all such results as may be gained by the 2.A.C.

There shall be no premature firing before appointed day and hour. The sectors are to maintain their customary appearance. It is to be avoided, at all costs, that prisoners be taken by the enemy.

DEGOUTTE.

The movements on the nights from the 16th to the 17th and from the 17th to the 18th were painstakingly executed. Everybody worked so hard at it and showed so much good will, so much "stick-to-it-ive-ness," that during the night from the 17th to the 18th all the artillery of the U. S. 1st Division got into place; some batteries of .155 C. arrived only two hours before the moment of attack.

These men, officers as well as privates, had lived through terrible weeks at Cantigny. Sanitary conditions were unspeakable. There were lines of forest to penetrate, as well as muddy roads. There was a plague of flies by day and a dearth of trucks at all times. Only the amazing mobility of the Americans made this movement possible.

There was a confusion of orders throughout these preliminary marches which must have had fatal consequences but for American alertness. The men got the "forward" idea. They always acted upon it. Even when we French paused in bewilderment, the Americans were streaming on.

Nor could I help admiring the fortitude of the Americans in submitting to privations to which, in their own country, they had been wholly unaccustomed. In the United States, the humblest people enjoy every sanitary convenience. The theatre of our operations was now so crowded that the filth alone was a plague. How the Americans contrived to keep as clean as they did I cannot imagine.

"General," pleaded an American commander, as he saluted General Mangin, while I stood by, "I have a favour to ask."

"I shall grant it if I can," my chief replied. "What can I do for you?"

"Leave to visit Paris for a few hours."

"To Paris? But why?"

"To get a bath, General."

"The attack is about to open," General Mangin said sympathetically; "otherwise I would let you go with pleasure."

It was perhaps a jest to the American but General Mangin did not think of smiling. He was overwhelmed by the spectacle of suffering and strain to which the Americans were subjected. They endured everything without a groan or a grimace. They even jested at the stalling of trucks. They sang in chorus. They were unhappy only when they could not move. They even marched in single file along blockaded roads. They scrambled on hands and knees through dense forest growths. They left nothing behind them. Guns, trucks, blankets, ammunition, harness, horses—all these they bore with them in a steady stream. They were not once foiled by ditches or disconcerted by obstructions at crossings. Nor must I omit to mention the achievement of the commissary. The men were fed on the American side with a regularity that could not be compared, naturally, with conditions in the rear, but it spoke of efficiency. The men ate, and that fact alone is eloquent.

The "Rainbow Division" lost none of its prestige in these tremendous hours. Under General Menoher, it had already seen stern service elsewhere, but in the Soissons operations it repulsed seven assaults of the enemy. This division, although perilously placed and subject to a rain of shells, was alert in counter attack. I think the Germans were themselves amazed at the mobility of this division, the swiftness with which it could recover from the shock of seeing a position captured, and the ease with which it recovered lost ground.

This "Rainbow Division" was, to be sure, conspicuously placed wherever it participated, and it had by this time been so long in France that we knew it somewhat better than the others. It had suffered cruelly in defending France. It seemed to me to show somewhat less impatience at what its officers may have deemed our "slowness."

Allowance must be made, in considering differences of opinion between the Americans and the French, for the eagerness of our allies to go through the enemy's lines. That we found to be the great American idea. We must go through the enemy's line without delay. We must "speed up."

Such was the spirit of the Americans at Soissons, and to this spirit I attribute the decisiveness of the result there. In the movements for position, prior to the opening of the offensive on the 18th of July, the speed of the Americans made it possible to realize the purpose of Marshal Foch at Soissons.

Most military observers will agree that the action at Soissons in July of 1918 was one of the world's decisive battles. It must, I think, be more than a coincidence that the first battle of the World War in which the American forces participated on a great scale turned the destinies of the conflict.

This tremendous struggle was characterized by the unusual mobility of the forces engaged in it. All observers on the ground agree that the movement of the troops was not only incessant, but on our side well to the front. There seemed to be few of those disheartening pauses which in the progress of a battle leave so much to mere accident and the unforeseen.

American military experts, I know, think we were somewhat inert—the French, I mean, and the British. We are told that if the pace had been livelier the action would have resulted not merely in turning the tide, but in annihilating the enemy.

But nothing could have been livelier than the movement of the Americans to the front. One or two of their divisions simply rushed into the fray. Thousands of the Americans had not slept for more than twenty-four hours when they came under the enemy's fire.

Many Americans fail to distinguish—in the following accounts of the battle near Soissons—the difference between strategy and tactics. It is not always best from even a tactical standpoint—to say nothing of strategy—to force the pace in battle. Napoleon was so deliberate at Austerlitz as to amaze his staff, but he gained his purpose. Speed would have defeated it. The same consideration applies to Marshal Foch's handling of the Germans at the Château-Thierry salient. On the British side, as well as on the side of the French, the war was one of waiting, waiting, waiting. It was because we were in a position to wait the longest that the Allies won.

Naturally, all these considerations failed to impress the Americans. They were fuming and fretting at the delay. They did not neglect the opportunity afforded them by Soissons to push the enemy hard. It may well be that had the Americans been allowed their own way here the enemy might have been disposed of then and there. General Bullard thought so.

Most of us were amazed by the displays on the part of the Americans of what they call, I believe, "hustle." The reports before me as I write, the bulletins from headquarters, the tales still told in war school lectures, are filled with episodes illustrating these American traits. I am at a loss how to arrange them. I shall cite a few instances of what I mean, and I shall not confine myself to the operations in the immediate vicinity of Soissons. The Americans were literally pouring toward the front from points all along the long line that advanced steadily in those July days.

Not many days before the great offensive opened, General Bullard, commanding the American 1st Division, had been promoted to the command of a corps. His place at the head of the division was taken by General Summerall. General Bullard, who had great influence with General Pershing, was the champion of the idea that we were tactically too deliberate. He seemed to favour the strategy of Marshal Foch, but he suspected that we did not realize the strategical conception because we did not fight fast enough.

When General Summerall replaced General Bullard near Soissons, we thought we would have a leader more in touch with our own methods. But I found that General Summerall—a gifted commander and a gallant fighter—wanted to force the pace. I never supposed, in view of the condition of his men and horses, that he would be in line by the day the action opened. His words were by no means optimistic, but he was always better than his word.

"Tell General Mangin," he exclaimed, "the state of my horses!" It was General Mangin who commanded at this point. "I cannot guarantee," General Summerall added, "that all my guns will be at the battle of the 18th of July. But I shall do everything that is humanly possible."

I had heard intimations of the same sort from other Americans. I always felt that they would rush whatever was to be rushed. It transpired that the guns, and General Summerall as well, were on time. It is true that some batteries got into place barely two hours before the attack opened. All the artillery of the American 1st Division, horses or no horses, got into position during the night preceding the opening of the battle.

Let us now turn to the 2nd Division, U. S. A., which fought for forty days. General Harbord, victor of Belleau Wood, took over its command, instead of General Bundy, who was appointed head of an army corps. Certainly they were tired, very tired, but Pétain wanted the American army corps associated with the great offensive. He wanted to put them, if only for a few days, in the "most visible" place of this great offensive action which was the beginning of our victory. Quickly, he moved the two divisions, which were the best American troops, to the left of Mangin, joining them to the Moroccan division—one of our best divisions. He planned to put them all under the orders of the new army corps commander, General Bullard, commanding the American Third Army Corps, but General Bullard, then at Rirement, could not arrive until the morning of the 16th, and his general staff was too restricted to function. Instructions for the army and the army corps had already been issued. To launch such an attack, supported by all the artillery and tanks, with the necessary munitions, and the help of the quartermaster corps, it was indispensable to give orders early. The commanding general of the U. S. Third Army Corps was to function as an assistant to General Berdoulat. As soon as the offensive succeeded, he was to take his army corps to another active part of the front.

My late chief, General Mangin, was delighted to receive American divisions to coöperate in his offensive. He wished to see all the units before they entered into line. An American general presented his troops, and proved to him the marked enthusiasm of each of his regiments for the impending attack. General Mangin congratulated his American ally, expressing his satisfaction at the fine troops, whose courage was already famous with the French.

"We were held up during the whole day of the 15th," a liaison officer reported to me, "because we had to be on the alert against a possible German attack. At last, our infantry was taken away in trucks in the direction of the forest of Villers-Cotterets. Our mounted troops got there by the roads."

"It was with the greatest spirit of sacrifice," another liaison officer told me, "that the Marine Brigade and the 3rd Brigade, forgetting their fatigue, hastened to the forest of Villers-Cotterets and went through it, despite the greatest difficulties.

"The American infantrymen, in their deep yellow uniforms (very deep yellow, when belonging to the Marines), finding no more room on the overcrowded road, marched in single file along the ditches of this big road and slipped between the trees of the forest. At every crossing of the roads were encumbrances disentangled by the gendarmes and the M.P.'s. While the infantrymen sneaked through the woods, the artillerymen displayed great initiative and courage in getting their guns up to the firing positions, which the chief officers had decided upon the day before. They prepared their firing minutely after plans and maps, since it was forbidden to fire ranging shots. On the 17th of July, at four o'clock in the morning, the whole 2nd Division, *nearly* complete, was ready to rush to the attack."

My chief, General Mangin, had been entrusted with the task of surprising the right flank of the Germans and cutting them off from Soissons, thus helping to empty the pocket of Château-Thierry. In the course of this enterprise, many incidents developed clearly demonstrating the spirit which animated the American troops.

General Savatier of the staff of Marshal Foch was visibly surprised when I informed him what was expected of the Americans.

"They will coöperate in the surprise attack on the German right flank!" As I spoke, I wondered if the Germans would be as surprised as my colleague was then. "They will be used," I went on, "to cut the Germans off from Soissons."

General Savatier spoke emphatically: "That's it! The Château-Thierry salient must be straightened out. The American rush at Soissons will make this certain."

I learned that the 1st and 2nd American divisions

were already strung along, some right next to the Moroccans, others by the side of our own troops.

At four o'clock on July 18th, General Mangin and myself reached a high tree, where an observation post had been installed for him at the border of the woods. I remained at the post of command, near the telephone, when there came a call from the Twentieth Army Corps.

"Hello. This is the Twentieth Army Corps. An American division which we thought completely ready for the attack informs us that its column of machine guns has been cut off and will not be able to join the division to-night."

"*Diable*," was the reply. "What do the Americans say about it? Will they be able to attack anyhow?"

The answer came back: "They say that with or without machine guns they'll attack, and if they do not receive them, they'll take them away from the Boches."

I could hardly believe the report. To my amazement, General Berdoulat, commanding the corps of which the American division in the forest formed a part, confirmed every word when I rang him up.

It seemed to me as if the very next moment every gun along the front, from the Aisne to the Marne, was roaring to heaven. But I had not reckoned with the resourcefulness of the Americans. General Berdoulat told me later that the Americans picked up what guns they could as they sped among the trees to the open. Between them and the enemy was a network of wire entanglements and a medley of shell holes.

From the height of his observation post, General Mangin and myself followed the advance of the first line. In order to make the most of this first success he ordered me to put the light tanks, which he had kept with the army reserves, at the disposal of the Twentieth and Thirtieth Corps. He also commanded the Twentieth Cavalry Corps to come nearer to the first line to take advantage of the breach made in the enemy's first line. But this cavalry had the greatest difficulty in getting out of the woods and realized that nothing could be done on horseback. The enemy, as quickly as possible, reënforced his right. He did not want his lines of communications cut off from Soissons.

"I had a good view of the scene," General Berdoulat told me later on. "The air was clear, for the rains had washed it thoroughly. It was dawn when I scanned our line at the opening of the attack. Our tanks made a din. The whole front was lit up. First came a flame, then the guns. It was like lightning followed by thunder. Then I saw the flash of the signal rockets. Our infantry was asking the artillery to lengthen the range."

"Ha!" I could not resist an expression of my delight. "That meant the infantry were on the go. The Americans!"

General Berdoulat nodded. "The Americans had gone on out of the forest through the barrage. It was as early as six o'clock when they got to the linden tree of La Glaux. That was the 1st Division. The 2nd reached the Beaurepaire Farm[41] in a run. By seven o'clock the Americans were in the ravine of Missy.[42] In fact, a great many of them were as far as Vauxcastille. In two hours more, they were masters of Ploisy,[43] holding many German prisoners."

Familiar as I was with the swiftness of the Americans by this time, the persistence of their rush and "go" later on in the course of this same advance again took me by surprise.

General Summerall had advanced his headquarters to Cœuvres within three days. No wonder General Harbord got as far as Vertefeuille Farm[44] in the same time. As for General Bullard, he kept on and on. He and his men were on the outskirts of Tigny by the time I had moved ahead to Montgobert. What a toll of prisoners the Americans had taken!

I do not wonder they got out of touch with the Moroccans. We were quite unprepared for such fury in an attack. I was anxious to have the Americans relieved. They had been under a strain for days.

"General Bowley"—I had an American at the other end of the telephone wire—"you will be relieved this very night."

"Impossible!" he replied. "It is a question of honour. We have hundreds and hundreds of shells sent to us by the enemy. We want to return the compliment before we go."

The Americans were the chief subject of discussion wherever the French and the British exchanged impressions of this offensive.

"You mustn't suppose," I heard one of my officers say, "that the Americans had easy ground to cover. Nor did they have behind them an artillery that played on the enemy to facilitate their advance. The Americans had to flounder across ditches that were piled high with dead horses. They crossed ground raked by the fire of the enemy. They were a day without water in a terrific heat. They lost in some instances all the commanding officers of a regiment except the non-commissioned ranks."

As far as this phase of the campaign is concerned, General Berdoulat, commander of the Twentieth Army Corps, to-day more than ever, is of the opinion that the most striking development in the course of the whole enterprise was the enormous advance of the first day, with its relatively slight losses, and the slight results afterward obtained at the cost of great losses. The reason for this is that, on the first day, we profited by the primary asset of every success in war—*surprise*. Moreover, the attacking troops were well under the control of their chiefs, advancing in order and directly supported by the fire of their artillery.

From the second day on, our artillery failed to locate exactly the advanced columns because, through lack of practice, the American troops could not point out the first lines to the aëroplanes. In consequence, the enemy was able to bring out his machine guns, either from the ravines or the caves, so numerous in the region of Villemontoire, without being fired upon by our artillery.

Against machine guns bravery is futile. Every troop coming under their fire was instantly destroyed, unless they sheltered themselves at once and fired effectively upon the adversary.

There was no heed of large effective forces, but of small, almost invisible supply columns, creeping along the recesses of the ground, supported mutually and successively by the fire of their heavy and light machine guns.

The two American divisions were in marvellous form, and their conduct gained for them the following appreciation in an official document of July 22, 1918.

Their offensive spirit is indisputable; it has, in fact, been noted by the enemy in a written document found a month ago, referring to the 2nd D.I.U.S.

To this ardour we must attribute the heavy proportion of loss suffered. In his desire to come immediately into a hand-to-hand fight, the American officer (as well as soldier) often loses sight of the precautions necessary to avoid useless losses. The attacking units are not scattered enough. Evidently, they are still somewhat lacking in experience.

The necessary liaison practice has not been acquired, either for the work outside or in the division itself. The communication system is not thoroughly carried out. Its absence is the inevitable consequence of an insufficiently organized liaison. It must be said here that telephone communications were extremely difficult; that their frequent interruption, combined with the blocking of the roads, made the transmission of certain reports very slow and difficult and even altogether impossible.

The ammunition supply worked well. That of food was less satisfactory. This is due, in the main, to difficulties of traffic, and to the order that ammunition was to have the right of way. Certain units of the 6th Marines received no food supply during two days of battle and were forced to live on their reserved rations.

The supplying of water was also very difficult. Many water tanks arrived empty. As the water resources of the region were deficient, owing to the recent drought, the 6th Marines were not supplied with water during forty-eight hours.

This simple quotation shows the necessity for a troop to be well instructed—something which cannot be attained without sufficient time. In the furnace of battle there is no facility for explanations; the chief must know his job thoroughly and be understood and followed by his soldiers upon the merest sign. The comment also gives an idea of the energy and self-sacrifice required, in order that those new American troops should, in a few hours, gather their magnificent trophies: 6,250 prisoners and 146 cannon.

At the two extremities of the big offensive, which shortened the duration of the war, all combatants, Allies and enemies, were witness to the fact that the American army corps spent, without stint, their young ardour and their fine courage!

General Degoutte, commanding the Sixth Army, in a General Order of August 9th, clearly emphasized the important part played by the Americans. In this General Order General Degoutte said:

General Order

Before the big offensive of the 18th of July, the American troops, which formed part of the French Sixth Army, distinguished themselves by taking from the enemy the Woods of the Marine Brigade and the village of Vaux, stopping the offensive on the Marne and at Fossoy (6 kilometres east of Château-Thierry).

Since then, they played the most glorious part in the Second Battle of the Marne, competing in ardour and bravery with the French troops. During twenty days of incessant fighting, they freed numerous French villages and made, through difficult country, an advance of 40 kilometres, which took them beyond the Vesle. Their halting places will mark the names which, in the future, shall illustrate the military history of the United States: Torcy, Belleau, Plateau d'Etrepilly, Epieds, Le Charmel, l'Ourcq, Seringe-et-Nesles, Sergy-on-the Vesle, and Fismes.

The young divisions, which had their baptism of fire, showed themselves worthy of the ancient warlike traditions of the regular army. They were possessed of a firm determination to beat the Boche and ruled by that discipline which always demands the execution of any order given by the chief, no matter how many difficulties must first be overcome or sacrifices made.

The splendid results attained were due to the energy and skill of the commanders, and the bravery of the soldiers. I feel proud of having been in command of such troops.

DEGOUTTE.
Commanding General of the Sixth Army

What led to most comment, after the big offensive, was the fact that together with the old troops of Summerall and the Marines of Harbord, such young divisions as Haan's, not even trained in battalion schools, threw themselves spiritedly into the battle at the right wing of Degoutte. The National Guards of Pennsylvania, who made up this division, had their hearts in the right place. Their morale was peerless. General Muir, or "Uncle Charley" as his men called him, was anxious to see his division reorganized and put into action.

The training of the Americans was lamentably inadequate. The officers had little experience in war; consequently, they showed a tendency to attack with infantry in too close formation, which resulted in heavy losses. The general staffs proved even more inexperienced. All this was inevitable, but because of it the Americans are deserving of all the more praise.

The Old Guard of Napoleon said: "It is with our legs that he wins his battles!" The young American divisions won their battles and ours with their morale!

PART FOUR

AMERICAN OPERATIONS IN THE ST. MIHIEL SALIENT

AMERICAN OPERATIONS IN THE ST. MIHIEL SALIENT

I

INTRODUCTORY NOTE

THE triangle in which the St. Mihiel battles were fought rests on St. Mihiel, Haudiomont, and Pont-à-Mousson. The apex of the triangle, the reader may recall, was St. Mihiel, while its base extended from the neighbourhood of Haudiomont in a southeasterly direction toward Pont-à-Mousson. This salient, "sticking out like a sore thumb," was a remnant of the first stage of the war, when mobile warfare gave way to trench warfare.

The German supreme command had considered repeatedly the abandonment of this unnatural position, which constituted the weakest link in the iron chain drawn by the Germans across France and Belgium. In the fighting in the Aisne-Marne region the German supreme command took the initiative. After the American counter drive of July 18th the Germans came to understand that the new opponent from across the sea was determined to assume the initiative himself. American activities in the Château-Thierry–Soissons–Fismes triangle and on the Ourcq had hardly died down when the A. E. F. undertook to wipe out the St. Mihiel salient.

The resulting battles are depicted graphically by General von Ledebur and General Savatier. It was at

St. Mihiel that, according to Ludendorff, Pershing for the first time gave his measure as an army leader, in the course of an independently executed offensive movement.

The success of the American counter drive of July 18th convinced the Germans that the St. Mihiel salient would be Pershing's next objective. They determined to straighten out the salient in order to strengthen the front as a whole. This operation required great circumspection. Under no circumstances must the enemy overrun them before the new positions were sufficiently prepared. The German staff worked out detailed plans for the evacuation of the salient and the withdrawal to a prepared line of defense, the so-called Michel Position. The German command was determined to duplicate its surprising exploit now known as the Siegfried Movement. They needed time to prepare the new line and to move vast stocks of war material. They could accomplish their purpose according to schedule only if the expected attack did not take them by surprise. But the attack did come as a surprise! It burst upon Army Unit C on September 12th and did not relax until General von Ledebur's panic-stricken men were driven to the Michel Position. It was not a strategic retreat but a rout.

General Ledebur, who was acting as chief of staff to the late Lieutenant General von Fuchs, the commander of Army Unit C, describes in detail both the laborious preparations for the German withdrawal and their precipitous retreat. The Germans, in their reckoning, miscalculated the factor of time. The attack came at what General von Ledebur terms "the most unfavourable moment imaginable." The German general adds a variety of explanations for the St. Mihiel defeat, which he attributes in part to the whirlwind attacks of the Americans.

General Savatier reviews the battles around St. Mihiel from his own observations, with the aid of data supplied for this purpose by Captain Crochet of the French Liasion Service. The impetus of the American onslaught was so terrible that the Germans first believed that they were facing battle-hardened French or British contingents. The American operations at St. Mihiel taught the Germans that their new enemy was the most formidable force in the "big push."

II

RUSHING THE ST. MIHIEL SALIENT

By Major General Baron Otto von Ledebur, former Chief of General Staff, German Army Unit C

UPON his arrival in France in the summer of 1917, General John J. Pershing expressed his astonishment that the Allied armies had not yet attacked and wiped out the St. Mihiel salient. It still protruded into the lines of the Allies not unlike a sore thumb. As a matter of fact, this salient was a most tempting objective for an attack. This part of the front constituted one of the few points at which it was possible for the Allies to stage an encircling offensive movement.

To the south of Verdun, our front line projected like the somewhat flattened apex of a wedge, from the Woëvre Plain up to the Heights of the Meuse. Both flanks of this position were bent sharply back; in the north toward the fortress of Verdun, to the south against the Nancy–Toul line of fortifications.

How was it possible that the Germans had chosen such a dangerous, and as General Ludendorff himself expressed it, such an "unnatural" position, holding on to it for four long years?

A word of explanation is in order here.

This position was not chosen by the German supreme command. It simply developed in the course and during the last stages of mobile warfare in the autumn of 1914. At that time—toward the middle of September—more than two German army corps, both their flanks covered against attacks by the French from the direction of the fortified Heights of the Meuse, the so-called Côtes Lorraine, advanced from the Woëvre Plain to force the crossing of the river. The ultimate goal of this enterprise was to join the army of the German Crown Prince on the other bank of the Meuse, thus separating the fortress of Verdun from the region beyond it. Had this movement succeeded, the capitulation of the isolated corner stone of the French front would have been merely a question of time.

The first part of this difficult task—forcing the Heights of the Meuse—was successfully accomplished by the Germans, albeit with severe losses. They even succeeded in taking, by storm, the defensive works of the Camp des Romains near St. Mihiel, thereby gaining a bridgehead over the Meuse. However, a further German advance on the other bank of the river was forestalled by the arrival of new enemy forces. At the same time, strong French counter attacks from the north and south prevented an extension of the base of attack. Thus, what was originally a stage of the German advance, in the course of a gradual change from mobile warfare to trench warfare, degenerated into nothing but an unfavourable, wedge-like position.

There were various reasons why the German supreme command did not renounce the unfavourable position thus forced upon it. An essential factor was the expectation that whenever the offensive on the west front should be resumed, the St. Mihiel salient would serve as a postern gate for a sortie. This, if sufficiently supported between the Meuse and the Argonne, would aim once more at cutting off Verdun. Another reason presented itself in the fact that withdrawal of the German position from the Heights of the Meuse to the Woëvre Plain would expose the war-economically important Briey-Longwy Iron Basin, including the Metz–Longuyon railroad to the long-distance artillery fire of the enemy.

In the spring of 1915, the forces under General Hermann von Strantz, stationed in the St. Mihiel sector, proved the objective of severe French attacks. These apparently aimed at "pinching off" the salient. For this reason, the enemy mostly directed his endeavours against the bent-back flanks of the German position. Along the heights of Les Esparges-Combres as well as along the south front near Thiaucourt and the Bois le Prêtre, very severe and bloody battles ensued, lasting for weeks. This fighting eventually ceased, with the definite repulse of all French attacks by the Germans. Moreover, on the Heights of the Meuse proper, splendidly localized German attacks had succeeded in improving our positions opposite the south front of Verdun.

In the course of the later German offensive against Verdun, commencing in February, 1916, and lasting well into the summer, the German supreme command renounced any intention of reaping advantages from the St. Mihiel salient. There were not enough troops available to support an attack against Verdun from the north sustained by pressure simultaneously exerted by von Strantz from the south, together with an additional forcing of the Meuse. Thus it happened that the St. Mihiel sector developed into a decidedly quiet part of the front, where no developments of any importance occurred during 1916 and 1917.

Once more, in the later stages of the war, the German

supreme command took under consideration the advisability of utilizing the St. Mihiel salient as the base for a larger offensive movement. This was in the winter of 1917–1918 when General Ludendorff drew up his plans for the last great offensive. It was intended to bring about a decision in the western theatre of war before America's entrance made itself felt. At that time was discussed a plan which aimed at cutting off Verdun—thus forcing the capitulation of the fortress—by two attacks to be launched in corresponding directions from the Champagne, and from the Heights of the Meuse.

In my position as chief of the general staff of General Fuchs, who by this time had taken over the command of Army Unit C, I felt it incumbent upon myself to oppose the employment of these forces in connection with this project. The suggestion was referred to as the "Castor and Pollux Plan," details of which were being worked out. My opposition was based on the fact that the flattened apex of the wedge-like sector of St. Mihiel did not possess a sufficiently broad base to serve as jumping-off positions for a simultaneous launching of strong forces across the Meuse. My point of view proved a factor in General Ludendorff's ultimate decision to abandon this plan.

On the other hand, the German supreme command was long aware that it would prove impossible to repel a serious attack by strong forces in the region of the "faulty triangle." What was still a possibility in the spring of 1915 must ultimately prove futile on account of the destructive energy of weapons employed in a modern attack, an energy ever tremendously accelerating.

Thus, it had been resolved, that in the case of a major

offensive of the enemy no decisive battle was to be accepted in the St. Mihiel salient, but rather that the latter was to be given up in good time. To this end, as early as 1916, an essentially shortened tangent position along the general line of Ville-en-Woëvre–Harville–Jonville–Rembercourt was laid out straight through the Woëvre Plain, to be subsequently reënforced. This line was known as the Michel Position. Detailed plans for withdrawal to it had meanwhile been prepared by our superior army command. The retreat was to be conducted similarly to the well-known "Siegfried Movement" in the spring of 1917 when we surprised our opponents by withdrawing the German defensive front from ground rendered untenable against persistent attack by shell craters and mud during the Somme battle. This withdrawal was to the much shorter and effectively fortified Hindenburg Line.

Analogous to the "Siegfried Movement," the salient of St. Mihiel was to be given up only then when there were unmistakable signs of an imminent major offensive by the enemy. Here, the greatest difficulties for a successful conduct of the retreat manifested themselves. Everything depended on the timely recognition, beyond all doubt, of the objectives of the enemy attack and of such preparations as our opponents might be making.

Even by spring and at the beginning of summer, 1918, the St. Mihiel salient remained a quiet sector. To the north, inaugurated by the German offensive, tremendous battles were in progress. Thus it happened that in summer, 1918, our Army Unit C was exclusively made up of such divisions as had either participated in the great battles in the north and had been transferred to our quiet sector to regain their fighting stamina, or else of such divisions as were only suited for quiet trench operations, like the 5th, 81st, and 13th Territorials Divisions. In addition to these troops, the Austrian 35th Infantry Division was, since the beginning of August, stationed southwest of the Combres Heights for the purpose of acclimatizing itself to the conditions in the western theatre of war.

The condition and fighting value of enemy units opposing us presented probably the same picture, at least as far as our west front and the St. Mihiel salient (up to the region adjacent to Fort Liouville) were concerned. Here, French troops had been stationed. However, in the south, our Army Unit C faced new American divisions which even extended down the front of our neighbour to the left, the Nineteenth Army, as far to the east as the Moselle. By that time, the Americans were no longer unknown opponents of ours. Already as early as April, 1918, the American 2nd Division had been employed against the protruding corner of our St. Mihiel position, while the 26th Division, A. E. F. (which later on, under the leadership of General Edwards, participated with distinction in the battles in northern France), had been employed against our south front.

Naturally, of course, we sought to ascertain the fighting value and the stuff of which the American soldier was made, by capturing as many prisoners as possible. About the third week of April, by advancing against the American 2nd Division without any preparatory artillery fire and with only a few companies of infantry, in the neighbourhood east and southeast of Maizey, we succeeded in capturing twenty-five men of the 9th Infantry Regiment, A. E. F. These prisoners made a good impression, from a military point of view. They were all well fed, strong individuals, doubtless possessing valuable military potentialities. Those who were not actually taken by surprise in their dugouts, gave a very good account of their fighting spirit, not only by effective machine-gun fire but also by the employment of cold steel in hand-to-hand encounters. Still, they utterly lacked practical war experience. According to their own statements, they had been prepared for trench warfare, but they were not, by any means, completely trained for it.

On April 20th, while attacking the 26th Division, A. E. F., we succeeded, with the aid of gas and a short preparatory artillery fire, in advancing to the third line of our opponent. This was eventually taken, together with the village Seicheprey, after we had overcome very stubborn resistance.[45] The attack yielded four officers, one chief surgeon, and about one hundred and eighty men of the 102nd Infantry Regiment, A. E. F., as prisoners.

Here, I wish to quote a report in regard to the fighting value of the American soldier:

> Almost all the way through, the American soldiers make a good military impression, and, to a certain extent, put up a strong resistance. Officers, as well as enlisted men, remarked: "That we are lacking in training and actual war experiences we may have proved to you to-day, but we are surely not lacking in courage." This self-estimate undoubtedly contains much truth. As soon as the American soldier, after more thorough training and greater experience, gains greater confidence in himself and his officers, he is sure to prove an opponent not to be underestimated in trench warfare. For actual offensive purposes, the American soldier is hardly to be considered formidable for the time being. The repeated statement is made by prisoners that they are utterly lacking in war enthusiasm and confidence in the success of their own arms. Their growing understanding of superior German generalship and fighting value is manifesting itself.

Quite interesting, too, is the following deduction in regard to the war which seemed to prevail generally among the American prisoners:

> Their political views fully coincide, maintaining that America, i.e., Big Business, merely entered the war for the purpose of recovering the money advanced to the Entente nations.

I, myself, remember these words of one of the prisoners: "This is a hell of a war. We have just about enough of it!"

The front of Army Unit C consisted of three distinct group sectors: Combres, Mihiel, and Gorze, with the right wing of the Combres sector linked up with the Fifth Army to the south of the Verdun–Etain highroad. The front line of the Combres sector was held by three divisions, whereas the two other groups had only two divisions each in their advanced positions. It is evident that the higher commanding officers of Army Unit C, in view of the unique projecting position which the troops held in the St. Mihiel salient, and which seemed to invite an encircling movement, were continually on the lookout for possible preparations for an attack by the enemy.

I have already mentioned that as soon as the intentions of the enemy to launch a major offensive became obvious, it was decided to give up the St. Mihiel salient. A memorial, given out by the superior army command under date of June 21, 1918, and entitled "Instruction for Defensive Action Michel," contained most minute details for the execution of these operations. They were worked out on the assumption that the enemy, in case of a major offensive, would either simultaneously, or with very little difference as to time, advance against both fronts of Army Unit C.

"While action is developed around the projecting corner of St. Mihiel," said the memorial, "attempts at opening a wide breach might be directed against groups Combres and Gorze." The principal attacks of the enemy were expected on the west front: in the plains from the direction of the Haudiomont–Trésauvaux line toward the Harville–Woël-Avillers line, simultaneously with an attack against the Côtes between Combres and Mouilly, and an auxiliary attack to be launched through the open country, from the neighbourhood of Lamorville, in the direction of Hattonchâtel. On the south front the onslaughts were anticipated from the line Seicheprey–Regniéville in the direction of St. Benoit-en-Woëvre–Dampvitoux.

In regard to the planned withdrawal to the Michel Position, two possibilities were taken into consideration: The first was a withdrawal according to plan, in case the major offensive of the enemy were recognized in time. Next would come measures for withdrawal to the Michel Position, in case the major offensive of the enemy developed as a surprise.

In the first case, eight days were allowed for the removal of war material and destruction of defensive works, while the ensuing withdrawal to the Michel Position was to be executed in the course of four consecutive nights. Details of these retreat operations already existed under the code name "Loki." During the eight days allowed for the removal of war materials and the destruction of our defensive works, the salient was to be held in order to cover these operations. There was no intention of reënforcing the first line by bolstering it up with additional divisions. To prevent deep breaches through the flanks of Army Unit C, four divisions ready for immediate action were considered necessary. They were to be employed in such a way as to flank the advancing enemy, if possible, thus forcing them to retreat. Of course, reënforcements of artillery and flyers of all kinds were available.

When relinquishing the St. Mihiel salient, not only the removal of great stocks of war material was to be stressed, but—analogous to our procedure during the Siegfried Movement—it was also planned to destroy all defensive works as thoroughly as possible. Moreover, the terrain to be abandoned to the enemy was to be left as impassable and devastated as possible, to make things in general difficult for him. Batteries not provided with teams of horses, as well as heavy and light mine throwers, were to be removed from the front to the Michel Position as early as feasible. Unreliable elements of the population were to be transported to the rear and sent inland in good time as a means of keeping our plans secret.

The actual withdrawal during the four "Loki nights" was to be performed by sectors, the single groups being expected to cover each other. Also, to conceal our intentions, numerous officers' raiding parties were to be employed, reënforced by machine guns and light field pieces. These raiding parties had orders to retreat only when actually pressed by the enemy, and were supposed to keep in constant touch with him.

While our right neighbour, the Fifth Army, was prepared for a general attack of the enemy along the left wing of its main position, our left neighbour, the Nineteenth Army, was instructed that all its forces stationed on the west bank of the Moselle must withdraw to the Michel Position, in accordance with operations of Army Group Gorze.

Things in general, however, would be entirely different if the enemy's major offensive should come as a surprise, like the Cambrai battle and the first German offensives in 1918. If the enemy drove a deep wedge into one or the other part of the salient, and if this were not balanced quickly enough by counter attacking, it would prove necessary to retreat to the Michel Position precipitately. In this event, the retreat was to be executed in only two nights, with the work of removal of war material and destruction of defensive works greatly curtailed. In case of a quick, deep break through our lines (naturally interfering greatly with a systematic evacuation) efforts must be concentrated upon holding open at least a part of the rearward lines of communication, for the retreat of the flank not penetrated by the enemy. To this end, we expected to utilize the wooded lake country behind the centre of the salient between Hattonchâtel and Lachaussée, which appeared very suitable for such defensive purposes.

All these suggestions were in the nature of mere hints to guide subordinate commands in their preparations for such difficult situations as might possibly present themselves. Should occasion for such measures arise, it was understood that all operations would be executed in strict accordance with orders from the superior army command.

About August 20th, the attention of our superior army command was aroused by extensive erection of barracks near Chaumont, Rimaucourt, Liffol, and Bazeilles, as well as by lively building activities close to the railroad stations at Abainville. Opposite our south front, the employment of American divisions seemed to hint at a replacement of units. According to statements elicited from prisoners on August 23rd, it appeared that the 82nd Division, A. E. F., which only a short while ago had been assumed to occupy the sector west of Xivray[46] as far as the neighbourhood of Limey,[47] was now stationed on both banks of the Moselle, with the 90th Division, A. E. F., extending farther to the west.

Here in front of Army Group Gorze, holding a sector from the edge of the wood, three kilometres east of Loupmont[48] down to the left as far as Fey-en-Haye,[49] an unmistakably intensified activity of enemy flyers had become noticeable. Even as high up as six thousand metres, German reconnoitring flyers were molested by enemy pursuit fliers. However, we assumed that this air blockade was merely maintained by the enemy in connection with the replacement still under way. For the time being, there were no signs of imminent smaller or bigger offensive movements.

Toward the end of the month, our reconnoitring flyers reported additional building of barracks along the railroad Bar-le-Duc–Gondrecourt–Chaumont–Neufchâteau, as well as in the Neufchâteau–Toul–Commercy sector. The activities of enemy raiding parties, in front of the German positions, became more pronounced. Also, intensified traffic in the enemy's rear was reported, and assumed to be in connection with the arrival of new American contingents.

To be sure, the reported rearrangements of sectors on the west front of the St. Mihiel salient, as well as the appointment of a new general command, could be taken as an indication of imminent offensive intentions. There was a rumour that on the south front of Army Group Gorze, to the west of the 90th Division, A. E. F., the 99th Division, A. E. F., had also been stationed. However, from captured war material it was soon ascertained that this was the 89th Division, A. E. F.

We assumed that these American divisions were placed at this part of the front to receive additional training and to become acclimatized to service along the front. From all this we drew the conclusion that an attack on a greater scale need not be expected here for the time being. This, of course, did not at all imply an underestimation of the American troops. I mentioned before that, as early as April, 1918, we respected the Americans as opponents. No confirmation was obtainable in regard to the reported changes within the enemy sectors along the west front in the course of the next few days. However, our attention was directed equally to both fronts of the salient inasmuch as the situation there might change very quickly.

At last, on September 1st, the superior army command of Army Unit C, subordinated to the command of Army Group Gallwitz, received information that seemed to disclose the intentions of the enemy. The bulletin stated:

> The Supreme Command just wired: "Reports to the effect that the Americans intend to advance *along both banks of the Moselle toward Metz* become more numerous. . . ."

At the same time, General Ludendorff ordered Army Group Gallwitz to speed up the approach of the 123rd Division of Infantry, held in reserve until then. These troops were to be placed along the boundary between

Army Unit C and the Nineteenth Army, to the east of it, and kept in readiness to reënforce the latter when necessary.

Additional reënforcements came to Army Unit C, when the supreme command ordered, first the 107th and, a little later, the 88th Division of Infantry to join us. The new troops were stationed in the sector Gorze–Briey–Fentsch and to the west of it. These reserves were further strengthened by the 31st Division of Infantry until the latter, during the first days of September, as a part of the Mihiel sector effectives, was relieved by the 192nd Saxonian Division of Infantry. All these divisions were greatly exhausted. To make them fully fieldworthy once more, several weeks of rest and training behind the front would be necessary.

Thus, the number of divisions at our disposal was eleven, including three divisions of territorials. Of these effectives, seven were to be employed in the first battle line. In addition, our artillery was somewhat reënforced by pieces of different kinds and calibres. And, for the purpose of dealing effectively with a possible major offensive of the enemy, our air forces were reënforced on September 2nd by Pursuit Squadron 2 and by one group of combat planes, both consisting of four units (*Staffels*) each. Three flyer detachments were also ordered to support us.

In view of the threatening situation in general, the commander-in-chief of our Army Unit C, Lieutenant General Fuchs, once more submitted to the supreme command his suggestion of August 25th. This suggestion aimed at changing the boundary between Army Unit C and the Nineteenth Army in such a way that the 255th Division of Infantry, stationed in the sector left of Army Unit C as far as the Moselle, was to be subordinated to his, Fuchs's, command. Thus, in case of an attack against the south front of Army Unit C, all troops to the west of the Moselle would be under a unified command. Such a procedure appeared the more essential (in case the prepared systematic Michel Movement were actually made) to insure unity of action at the most vulnerable spot of the whole operation. This would be south of Pagny, and the very pivot of the entire Michel Movement. However, at that time, it was the opinion of the supreme command that a rearrangement of boundaries between the different armies might be dispensed with.

In the meantime, in view of the fact that preparations by the enemy for a general offensive were becoming more and more obvious, we started with the removal of war material from the St. Mihiel salient on September 2nd. Rail connections not absolutely indispensable for replacements and for a general Michel Movement were taken up. All supplies and material stored in the salient not absolutely essential were withdrawn behind the Michel Position. As far as artillery ammunition was concerned, sufficient stores for only two days were left in front of the Michel Zone, while ammunition for small weapons was supplied for the usual eleven days' period. Even as far as food was concerned, it was understood that in front of the Michel Position only such stores should be left as were sufficient to take care of immediate needs.

During all this time, the superior army command energetically endeavoured to collect all possible information on the general situation by resorting to every available means of reconnoitring, on the ground as well as in the air. According to reports received during the first days of September, confirmation appeared to be lacking in regard to an imminent and far-reaching general offensive against both sides of the Moselle by the Americans. In spite of this, our defensive preparations continued with energy, especially as the possibility of smaller surprise attacks was clearly perceived.

General von Gallwitz himself at this time held the opinion that such signs as manifested themselves—especially the replacement of troops observed opposite our south front—did not seem to indicate that a general, far-reaching attack against Army Unit C was contemplated by the enemy. Under date of September 3rd, General von Gallwitz expressed this view in a report to the supreme command. At the same time he inquired whether he was to embark upon the Michel Movement in the event of an attack of limited extent; for example, an attack directed against the eastern part of the south front of Army Unit C, perhaps in connection with operations against the Nineteenth Army. Von Gallwitz was of the opinion that an attack against the greater part of our south front could be repelled successfully only in case the supreme command guaranteed him essential reënforcements in good time. This much was certain: in case it proved impossible to repel such an attack completely, the St. Mihiel corner, as well as the west front of Army Unit C, would be seriously jeopardized.

The decision rendered by the supreme command stated that sufficient forces for repelling an attack, launched on a broad base against the greater part of the south front of Army Unit C, were not available at the time. Accordingly, an attack of this kind was not to be accepted along the present front line. In case such an emergency should arise, withdrawal to the Michel Position would seem advisable, analogous to that prescribed in the event of an attack against both our fronts. This decision of the supreme command, handed on to us by General von Gallwitz on September 4th, wound up by ordering Army Unit C to enter immediately upon suitable defense preparations. Any minor attack against the eastern part of our south front, extending only as far as the neighbourhood of Flirey, was to be accepted along our most advanced lines.

Thus, the views which already prevailed for these last few months were not in the least changed. At any rate, it would prove very hard to discern from the enemy's preparations whether he was embarking upon a general offensive or merely indulging in a localized attack, especially if the enemy succeeded in cleverly covering up his preparations.

General Fuchs, even before receiving this decision of the supreme command, entered upon the necessary preparations along the lines indicated. Up to September 5th, the situation in front of our sector developed as follows: Along the west front of the salient position, the enemy throughout these last few days remained comparatively quiet. On the other hand, along the south front opposite Group Gorze, enemy artillery was active since September 1st. After quite an interval, the enemy once more indulged in nocturnal artillery fire, partly for the mere purpose of molesting us. This artillery fire seemed to direct shots at our battery positions and our communication lines. Some of this ranging fire was directed by aëroplanes. However, we saw no reason to assume that the enemy's artillery was now reënforced. On the west front, a noticeable increase in the enemy's reconnoitring activities in the air grew apparent, over his own lines as well as rearwards.

Opposite our south front, from early in the morning of September 2nd until two o'clock in the afternoon of September 3rd, a very distinct intensification of all traffic on field, narrow, and standard gauged railroads, especially in the sectors Toul–Francheville–Royaumeix, became evident. It seemed that all this activity, extending approximately as far as the neighbourhood of Royaumeix, generally directed itself toward ammunition dumps and railroad sidings opposite our south front. On the same day, very heavy truck traffic and other vehicular transportation were reported from Boucq in the direction of Raulecourt, and from the south toward Commercy. During the night of September 4th–5th, extremely heavy traffic became audible in the neighbourhood of Bernécourt, and to the west of it. It appeared that railroads, motor trucks, heavy guns with caterpillar wheels, and perhaps even tanks were being moved. Also, heavy traffic by way of Clermont–Revigny toward Verdun and Souilly seemed under way. In addition, intensified local and long-distance traffic was observed in the neighbourhood of Bar-le-Duc, Longeville, and Toul. Inasmuch as the enemy camouflaged his movements very cleverly, it proved difficult to gain a clear picture of what was taking place.

From all these reports our superior army command drew the conclusion that, especially opposite our south front, and to a certain extent also opposite our west front, ammunition replacements and other preparations for a more extensive attack were under way. But whether this attack was actually imminent, we did not know, as it was impossible to gain sufficient information in regard to the enemy units stationed opposite our south front. The enemy's infantry being in great depths and the foreground very extended, it proved impossible to capture prisoners, in spite of the fact that numerous raiding parties went forth for this particular purpose. In view of such a state of affairs, it seemed all the more essential to focus attention on the activities of the enemy, as he had very useful rail connections at his disposal, making it possible for him quickly to assemble his forces. Also, extensive woods covered up artillery and tanks to quite a large extent.

Meanwhile, preparations to repel local attacks were continued by ourselves. Work on the Michel Position progressed uninterruptedly. While the building of defensive works of reënforced concrete was not especially stressed any more, great value was attached to the wiring of the foreground and the adjacent fighting zone.

The continued uncertainty in regard to developments opposite our front in those days proved a heavy burden on the shoulders of the responsible leaders of our superior army command. It was to be assumed, from reports received, that the Americans were preparing for an early attack, storing up ammunition and other war material, perhaps even guns, opposite our south front. But just how far this attack would extend to the west, how far across the Moselle this attack would include the sector of the Nineteenth Army, and how far along its west front Army Unit C would be attacked simultaneously (or later), remained an unsolved riddle.

About September 6th, came the first indications of analogous preparations by the enemy to the east and southeast of Verdun. This led to the conclusion that the opponent would not be satisfied with the mere tactical success of flattening out the St. Mihiel salient, but rather aimed at a much farther flung strategical goal. To this end, it was assumed that the enemy would employ a French attack to both sides of the Verdun–Etain highway, as well as an American attack along both banks of the Moselle, in the direction of Metz.

We decided to interfere with the plans of the enemy, and attempt to force him to abandon his intentions, at least for the time being, by embarking ourselves upon an offensive counter thrust, with an immediate, limited goal.

Therefore, on September 8th, General Fuchs suggested to Army Group Gallwitz to advance against the line Xivray–Noviant-aux-Prés–Blénod. In case the foe were pushed back along this line, we should gain an additional advantage, greatly facilitating the subsequent Michel Movement. This advantage would consist in pushing the enemy farther back from our most vulnerable spot, also in extending the salient position proper.

As may be gathered from a memorial addressed to the supreme command under date of September 11th, General von Gallwitz shared the view that the enemy, in attacking Army Unit C, was perhaps aiming at a larger strategical goal. The theory emerged on the basis of our own deductions:

It must, unquestionably, we felt, be the intention of the enemy's supreme command to carry the war to German soil as soon as feasible. After the withdrawal of the German fighting front in northern France by sectors (only to be reëstablished more to the rear) the enemy still faced a very big task in attempting to push us back beyond numerous river positions and fortified lines on French and Belgian soil. This way led through the enemy's own devastated country. Thus it seemed plausible that the enemy, instead of hammering against the German front in northern France, would employ all his strength in Lorraine, perhaps against the Nineteenth Army, while simultaneously advancing from Verdun, with the intention of getting on German soil quickly and easily.

In this way, the enemy would be able to prevent us from exploiting the Briey Iron Basin. He would also be in a position to threaten one of our most important lines of communication, the railroad Conflans–Metz, as well as the coal and industrial region of the Sarre. Here, the enemy, by encircling Metz, would perhaps find himself in a position to drive a wedge into Germany proper, a procedure which, in turn, would naturally react on our northwest front. Doubtless Marshal Foch had to be credited with sufficient strategical discernment necessary to conceive such plans. Moreover, in view of his strong American reënforcements, Foch must have enough effectives at his disposal.

In spite of the fact that General von Gallwitz shared General Fuchs's views in regard to these possible strategical plans of the enemy, the suggested preventive attack did not come off. In agreement with Army Group Gallwitz, we soon abandoned this idea. The preparatory activities of the enemy were becoming more pronounced each day and we would not have time enough to prepare the suggested preventive attack.

General von Gallwitz, however, issued orders that the necessary measures be taken for an early withdrawal to the Michel Position in accordance with plans drawn up. This order stated:

The removal of materials, etc., is to be carried on with all possible energy, inasmuch as an aggravation of the situation, necessitating an earlier onset of the Loki movement, may tend to cut down whatever time is at our disposal. As far as the country is to be devastated, only the absolutely necessary destruction work must be attended to, first, in order not to arouse the suspicion of the enemy, and, second (if the situation as a whole should improve), because the supreme command may possibly postpone the Loki movement. Before the Loki movement is embarked upon, agreement of the Army Group must be secured.

Speed, then, was of utmost importance! According to the majority of reports received, it appeared that the enemy's preparations for attack progressed rapidly, especially along the south front of Army Unit C. Moreover, to all appearances, the enemy, along the west front, made ready to proceed against the left wing of the Fifth Army and the right wing of Army Unit C.

On September 10th and 11th, orders were issued to hold the respective units in readiness for defensive action. Work in the rearward battle zones was to be speeded up by the respective army groups. For this purpose, Group Combres was reënforced by the 88th, and Group Gorze by the 31st Division of Infantry. All available forces had been ordered to speed up the work outlined. For the same reason it was decided that the 88th Division must occupy the country west of the line Brainville–Ozerailles not later than the night of September 13th, while the 31st Division, at the same time, must reach the neighbourhood west of the Rezonville–Gorze–Onville position. Until further notice, the 107th and 123rd Saxonian Divisions of Infantry were to remain at the disposal of the supreme command, fully prepared to rush into action at short notice. In order to get closer to the fighting line, the 107th Division was to be moved to the neighbourhood of Labeuville–Jonville, and the 123rd to the east of Rezonville–Gorze–Onville. The latter had to reach this position not later than the evening of September 13th, prepared for a speedy concentration around Arnaville–Pagny–Prény. As early as September 8th, part of the heavy artillery at the disposal of the army attached itself to the Army Groups Combres and Gorze for employment behind the Michel Position.

Now the time had come to withdraw from the front such batteries as lacked teams, replacing them with such as could be moved at short notice. In making this change on the south front, we prepared to outflank the enemy, in case he attacked Group Gorze. Beginning with the morning of September 12th, Army Groups Mihiel and Gorze must have their batteries prepared to disturb such preparations for attack as the enemy might be busying himself with at that moment. In the advanced fighting zone, only preparations to repulse tanks were to continue and with all possible speed. Measures of an appropriate kind must conceal the necessary rearrangements of troop units from reconnoitring activities by the enemy on land and in the air.

Simultaneously, orders were given to remove all stocks of war materials from the St. Mihiel salient, beginning with September 11th. In view of the tension prevailing, we adhered to the instructions issued for the removal of materials, although this work might proceed in much shorter time than scheduled, since preparations had meanwhile begun. Accordingly, under date of September 9th, new directions were issued for the removal of war material and devastation of the region abandoned. Although we expected the enemy to launch his attack soon, perhaps within a few days, it was impossible for us to surmise exactly when this attack would begin.

Heavy precipitation which, since September 8th, alternated with clouded skies and storm-like winds, had greatly interferred with air reconnoitring, thus favouring our preparations. But at the same time, weather of this kind made it impossible for us to ascertain how far the enemy's efforts had meanwhile progressed.

On September 12th, at two o'clock in the morning, heavy artillery fire set in along the whole army front with surprising suddenness. Most of its fury was directed against Army Group Gorze. It was not quite so heavy opposite Army Group Combres, and still less fierce along the line held by Group Mihiel. Farther up to the north, along the Verdun front, activity of the artillcry was directed against the Fifth Army, with the obvious intention of harassing units employed there. Opposite the left wing of the army, the fire of the enemy artillery also extended to the sector held by the 255th Division of Infantry, which formed the right wing of the Nineteenth Army toward the Moselle.

The enemy's fire directed against Group Combres, maintained by about fifty batteries, was aimed especially at the rear, in the neighbourhood of Etain and Warcq. However, within the next few hours, artillery activity gradually slowed down, remaining lively only in the terrain around the Combres Heights. Desultory fire continued toward the rear of the 35th Austrian Division of Infantry, stationed to the south of the Combres Heights. The fire aimed at Group Mihiel was apparently intended only to disturb us, covering, however, in our rear crossroads, especially. Heavy fire of large-calibred pieces covered Chaillon, Creüe, Heudicourt,[50] and the Varneville-Buxières highway, in the northern part of the sector. Around four o'clock in the morning, the fire along the whole Group Mihiel sector ceased.

Army Group Gorze was attacked by the enemy's offensive fire at the most unfavourable moment imaginable! On the afternoon of September 11th, it had been ordered that the effectives in this sector—the 10th Division of Infantry and the 77th Reserve Division—in case of an attack, were to occupy covered positions which had formerly served the artillery; in the region of what had previously been our main line of resistance, only combat companies were to be left to serve as foreground garrison. This procedure seemed advisable not only as a means of removing part of the troops from the zone of the most effective enemy artillery fire, but also because it was expected that a deeper formation would assist in more successfully stemming an enemy onslaught. The new main line of resistance was merely under construction at this time; there were difficulties to overcome along the whole line, with the better part of the front comprised of destroyed trenches. For the time being, there was a lack of dugouts and cover against artillery fire. This new position was scheduled for occupation by four o'clock in the morning.

While occupation of the main line of resistance on the right wing of the 10th Division of Infantry was for the most part successfully accomplished, units at the centre and the left wing of this division on march found themselves exposed to heavy fire. In the darkness of the night, companies and batteries dispersed, suffering great losses. Teams of horses, intended to pull out batteries, were prevented by the heavy fire from reaching their goal. As far as the 10th Division of Infantry was concerned, comparatively few batteries were lost because, during the previous days, the commander of this division, General von Diepenbroick-Grüter, with great foresight, arranged his artillery in deep echelon formation. On the other hand, the artillery of the 77th Division of Reserves suffered so much the more, inasmuch as their gross changed position just at that time.

Before long the roads were torn to pieces by the enemy's artillery, and littered with blown-up vehicles and dead and injured horses. The leader of the 77th Division of Reserves, under the impression that it was his duty to accept the attack in the zone of his previous main line of resistance, left two thirds of his infantry in the old positions, contrary to orders issued by the Army Group Command. Only a few batteries, within the divisional sector, were in a position to support the defensive. In this way, the infantry were mostly left to themselves. Towns in the rear of the Gorze sector, especially Thiaucourt,[51] Bouillonville,[52] Xammes,[53] and Pannes,[54] as well as the main connection roads, came under the fire of heavy-calibre guns. Additional difficulties for those in command arose from the fact that the very first shells destroyed almost the entire telephone net. Thus, orders could be communicated only by Morse lamps and runners—a decided handicap, in view of the fact that within divisional sectors of from 9 to 13 kilometres distances are comparatively great. This fact added to the unfavourable developments of our defensive actions.

Soon after the onset of the enemy's artillery fire, the 31st and 123rd Saxonian Divisions of Infantry, stationed behind the front, received orders from the leader of Group Gorze, General von Hartz, to advance to the prepared points of concentration. Regiments belonging to the 31st Division, at this moment stationed around Lachausée, St. Julien, and Mars-la-Tour, were to report ready for action north of Charey, while the 123rd Division, from the neighbourhood of Gorze, was to advance to Onville, and to the east of it.

Despite the fact that all resting divisions within the region of Army Group Gallwitz held themselves at the disposal of the supreme command, our staff assumed the responsibility of drawing upon these units. The proceeding was based upon the conviction that the heavy artillery fire along the whole front of Army Group C must be the introduction of the expected offensive. The 88th Division of Infantry was also in readiness, receiving from the superior army command the order to stand ready in the direction of Allamont. Later on, the 107th Division of Infantry got orders to start toward Buzy, by way of Fléville-Lanhères.

Thus, all divisions held in readiness for action were moved to the rear of those sectors which, in view of the situation as a whole, and the heaviness and extension of the enemy's artillery fire, were suspected of constituting the opponent's objectives. Acting upon the instructions of our superior army command of September 2nd, the 255th Division of Infantry was put at the disposal of Army Unit C, at 5:40 A.M. on September 12th, thus extending our sphere of command to the Moselle–Arnaville–Gorze line. As mentioned before, this measure had appeared to be one of the utmost importance. But at this very moment of extreme tension its execution only served to add to the difficulties facing us.

At about 5 A.M., the activity of enemy artillery against the centre and the left wing of the 10th Division of Infantry developed into drum fire. Supported by gas, this drum fire concentrated especially against our front lines, the covered positions of our artillery, and intermediate terrain. It became clear that here the enemy would launch his main thrust.

At 6 A.M.—it was meanwhile daylight—yellow flares went up above this sector.

The American infantry went over the top!

Along a stretch of the front measuring approximately 20 kilometres, between St. Baussant[55] and the woods to the east of Regniéville-en-Haye,[56] the American infantry charged the German position. Tanks added pressure to the attack.

Utterly lacking in artillery support, the infantry of the 77th Division of Reserves was soon overrun. In the sector of the 10th Division of Infantry, however, the 47th Regiment resisted valiantly to the north of St. Baussant, as did the 6th Regiment of Grenadiers on the heights to both sides of Essey,[57] along our new main line of defense. Early in the action, connection to the left with the 77th Division of Reserves was lost. Up to 11 A.M., the front of the 10th Division of Infantry remained unshaken, although the Americans now succeeded with their thrust against the 77th Division of Reserves, and already occupied Thiaucourt. Subsequently, the opponent, after several ineffective attempts, broke through the front of the 10th Division of Infantry to the north of St. Baussant.

Simultaneously, the Americans, from the neighbourhood south of Thiaucourt, commenced to exert pressure against the flank and the rear of the left wing of the 10th Division of Infantry with the result of bending it still farther back to the north of Essey. At the same time, numerous flyers launched attacks with bombs, machine guns, and hand grenades against the still-resisting, but already greatly depleted, ranks of our infantry. At 12 A.M., the centre and left wing of the 10th Division of Infantry gave way after brave resistance, retreating, but fighting, toward Pannes. The right wing of the 10th Division, south of Montsec, was not attacked for the time being, and remained in its position. As most of the telephone lines within the sector were down, the superior army command, for the longest time, was unable to obtain definite news of the fighting on the Group Gorze front.

Right here I wish to quote a few lines from a private letter which I wrote only a few days later:

> On the night of September 11th, I turned in without being in the least disquieted. At 2 A. M., the thunder of guns, audible along the whole front of 90 kilometres' length, awoke me. Immediately I knew what was up! I rushed to Headquarters. I seized the phone and did not even so much as lay the instrument down for fully twenty-four hours. Up to 6 A. M., the American drum fire went on madly, not only along our front lines, but also far toward the rear. Every three minutes, heavy shells crashed into the railroad station of Conflans, close by to our Headquarters Moucel, as well as upon the bridges across the Moselle near Metz.
>
> Reports from the front came in one after another. At 6 A. M., the charge of the infantry set in. Around 8 A.M., I came to the conclusion that as far as the Groups Combres and Mihiel were concerned, we had succeeded, in spite of our thin front, in repelling local attacks of the enemy. However, I did not obtain definite news from Group Gorze. All I knew was that the Americans had launched an attack against this group along a front of 25 kilometres length.

As soon as we were informed of the attack by American infantry, our pursuit, as well as our combat squadrons, received orders to get into the fight. Also, the Nineteenth Army was called upon to support us.

At first, high winds seemed to interfere with our flyers participating in the fighting. Low clouds and heavy downpours drenched the field of battle. Nevertheless, the combat units succeeded in ascending, during the morning, with only 300 m. ceiling (height of clouds) to take part in the bitter fighting of the 77th Division of Reserves. But all day the bad weather interfered greatly with the success of our reconnoitring planes. Thus it happened that the superior army command did not receive any information, in regard to the retreat of the 77th Division, before 10:30 A.M. Immediately, the 10th and the 77th Divisions were supported with one regiment each of the 31st and 123rd Divisions, for the purpose of holding their positions. The regiment dispatched by the 31st Division was to be thrown forward in a counter thrust to the right of Beney[58]–Essey. The right wing of the 255th Division of Infantry, too, had felt the American attack. Here, right at the beginning, strong enemy forces invaded the foreground, but the division, to all appearances, now held its own.

The situation along the rest of the army front had meanwhile developed as follows:

Opposite Group Combres, advances by the French, about 7:30 A.M., against the sector held by the Austrian 35th Division of Infantry, began along the Heights of the Meuse. These operations, at first, proved local only, and lacking in stamina. However, just as expected, after extensive artillery preparation, at 10:30 A.M., strong enemy attacks developed against the Combres Heights, and to the west of it. Here, General of the Infantry, Baron von Gayl, resisted valiantly with his 13th Division of Territorials.

Group Mihiel, as early as 7:00 A.M., after a short intensification of preparatory artillery fire, partly supported by gas, coped with advances in the neighbourhood of Apremont, against a sector held by the 5th Division of Territorials. At this point, however, the opponent was thoroughly repelled. Such of their troops as invaded the foreground were quickly driven back. Renewed advances at about 9:00 A.M. also proved abortive. In general, enemy artillery fire against Group Mihiel remained well within bounds up to 11 A.M. One part of the front of the Nineteenth Army occupying the line east of the Moselle had also been subjected to heavy artillery fire. However, attacks had not been launched in that neighbourhood.

At 11 A.M., the superior army command received a report from the 255th Division that its centre and left wing still held the foreground, while its right wing was interfered with, on account of developments along the front of the 77th Division of Reserves. Things there were in rather poor shape. But up to that time we had not received any definite information from the 77th Division directly, in regard to prevailing conditions. In reference to the 10th Division, we were also insufficiently informed.

Then, at 11:15 A.M., the extreme seriousness of our situation became clear in a flash, from a report which informed us that the line of the 77th Division was broken and that the enemy, to all appearances, had already reached Viéville.[59] The 31st Division, with two regiments, received an order to counter attack, by way of Thiaucourt, while the 123rd Division was to be launched against the enemy from the region south of Waville. The 10th Division seemed to hold the covered artillery positions.

These reports came like a thunderbolt to the superior army command. Up to then, we never doubted our ability—with perhaps hard fighting—to repel the enemy from our present positions, until our abandonment of the St. Mihiel salient in general, and the retreat of the army to the Michel Position in accordance with our plans. This news, therefore, proved a very heavy blow to us. Nevertheless, we had to make the best of matters, and act quickly.

Our first thought naturally was to reëstablish the old situation at the point of the breach. Thus, the 88th Division of Infantry, held at the disposal of Group Combres near Allamont, was immediately attached to Group Gorze, and ordered to stand ready in the direction of St. Julien. We hoped that, meanwhile, activities of the 31st and 123rd Divisions would bring about favourable developments. However, such developments had to come quickly! If this proved an empty hope, not only the whole salient position of St. Mihiel would become untenable for the army unit, but also the other troops, especially Group Mihiel, were in the gravest danger of being cut off.

At 11:50 A.M., Group Gorze reported:

> The enemy now stands southeast of Thiaucourt–Tautecourt Ferme. Apparently, the 77th Division has been annihilated. No report has been received so far, in regard to counter thrusts by the 31st and 123rd Divisions.

Now, the fateful resolution to retire the army immediately to the Michel Position could not be postponed any longer. Although General von Gallwitz reserved for himself the prerogative of ordering the retreat to the Michel Position, it now proved impossible to lose any time. Thus, Lieutenant General Fuchs assumed the whole responsibility in this extremely difficult situation. We knew that by abandoning the salient position we must leave great stocks of war material to the enemy. We also had to figure on the possibility that now, fighting at close quarters almost along the whole army front, it would be difficult to shake off the opponent without heavy losses. Especially on account of the deep breach through our lines near Thiaucourt, the roads farther south in the salient could no longer be utilized by us for the retreat. At any rate, all this had to be accepted as unavoidable, if we were not to expose the whole army to a catastrophe.

At 12 A.M., Group Mihiel received the order: "Loki movement to be started immediately." At this very moment, as reported by General von Below, leader of Group Combres, heavy fighting was in progress on the Combres Heights. St. Rémy had been lost; the Americans had broken through here on two points. The thrust through the right wing of the Austrian 35th Division of Infantry had not yet been blocked. This group was informed about the start of the Loki movement of its left neighbour with the additional order:

> Position at Combres Heights must be held with all available strength.

The heavy attacks against Group Combres proved clearly the enemy's intention to cut off, and force into capitulation, those of our troops fighting at the apex of the salient. For this purpose, the Americans were intent upon breaking through our south front. Perceiving this situation, our convictions became strengthened that the salient had to be abandoned immediately.

To prevent a possible break through Group Combres, the 107th Division of Infantry was turned toward Olley and put at the disposal of the group for employment in the Michel Position. The 28th Division of Reserves, rushed to our aid by order of the supreme command, was substituted in the direction of Buzy.

The most important thing to do now was to block the breach through Group Gorze. Anxious hours ensued. The 31st and 123rd Saxonian Divisions of Infantry were still too far off to stem the American advance at Thiaucourt. About 1 P.M., the situation there was about as follows: The 10th Division with its right wing still held its old position south of Montsec,[60] although bent back via Pannes toward Bouillonville; the one regiment of the 31st Division, put at the disposal of the 10th Division, marched toward Pannes. The 77th Division had actually been annihilated; fragments of it were now retreating north of Thiaucourt.

General von Hartz, in charge of Group Gorze, arranged the divisions meanwhile put at his disposal in such a way that attacks might be launched by the main forces of the 31st Division from the region northwest of Thiaucourt, in a southwesterly direction. The 123rd Saxonian Division of Infantry was ordered to advance beyond the general direction from Waville toward Viéville. It was expected that these divisions would get into the fight about 2:15 P.M. Meanwhile, the 255th Division, its right wing greatly bent back, still held its main line as far as the Moselle.

Our situation appeared even more critical when, at 1:45 P. M., a report from Group Combres arrived to the effect that on the right wing of the 35th Austrian Division of Infantry the cover of the artillery had been broken through.

On the south front, there was a very noticeable loss of time until the two divisions sent there for support went into action. On account of bad roads, both divisions made only slow progress. Thus, the 10th Division of Infantry, facing a numerically much superior enemy, was pushed back on Beney, where its fragments made a new stand. To the left, connection with the one regiment of the 31st Division of Infantry, put at the disposal of the 10th Division, was successfully established.

However, when the latter belatedly arrived at Xammes, about 3:30 P.M., the enemy was already advancing against this point from the direction of Thiaucourt. Nevertheless, the advance of the opponent was checked. At last, about this time, other parts of the 31st Division and the 123rd Saxonian Division of Infantry entered the fray. Although the former was unable to carry the attack over to the enemy's line, it was nevertheless able to settle on the heights near Jaulny, thus blocking the enemy's further advance toward the north. The 123rd Division, meanwhile, advancing to the east of the Rupt de Mad,[61] and supported by the right wing of the 255th Division, succeeded in slowly pressing back the Americans in the direction of Viéville.

In this way, progress of the Americans at the southern breach through our lines had definitely come to a standstill. Undoubtedly, we were entitled to look upon this development as a success, especially as we had kept the enemy away from our line of retreat through

Heudicourt, St. Benoît,[62] and Dampvitaux. I shall not deny here that we were only able to do so because of the assistance the enemy inadvertently lent us. To all appearances, he lacked the necessary skill in exploiting his great initial successes, possibly because his leadership was overwhelmed by the vastness of the results obtained. At any rate, the grave dangers which hung over Army Unit C had fortunately passed. The retreat to the Michel Position was safeguarded. Meanwhile, Group Mihiel marched. Its north wing was covered by Group Combres, which held on to its positions tenaciously.

After their success before our south front, the Americans, starting as early as 11 A. M., became more lively in the Group Mihiel sector. They commenced with an advance against the right wing of the 192nd Saxonian Division of Infantry. At the same time, low barrage fire of the enemy was trained on the St. Benoît–Beney road. Shortly before noon, the Americans, while attacking the centre of the 5th Division of Territorials, succeeded in entering their foreground, but were driven back later on. At 1:10 P.M., the Saxonian Lieutenant General Leuthold, leader of Group Mihiel, ordered the defense to retire to a more rearward intermediate position, in accordance with the Loki plan. However, in view of the dangerous situation still pending at the breach near Thiaucourt, the superior army command interfered, instructing Group Mihiel not to make a stand in an intermediate position, but rather to retreat, without any stop, right back to the Michel Position.

At 2 P.M., the enemy renewed his attack against the sector held by the 192nd Saxonian Division of Infantry. Along the outer right wing, the enemy had been annihilated among the wire entanglements, but there was still a possibility for the Americans to break in farther down to the south, where they were pushing on toward the east.

But in spite of all this, we succeeded in shaking off the enemy. At 3 P.M., the 192nd Division started on the march to the rear. The 5th Division of Territorials, too, could embark upon the retreat without being pressed by the Americans. To the left of the territorials, up to 3 P.M., the right wing of the 10th Division held its old position south of the isolated hill, Montsec. Inasmuch as the Americans did not force their attack here, we succeeded in remaining in touch—even if only somewhat loosely—along the line Nonsard[63]–Lamarche,[64] with all those parts of the division that were pressed back toward Beney. The 5th Division of Territorials, too, had detached forces in the direction of Nonsard, apprehensive that American infantry and tanks might block its line to the rear in the neighbourhood of St. Benoît. After the left wing of Group Mihiel started on the march back, the right wing of the 10th Division withdrew to cover the retreat.

When, toward 9 P. M., the opponent occupied Beney (where the greatly depleted 10th Division rendered resistance up to then), the 5th Division of Territorials, with the greatest part of its troops, had reached the Michel Position, while the head of the 192nd Division also approached.

In the course of the afternoon, Group Combres fought severely against the French along the Heights of the Meuse. Especially on the Combres Heights, where, in 1915, rivers of blood were shed, as well as in the region of St. Rémy and to the west of it, the

Americans, time and again, renewed their attempts to break through toward the south. The French, fighting against the stubbornly resisting 13th Division of Territorials, finally gained some ground to the west of Combres. St. Rémy, too, as mentioned before, had been lost around noon.

On the right wing of the Austrian 35th Division, owing to an enemy thrust, the defensive was withdrawn at about 11 A.M. to the covered positions of the artillery. A report received by the superior army command shortly after noon, stating that the enemy had broken through at this spot, fortunately turned out to be incorrect. Only a slight indentation was affected there by the Americans, but the attack proved abortive because the Austrian and German troops fought side by side, in true brotherly fashion. When, at 5 P.M. or thereabouts, thc brave leader of the Austrians, General Podhoransky, withdrew his troops from their exposed position to an intermediate line, after a battle entailing heavy losses, the retreat of Group Mihiel, to his left, was already in full swing.

Accordingly, at 6 P. M., General von Below, in charge of Group Combres, ordered a withdrawal to the Michel Position. The 13th Division of Territorials and the 35th Austrian Division started for the rear at nightfall, without being disturbed by the enemy. The 8th Division of Territorials, at the right wing, still occupied its sector after a comparatively quiet day. Behind the right wing of the army, near Rouvres, the 28th Division of Reserves concentrated, by order of the supreme command, to be employed in case of emergency. Meanwhile, the divisions of Group Mihiel approached the Michel Position so closely that, at 10 P. M., Group

Gorze, too, could start on its march back which, in the course of the night, ended almost without interference from the enemy.

On the morning of September 13th, Groups Gorze and Mihiel stood ready for defense in the Michel Position with Group Combres continuing its march toward this goal. The enemy did not press them. Only the air activity of the enemy proved actually annoying and lively. As soon as the 13th Division of Territorials had reached the Michel Position, the left wing of the 8th Division of Territorials, too, withdrew without any difficulties. Thus the Loki movement had been accomplished.

Only hesitatingly, the enemy followed. Even during the ensuing day, he made no preparations to continue the attack. Thus we were led to believe that the enemy would resume his attacking on the Michel Position, only after having completed his formation in front of it. Meanwhile, through receiving additional reserves, especially artillery, the fighting impetus of Army Unit C was intensified. However, the expected attacks against our front did not materialize.

A few days later I jotted down in my diary:

> When, on the morning of September 13th, the Michel Position had been reached, a heavy weight was removed from my chest. There was just one more danger left: that the enemy might continue to attack, pressing hard against the exhausted divisions in the Michel Position. But nothing of the sort happened! Their attempts to advance against the 31st, 123rd, and the newly arrived 88th Divisions proved absolutely futile. The crisis has been weathered! Since then, our situation improved daily.

Summing up in retrospection this development of attacks, executed primarily with American troops and under American leadership, against the German position in the St. Mihiel salient, the following must be recorded: Right from the very onset, Army Unit C found itself in a highly unfavourable position. Inasmuch as it proved impossible to ascertain in good time the moment when the Americans would launch their attack, Army Unit C had to accept battle in advanced positions difficult to defend. This, in turn, necessitated a retreat under the pressure of an enemy greatly superior as regarded effectiveness of armament. Our difficulties became even graver when a section of our south front gave in too quickly. The calamity which developed here, because of the front of the 77th Division of Reserves having broken to great depths, doubtless could have been avoided. There can be no hairsplitting about the matter; this division simply failed us! If it had behaved correctly, we could, while fighting stubbornly, and retreating by sectors only, have offered resistance long enough for reserve divisions to arrive and enter the fight.

An essential reason for the deficiency of the 77th Division of Reserves was the undeniable fact that at this stage of the war the resistance of certain parts of the German army was greatly decreased, their nervous energy being exhausted, and their morale lowered by inferior replacements.

That despite all this we succeeded in withdrawing, to the greatest extent, the German troops on the Heights of the Meuse to our new tangent position, reflects glory of German generalship and furnishes a proof of the valour of the German army. All along the rest of the front, the army parried the enemy's thrust. There was no spot where he succeeded in breaking our line. To be sure, the enemy ceased battle quite early, apparently satisfied with the capture of approximately 15,000 prisoners and the considerable booty of 400 guns and other war material. The chief value of these developments to the enemy, however, was that they served to enhance the war spirit of the young American troops, imbuing them with justified pride in the successful outcome of their first independently conducted offensive action. And General Pershing displayed wise moderation in not attempting to endanger the moral gain of his success by continuing the attack against the Michel Position.

III

THE AMERICANS IN THE ST. MIHIEL SALIENT

By General Eugène Savatier, former Assistant Chief of the General Staff and Commander of the 34th Division, French Army

THE first decisive offensive that enabled the American Expeditionary Forces to demonstrate their prowess on a large scale began in the last week of July, 1918.

The Allied commanders were gathered around their new commander-in-chief, Marshal Ferdinand Foch, in a small park at Bombon. I well remember how, at that all-important conference, my chief, the Marshal of France, permitted the habitual gravity of his countenance to relax. "All goes well," he said. He was referring to the push against the enemy. He had talked with M. Clemenceau a day or two before. His government was firm in its belief that the Americans would turn the tide. "We continue to advance," Marshal Foch said.

Thus, this momentous conference began in the happiest mood. General Pershing was in fine spirits. I think he was touched and pleased when Marshal Foch himself brought up the subject of the Americans in the discussion that ensued.

"A quarter of a million Americans every month!" My chief was impressed and impressive. "The superiority is on our side," he continued emphatically. "The superiority may be small, but it is definite. It will soon be decisive."

The Americans were still uppermost in the thoughts of all. Marshal Foch had kept in touch with their achievements. Artillery was coming from the United States freely. Munitions were beginning to pile high on the wharves in the ports. I think it was General Pershing who asked that day about German man power.

Marshal Foch had kept in closest touch with the woes of the enemy on this score.

"The enemy has only recently emerged from a grave peril at home. Man power occasioned that upheaval. There is a worse situation now than ever in Germany."

The arrivals of American troops behind our lines had not been misunderstood by Hindenburg. Ludendorff was obliged to take strong measures at home to avert what might perhaps be called a panic. What added to the embarrassments of the German General Staff was a knowledge that the rise and progress of the man-power crisis were well known to Marshal Foch. The Marshal entered somewhat carefully into the subject, bearing, as it did, so closely upon the fate of the new drive.

The German army, we were told, wrestled with a twofold problem. There was the lack of effective forces and there was the demoralization resulting from a perception of this lack.

For a long time, the Germans had two kinds of divisions. They differed much in prestige and in importance. The ordinary German division held the front line. In addition, there was the division of so-called "shock troops." These last were specially prepared behind the lines for the rushes they made against our men.

The theory of this procedure was sound enough, but too much depended upon the circumstances under which it was followed, and the circumstances of the Germans were getting worse and worse. Marshal Foch seemed to think that the unexpectedly heavy reënforcements we were receiving from America had upset the calculations of the tacticians on the enemy side. There were two great drawbacks to their system of complementing divisions.

The divisions of the sector, holding the line and the trenches, discovered that they were regarded as inferior. This caused a loss of confidence among them and an ensuing loss of German morale. The morale of the shock divisions, to be sure, was raised. They knew they were chosen for attack. They contrived in some of their rushes to effect gaps in our line, especially where we lacked the benefit of the American reënforcements. The German shock troops were quite proud of what they had done so far. Their losses were very great just the same.

There were on the Marshal's table as he discussed these details reports which implied that the Americans took no great stock in the "shock" divisions. General Pershing seemed to share the view that their existence was a mistake on the enemy's part. At any rate, it appeared that the attacks of the "shock" troops were almost always carried too far forward in the same direction. Hence, they were not adequately supported by artillery fire. So at last the shock troops faced failure. This weakened their morale.

Another idea of the German difficulty with man

power was afforded by the fact that German soldiers of the class of 1920 were reporting for duty. The conscription of the 1921 class was even then hastening. When, however, the Allied commanders were gathered on this hot July day at Marshal Foch's headquarters, the German army was still a powerful weapon.

Nevertheless, my chief was convinced that the German army was now facing a very precarious situation.

"We have got them where we want them," he confided to General Pétain in my presence. "We shall deal them a blow that will prove fatal before November. The Germans will be kicked out of France. They must have a decision at once if it is to be favourable to them. They won't get it."

Before this gathering dispersed each member of it received a personal and secret document signed by Marshal Foch, and worded as follows:

THE COMMANDER-IN-CHIEF OF THE ALLIED ARMIES

GENERAL HEADQUARTERS
July 24, 1918.

Personal and Secret

The fifth German offensive, disorganized at the start, ended in being definitely checked. The offensive taken by the French Tenth and Sixth Armies changed the drive into a defeat. This defeat must be followed up with attacks executed with the utmost energy. On the side of the Allies there is an indisputable superiority in aviation, tanks, and artillery. This superiority is still small, but is destined to grow in proportion to the arrival of the American artillery.

Back of our lines the powerful American nation is pouring reserves of two hundred and fifty thousand men on the soil of France each month. As far as the enemy is concerned we know what exceptional measures have been taken to avert a crisis in man power during the month of May, and we see by their present difficulties that another crisis presents itself.

Morally we are gaining the upper hand. The Allied Armies have arrived at the turn of the road. In the midst of a defensive battle they have taken the initiative in operations; and not only their superior strength but also the principles of warfare make it imperative that they shall maintain it.

The programme of the next offensive actions will be as follows:

(1) Operations aiming at the liberations of the railroad tracks indispensable to the future manœuvres of the Allied Armies.

(a) Liberation of the Paris–Avricourt railroad in the region of the Marne, which is the minimum result to be obtained from the actual offensive.

(b) Liberation of the Paris–Amiens track. (British and French Armies.)

(c) Liberation of the Paris–Avricourt track in the region of Commercy by the reduction of the salient of St. Mihiel. (Preparations are to be made without delay, *and the operation is to be undertaken by the American troops as soon as they have the necessary means.*)

(2) Operations aiming at the liberation of the mining regions of the North and the removal of the enemy from the region of Dunkirk and Calais.

These actions must take place at short intervals, in order to hamper the enemy in manœuvring his reserves and reorganizing his units. They must above all contain the element of surprise which recent operations have shown is an indispensable qualification for success.

Foch.

With his army of raw recruits, few really trained, General Pershing had now to consider the reduction of the St. Mihiel salient. This was the tremendous task entrusted to him and his men in the general plan outlined at the Bombon conference.

The term salient was so loosely employed during the World War that I might note one thing about this St. Mihiel salient. It represented a break outward from the German line. The German line at that point was not straight. Instead of forming a "breaking inward" it broke outward, as I have said, forming what we French call a hernia or rupture. The most experienced commanders do not agree upon the best tactical expedient in attacking a salient. Should the attack be made at the point of rupture? Or should the operations be directed against the lowest point of the break?

After mature deliberation, General Pershing deemed it best to attack not the salient itself, but the two points at which it broke the German line. No one on the Allied side had any technical suggestion to make. Pershing came from West Point, the graduates of which have won prestige in engineering science.

By this time, the German forces had been in possession of St. Mihiel for nearly four years. What a transformation they had effected in the interval! Whatever could be of assistance to the French they had destroyed —roads, forests, bridges, houses. Villages were looted. The German policy was to leave the enemy only his eyes to weep with. They executed that policy at St. Mihiel with thoroughness and at their leisure.

Whatever at St. Mihiel could serve a German purpose was in a flourishing condition. There were miles upon miles of trenches dug by the Germans with a care almost loving. These trenches were walled like beautiful tunnels. They rose high above the head in some places, with well-graded steps for those who wished or were ordered to fire upon us. The word "dugout," at St. Mihiel, often designated what was in reality an underground house. The roads used by the Germans were well paved and clean. Lighting facilities, sanitary facilities, and transport facilities rendered St. Mihiel an exquisite illustration of the thoroughness of German military science.

But it signified as well the typically stationary character of their kind of warfare. They were prepared to stay at St. Mihiel until the crack of doom.

General Pershing cherished no illusions regarding the nature of the task assigned to him. The wire entanglements between him and his objective covered miles. The German artillery at this point was alert. The line was closely guarded. In the towns and villages covered by the area of the salient could be seen the French prisoners, toiling under the closest guard.

As his first step, Pershing saw to the posting of his artillery. Some thousands of guns had to be dragged to available positions. It involved the hardest labour. Fortunately, the American horses had been carefully treated since the return of the warm weather. The desperate state of these animals some months previously was to a considerable extent relieved. The men were hampered by a plague of insects and by the irregularity in the arrival of supplies. The Germans essayed to demoralize them with artillery fire.

It was easy to see, as the operations progressed, that the American engineers knew their business. We French thought them hasty in their improvisations, but in the matter of speed they were amazing. As early as the 12th of September, the artillery of the Americans was playing steadily upon the German positions. This served as a protection for the infantry attack. Two whole army corps of four divisions each were now on the move.

The principal attack was scheduled toward the south, with two army corps of four divisions each, while in the secondary attack to the north, one army corps comprising two United States divisions and one French division was to be used.

The artillery preparation began at one o'clock on the morning of September 12th with about three thousand guns, and at five o'clock the American First and Fourth Army Corps moved forward to the main attack. The enemy was unable to check them at any point, and when evening came all the objectives had been attained. The troops of the American Fifth Army Corps came into the secondary attack at eight o'clock, and progressed rapidly. The same evening, the American 102nd Regiment crossed the Heights of the Meuse and reached Vigneulles–Hattonchâtel[65] early in the morning.

The Fourth and Fifth Army Corps joined near Vigneulles–Hattonchâtel on the thirteenth, while the divisions of the Second Colonial Corps cleaned out the interior of the salient and occupied St. Mihiel.

In less than three days, the Americans had freed the Valley and the Heights of the Meuse, together with the greater part of the Woëvre, and had captured 13,250 prisoners, 460 cannon, and an immense amount of material.

It has been often asked who arrived first at Vigneulles, thus cutting off the enemy's retreat? It seems that the honour should go to the patrols of the 26th Division, and later the 1st Division in full force. But there was glory enough for all. The 2nd Division in a splendid rush took Thiaucourt, the 5th captured Viéville-en-Haye without loss in a very fine manœuvre, and the 90th conquered the quarries of Norroy[66] which had the reputation of being impregnable.

Although we French had shared the anxiety of the British regarding the outcome of the American operations, we had inferred from our reports that the A. E. F.

would do brilliantly. Our idea was that they would be at a loss with some of the artillery we loaned them for this attack. General Harbord, in command of the American 2nd Division, declared all along that his troops would be found at ease in the manipulation of any kind of machinery. He turned out to be right. His confidence and that of General Allen, General Liggett, and General Burnham in the versatility as well as the enterprise of the men they commanded was justified. General Pershing impressed them all with the importance of the element of surprise in this operation.

The surprise to the Germans resided in the discovery that those Americans whom they had been taught to despise were now the heroes of one of the most brilliant achievements in the "big push." The American attack had been so violent from the first that the Germans thought they must have British in front of them.

I transcribe here not my own impressions merely but those of Captain Crochet, thoroughly experienced as a tactician and one of the ablest pupils of Foch in the French army. He kept in close contact with the American forces from the opening of the St. Mihiel rush to its close.

"The operations," he assured me, "required both rapidity and secrecy on the part of the Americans.

"Silence has always been difficult to maintain in the American army, and as early as the middle of August officers and men told anyone who wanted to listen to them that the army was going to attack in the Woëvre in order to reduce the salient of St. Mihiel. Certain troopers even added that they were going to take Metz.

"On the twelfth of September, toward one o'clock

in the morning, the artillery preparation started; at five o'clock, infantry and tanks rushed forward. Along the front of the 1st Division everything went according to schedule, and toward ten o'clock in the morning the foremost troops had reached and passed Nonsard.

"We could certainly have pushed on toward Vigneulles had not the division stopped in the clearing at Nonsard to await the attack of twenty thousand German troops, who, according to a wild report based on a signal from the Second Bureau, were determined to make a breach in the American lines.

"It was not until ten o'clock that night that we were ordered to push on toward Vigneulles, even though a night march should be necessary. It was then too late to catch up with the Germans, who had passed through that point during the night in their hasty retreat. In the early morning we met patrols of the 26th Division coming from Mouilly and of the 39th Division coming from Apremont. It was a complete and perfectly executed reunion!

"Mention should be made of the terrific traffic jam that occurred on the roads which skirted the battlefields during September 12th and the following days. Some hours after the beginning of the attack, artillery batteries, files of machine guns, ambulances, trucks from the artillery parks, and convoys lumbered along the roads and became entangled. Everybody, being aware of the success of the attack, felt obliged to manifest his aggressive spirit by pushing ahead.

"Due to this haste and lack of discipline vehicles were forced to halt at places in the roadways which had been torn up by old trenches, and there occurred an inextricable tangle which stopped traffic for two or three days. There should have been more experienced staffs, and less independence on the part of the different branches, each of which tried to outdo their rivals. The enthusiasm which urged the lowliest cook to put his rolling kitchen into action the moment the zero hour had struck, was admirable, but should have been moderated."

"I dare say," I asked Captain Crochet after the action, "that the secret of the movement was soon betrayed to the enemy."

"The enemy," he replied, "never took the Americans seriously enough. Their operations on the eve of the attack ought to have been a fair warning. The Americans were so alert that they got to one crossroads before the French. More confusion! Perhaps we ought to have reckoned upon the Americans being ahead of anybody else! They were not disconcerted by false alarms. Two divisions of the American Fourth Corps had to spend hours in the dark and the rain expecting orders to attack. Their morale was not lowered."

PART FIVE

THE MEUSE-ARGONNE BATTLES IN THE FALL OF 1918

THE MEUSE-ARGONNE BATTLES IN THE FALL OF 1918

I

INTRODUCTORY NOTE

THE battleground of the Meuse-Argonne engagements constitutes the third of the three fateful triangles. These battles comprise the third and last phase of America's participation in the fighting of the World War. The triangle rests on Sedan, Stenay, and Samogneux.

General von Ledebur brings his account up to the middle of September when Army Unit C reached the Michel Position. Here General Max von Gallwitz, who was actually in command of the German troops which faced the Americans in the Argonne, takes up the thread of the narrative. It was in this region that on September 26th the American army entered upon the prodigious task of expelling the Germans from innumerable "pill-boxes," fortified positions, and other artificial and natural strongholds.

The star of Ludendorff was on the wane. Though Field Marshal von Hindenburg still dominated at General Headquarters, it was expected that he would hand in his resignation when Prince Max forced the resignation of Ludendorff. In that case the baton of the Field Marshal would have passed to General von Gallwitz.

Gallwitz, who bore the brunt of the American onslaught in the Meuse-Argonne triangle, gives a running account of operations from September 13th to November 11th, the day of the armistice. The fierce tenacity with which these battles were fought is apparent from his recital. He enumerates the names of villages, towns, hills, and woods which are now interwoven forever with American history. General von Gallwitz does not conceal his surprise that the Americans succeeded in penetrating his stronghold in the Argonne. He admits that he knew then, and had known for some time, that he was fighting for a lost cause.

Occasionally the General touches lightly upon the political situation and the notes flying across the ocean between Berlin and Washington. The armistice in which this correspondence culminated appears to him in the light of unconditional surrender.

The French parallel account of the Meuse-Argonne battles constitutes General Savatier's final contribution to this book. While, during the Meuse-Argonne battles of 1918 the A. E. F. were under the exclusive command of General Pershing, Pershing himself was subject to the regulations of the French General Staff, as was Marshal Foch himself. It was General Savatier's task as assistant chief of the General Staff of the French armies to coördinate American operations with the general plan of campaign.

From official documents and communications cited by General Savatier, it is evident that Foch and his officers were apprehensive that the American units, in their eagerness to march to Berlin, would advance beyond prescribed objectives. Savatier explains why American troops and not veterans were picked for the superhuman task of blazing the trail to final victory through the Argonne Forest.

The French general concludes his contribution, in the preparation of which he was greatly aided by Commander Collignon of the French Liaison Service, with pertinent comments on the A. E. F. from the point of view of the professional European soldier. He does not hesitate to criticize our troops. Nevertheless, he reaches the same conclusion as his opponent, General von Gallwitz. Both generals agree that the weight of America's sword inclined the scales of war in favour of the Entente.

II

THE RETREAT TO THE RHINE

By General Max von Gallwitz, Former Commander of a German Army Group

THE entrance of the American Expeditionary Forces into the great European war came about step by step, a procedure imposed by the necessity for organizing an army corresponding to those maintained by the older military powers, the training of this army, and its transportation overseas. Strong advance detachments, commissioned with preparatory work and general acclimatization, proceeded gradually increasing tactical units. Employment of American forces at the fighting front was also organized upon a systematically rising scale.

In January, 1918, I learned from reports that the 1st Division, A. E. F., was to be stationed opposite our front, between the Moselle and the Meuse. At first, officers put in their appearance, then enlisted men, but always intermingled with French effectives. Gradually, small American units formed in the trenches, alternating with French units. Later on, only American formations were active.

On January 30th, at Seicheprey, in the Woëvre Plain, we captured our first American prisoner, belonging to the 18th Infantry Regiment of the 1st Division. On April 20th, we succeeded in surprising the 1st Battalion of the 102nd Infantry Regiment, 26th Division, which had arrived at the front only two hours previous. On this occasion, 5 officers, 178 men, and 25 machine guns were captured.

The American front opposite us grew stronger continually. We knew that by May as many as eight American divisions had arrived in France. Speed of transportation overseas increased when the Allies, severely pressed by the German offensives, clamoured for assistance. By the beginning of August, we checked up on twenty-eight American divisions in France. Some fifteen of these appeared energetically in the front line. Americans more and more frequently emerged on different points of our positions. They attacked effectively, but always in coöperation with the French forces. It became clear that the growing number of American troops, together with an increasing feeling of national self-consciousness, would lead, not only to the formation of larger American units, but also to exclusively American enterprises with specific goals.

Now, I wrote in my diary as follows:

> I never expected such speedy developments. The Americans are becoming dangerous!

My apprehensions were confirmed on September 12th.

Between the French Second and Eighth Armies, opposite Army Unit C, then part of the forces under my command, an independent American army, under General John J. Pershing, came into being. Supported by the French, the Americans launched a big enterprise, attacking the "faulty triangle" of St. Mihiel. What happened there, and what conclusions we drew from these developments, have already been dwelt upon expertly by Major General Baron Otto von Ledebur, chief of staff, Army Unit C. It is left for me, however, to describe the situation ensuing after September 12th, because these developments reacted on other parts of my front. They created the very conditions from which developed the course of events on the opposite wing of my front, between the Argonne and the Meuse.

Previous to the attack against the German positions at St. Mihiel, reports have been received concerning a planned enemy drive against Metz involving both sides of the Moselle, and an invasion of Lorraine. To all appearances, an attack against so strong a fortress as Metz could not be considered tempting to the enemy. However, there was one possibility. The enemy might know that Metz had already been stripped of a great part of its defensive artillery for the reënforcement of our field army. It was natural enough for the enemy to invade the country to the northwest of Metz. There, the Briey–Longwy Iron Basin constituted one of the main sources of our armament. Of special importance to us were the railroad connections leading from Metz and Diedenhofen, by way of Longuyon, to the northwest. If these lines were actually disturbed, or even only threatened, communications with the armies in the west would be seriously interfered with. By flattening out the St. Mihiel triangle, Pershing's army got closer to these vulnerable points of our position.

It seemed obvious enough to look upon the American attack of September 12th upon St. Mihiel not as just an episode or an isolated stroke, but rather as the beginning of the frequently announced invasion of Lorraine. I was personally fully convinced that the results obtained there with comparative ease—we had immediately given way to the American attack—would be followed up without undue delay by additional attacks. Our new Michel Position, although much more desirable strategically than the St. Mihiel triangle, had not been completely finished, and offered, in parts, good opportunities to the approach of the enemy. I was greatly concerned about this wing of my army group, and endeavoured to concentrate there all the troops at my disposal, of which, however, there were not many. For the time being, problems of the Fifth Army, to the north and west of Verdun, had to be relegated to the background.

On September 13th, the enemy followed us only gropingly. An attack anticipated for the 14th did not materialize, and on the morning of that day I wrote in my diary:

> The enemy has granted us the great favour of giving us one more day of respite. This is quite valuable.

No attack occurred either on September 15th or 16th. The enemy, however, came closer and there was more activity in the foreground. I was reliably informed that, opposite that part of my front—the left wing of the Fifth Army and Army Unit C—where the opening thrust for the anticipated invasion of Lorraine was expected—nine American and six French divisions had been stationed, with six additional American and four French divisions held in reserve. It was also reported that there were not less than eleven hundred tanks at the disposal of the Americans, besides three hundred tanks in support of the French. However, farther to the west, along the Meuse, the enemy's forces had apparently not been reënforced.

Thus, there was no reason for us to assume that the

expected attack in the approximate direction of Conflans had been postponed. On the contrary, it seemed advisable for us, in view of such a possibility, to concentrate additional reënforcements for this event. That the enemy, for the time being, marked time, seemed sufficiently explained by the assumption that he was busying himself with systematically reconstituting his formations and reconnoitring our new position. A different interpretation was obtained from prisoners of the French 2nd Division of Cuirassiers. They maintained that the Americans, before launching another attack, meant to replace all the French now coöperating with them, in order to monopolize all the expected glory!

The following days, from September 17th to the 20th, did not yield any important developments, aside from lively fighting in the foreground. We found meanwhile sufficient time to establish ourselves. We looked forward to developments with equanimity. From the other wing, to the west of the Meuse, the enemy's sectors (as regards wireless or telegraphic communications) were reported to be suspiciously quiet on the evening of September 17th. During the next night, a continual noise of motors assailed our ears to the west of the Meuse. We were informed that in that neighbourhood Italians had appeared, but we did not interpret this news as a sign of an approaching attack, but rather as a mere measure of replacement. Nevertheless, to make sure, in the early hours of September 19th, three companies were thrust forward in the Meuse bend near Forges, for the purpose of bringing in prisoners. However, they returned empty-handed. A Frenchman, captured east of the Meuse, denied that the enemy had any intentions to attack, and a captured flyer stated that the great attack against Metz was timed for October.

Was the attack really postponed? It seemed so from the facts that the 2nd Division, A. E. F. (known to us as a crack unit, and stationed opposite the Michel Position), had meanwhile been replaced by the new 78th Division, A. E. F., according to statements of prisoners taken in advance-guard engagements. There were no tangible signs whatever of an imminent attack. Nor could such a development be expected in the near future, according to information obtained from prisoners.

I wish to point out here that captured Americans, as a rule, seemed to be quite candid in their statements, conveying a distinctly naïve impression when interrogated. Two flyers, belonging financially to the well-to-do element of their people, looked upon war primarily as a sporting proposition. They were gravely concerned when taken prisoners, and greatly surprised when well treated. One of them expected to be "beaten up." The other even anticipated being shot! Both stated unhesitatingly that the United States entered the war for financial reasons only. President Wilson, they added, was not at all desirous of humiliating Germany too much!

While quiet reigned supremely near Metz, the situation along the Meuse continued unsettled. Instead of the reported Italians, the 79th and 80th Divisions, A. E. F., put in their appearance on the west bank of the river. These divisions consisted of green troops. We at first assumed that their training was to receive the finishing touches on the hotly contested ground in front of Verdun. However, on September 23rd, opposite our Forges sector, members of the older 33rd Division, A. E. F., fell into our hands. We discovered next an extraordinarily strong replacement of fresh troops at the same point. We accordingly concentrated our attention upon this region. In addition, our neighbours to the west, belonging to the forces under the German Crown Prince, informed us that things in front of their sectors were getting quite lively. This information induced me to stop the 5th Bavarian Division of Reserves which, in anticipation of battles west of Metz, was now on the march to the east.

An aggravation of the situation manifested itself in a report, received on September 24th, to the effect that opposite the Third Army three new divisions had arrived. In the evening, I found that the Third Army, expecting to be attacked at dawn, relied on our support.

Thus I faced an altogether new situation.

The most obvious explanation seemed to be that the Americans, before launching their great thrust against the Briey–Longwy Iron Basin, were staging a manœuvre to deflect our forces to the west. But it was also possible that the Americans were preparing a decisive operation there while postponing the thrust against Metz.

General Pershing, by biding his time, had succeeded in keeping me in suspense and uncertainty.

Up to the evening of the 24th, I did not receive any enlightenment from our supreme command. On this day, an essential change in the situation developed. I ceased to act in the double rôle of commander of the Fifth Army and of the "Army Group Gallwitz." I remained merely leader of my own group, while the Fifth Army now came under its own commander, in the person of General of the Cavalry von der Marwitz.

The Fifth Army, stationed to the north of Verdun, had lost heavily through the heavy fighting in July and August. Later on, in September, rushing to the aid of Army Unit C, it attacked the St. Mihiel salient and was stripped of divisions, artillery and flyers to an extent that should be expected to occur only along a very quiet front.

This army now consisted of seven divisions only, organized in three groups. To the subsector west of the Meuse, between Vauquois[67] and the river, along a front of 14 kilometres, went the 117th and 7th Divisions of Reserves under the command of General von Oven. To the east of the Meuse there stood next the group of General Baron von Soden, with the Austrian 1st Division of Infantry touching the river and close to the German 15th Division of Infantry. The third group, consisting of three German divisions, under the command of the Austrian General Goiginger, forming the left wing of the Fifth Army, touched the right wing of the Army Unit C in the Woëvre Plain near Abaucourt.[68] Behind the front of this army, to the east of the Meuse, the 37th Division of Infantry and the 5th Bavarian Reserves formed a support. This reserve in theory included (behind the left group) an Austrian division which, however, I did not consider fieldworthy. Moreover, most of the German divisions, numbering only nine battalions, as compared to sixteen of American divisions, had fought heavy major engagements against the French and English but a short time before. These forces had now been retired to the temporarily quiet region opposite Verdun for rest and replacement. Until then, the enemy, too, rested there.

There were only two French divisions opposite Group Meuse-West. Two regiments of the 93rd (Negro) Division, A. E. F., reënforced them. Similarly, hardly more than two strengthened French divisions held a point on the eastern bank of the river.

The long period of repose along this part of the front ended during the next few days, beginning at the enemy's lines to the west of the Meuse. In answer to a request for support from the Third Army, on the evening of September 24th, I could do nothing else than put on the alert two battalions of reserves of the West Group, behind its outermost right wing. With the assistance of fleets of motor trucks, we brought back to the Meuse, near Dun, two thirds of the effectives of the 5th Bavarian Division of Reserves, stopped in their march toward the east. The last third, already farther advanced to the east, prepared to follow without delay.

The expected attack on the Argonne by the Third Army at dawn on September 25th did not materialize. However, signs indicated that such a coup was imminent. Also, in front of our West Group, activities increased suspiciously. They all pointed to the probability that this unit meant to take part in the anticipated fighting. It seemed that the enemy planned his attack to extend at least as far as the Meuse. Therefore, in the course of the day, I assigned the 5th Bavarian Division of Reserves, then assembling at Dun, to act as an "emergency unit" for the West Group, together with all such artillery and as many flyers as I was able to lay my hands on at that moment. It was understood that the 37th Division of Infantry, then behind the left wing of the army, was to advance by motor trucks toward Dun early the next morning.

It happened that on the afternoon of September 25th, a new American general command took over operations opposite our West Group. We counted not less than

382 aëroplanes in the airports behind the enemy's front. During the course of the evening, artillery became so active along the front, that at my headquarters at Montmédy window panes began to rattle.

As midnight approached, the activity of the artillery grew into drum fire. It extended along the whole front of the Third Army and from Group Meuse-West as far as Group Meuse-East. We soon convinced ourselves that our weak West Group would prove to be the enemy's objective. A patrol, advancing at two o'clock on this dire morning, near Béthincourt,[69] brought back one man of the 4th Division, A. E. F., which until lately stood opposite Army Unit C, and which now, obviously for attacking purposes, inserted itself between the 33rd Division on the Meuse and the 79th near Avocourt.[70]

The morning proved foggy. The sun did not pierce the clouds before 10 A. M. The attack broke on a front extending from the Champagne to the Meuse with the aforementioned three American divisions of 48 battalions against the 18 battalions of our West Group. Extending to the west, additional American forces dashed against the left wing of the Third Army in the Argonne. The Americans, with their much superior artillery, succeeded in galling our rear with a very heavy barrage fire. Thus they interfered with the dispatch of orders and blocked the approach of our reserves. General von Oven ordered one third of the only troops at his disposal at this moment, the 5th Bavarian Division of Reserves, to stand behind the 117th Division of Infantry, and another third behind the 7th Division of Reserves, while the last third, together with one regiment of artillery, was assigned to Nantillois.[71]

However, ten o'clock arrived relentlessly before these troops did. Meanwhile, the enemy's superior forces succeeded in penetrating our front lines. First, the 7th Division of our Reserves, thinly spread out along a front of 9 kilometres, yielded to the onrush of the 33rd and 4th American Divisions. A short time later, Cuisy, only 4 kilometres behind our most advanced line, fell to the enemy pressing on toward Septsarges.[72] The American 33rd Division soon succeeded in gaining ground beyond the woods near Forges and Gercourt in the direction of Dannevoux,[73] 7 kilometres behind our original line.

The 117th Division, occupying a limited area around and to the west of Malancourt, succeeded at first in holding their ground. However, the retreat of the 7th Division of Reserves presently made itself felt to the left, while at the same time the neighbour to the right, too, gave way. At the left wing of the Third Army, to the east of Varennes[74] near Vauquois,[75] the 1st Division of the Guards held for a while. This division, too, drew back later to the woods, 5 kilometres behind our first lines, succumbing to the superior forces of the Americans, especially the 73rd Division, A. E. F. When the Americans succeeded in breaking through near Véry,[76] the 117th Division, first bending back both of their wings, subsequently retreated to the village of Montfaucon,[77] which our men then held.

Meanwhile, General von Oven ordered counter attacks against the enemy, following us up in mass formation, and supported by strong reserves. Two regiments of the 5th Bavarian Division of Reserves were to advance, by way of Cuisy, toward Septsarges. Two additional regiments of the 37th Division of Infantry, which I had put at the disposal of General von Oven, were ordered to counter attack Ivoiry, to the west of Montfaucon. The third of the three regiments belonging to this division held itself in readiness to support the 7th Division of Reserves. To the west of it, the 5th Division of the Guards, belonging to the Third Army, now advanced within the sector of the 1st Division of the Guards. I also summoned the 115th Division of Infantry from Army Unit C, ordering these troops to entrain on whatever motor trucks returned after transporting the 37th Division to the front.

However, an ill omen seemed to attend the counter attacks thus directed. As far as the 5th Bavarian Division of Reserves was concerned, their transportation and formation was terribly handicapped by the barrage fire of the enemy. In this way the counter thrust, so impatiently awaited, did not come off before 5 P. M. Thus, precious hours slipped from us. As was to be expected under such circumstances, this action turned out quite unsatisfactory. In addition, the attack of the 37th Division did not develop according to our plan, as only one of their regiments was in front. The second regiment of this division, brought up on narrow-gauged railways, found its way blocked by traffic at Romagne,[78] while the third, ordered to support the left wing, did not get any farther than Dun. The 5th Division of the Guards, too, proved unable to regain the ground lost to the east of Varennes.

By this time we had been thrown back about 6 or 7 kilometres, with our new lines running from Charpentry by way of Epinonville[79]–Montfaucon–Septsarges, toward Sivry[80] on the Meuse. The enemy's plan therefore succeeded. His clever preparations, and especially the fact that our attention was deflected too long by developments at St. Mihiel, led to the insufficiency of our forces now surprised to the west of the Meuse.

On the east bank of the river, too, the enemy advanced against the Austrians without, however, launching a serious attack there. Nevertheless, the enemy succeeded in pushing back our line to the left of the river from Forges, as far as the north of Dannevoux. The Austrian Lieutenant Field Marshal Metzger accordingly bent back his line on the right bank of the Meuse and extended it, for which purpose two battalions of the 15th Division hastened to his right wing. The enemy blew up the bridge across the Meuse at Consenvoye.[81] He undertook the destruction of the bridges at Sivry and Vilosnes,[82] but wet fuses frustrated him. On the heights south of Haraumont, strong field pieces and a number of heavy batteries were concentrated to flank the west bank of the river. Here, during the night, American forces once more established contact with the depleted remnants of the 7th Division of Reserves which, in turn, retreated to the bridge at Vilosnes.

Our supreme command, not at all elated by these developments, ordered the 236th Division of Infantry, as reënforcements, by railroad to Dun. In addition, the 28th Division of Infantry, belonging to Army Unit C, was ordered westward.

In the course of the forenoon, the enemy continued his attacks by way of Ivoiry and Septsarges. To all appearances, the Americans endeavoured to encircle Montfaucon from both sides, in order to pinch it off. General von Oven reported counter attacks, although lack of concentrated reserves prevented the individual battalions we employed here from developing sufficient shock power. The enemy meanwhile advanced up to Nantillois. I ordered that Montfaucon be relinquished and a new line established, running from Epinonville, by way of the heights to the north of Nantillois to Brieulles.[83] The foremost regiment of the 115th Division of Infantry was not expected to reach the West Group before the afternoon, while the arrival of trains at Dun, carrying the 236th Division, was anticipated at 4 P. M. In addition, the shock battalion of Captain Rohr, a crack unit of picked men, got orders to come forward.

At noon a welcome message came. Along the new line, a strong attack launched from Montfaucon was repelled! Subsequently, we took Nantillois. Beginning at 3 P. M., a number of powerful enemy attacks, supported by strong artillery and tanks, between the Argonne and the neighbourhood of Nantillois, proved abortive. Also, between 7 and 8 P. M., a strong attack with tanks from the direction of Montfaucon–Septsarges was repulsed. Our situation seemed satisfactory once more, with the only exception that it had been necessary to bend back the right wing from Epinonville to Cierges. This disconcerting detail is easily explained. The enemy bore hard upon the corresponding wing of the neighbouring army.

Along the Meuse, things as a whole seemed languishing. The bridge at Sivry did meanwhile blow up. The other at Vilosnes held. The enemy subjected the East Group to gas shells. According to the enemy Report of the Day, the Americans took five thousand of our men prisoners between the Argonne and the Meuse.

A captured flyer stated that the enemy with his attack in the Champagne meant to effect a breach in our lines and that the thrust on the west bank of the Meuse, where six American divisions concentrated, was merely a secondary enterprise. To the east of the Meuse, French effectives took up their station, but with no idea of attack. On the other hand, the English were expected to resume their forward movement by the beginning of October, simultaneously with a great drive toward Metz–Briey which was to be extended to the north, as far as the Verdun–Etain highroad. Frenchmen captured to the east of the Meuse unanimously declared that their attacks in that region were not serious.

All this sounded quite plausible. It eventually proved to be not absolutely correct. Nevertheless, I was of the opinion that I must not weaken my wing to the west of Metz too much.

In the morning, the Americans renewed their attacks against the two divisions of the guards adjacent to us. However, these attacks were not so successful as previous ones, because the 52nd Division of Infantry arrived meanwhile. The attack spread to our own front, reaching as far as Brieulles, in a few hours.

About this time, General von der Marwitz, who, after completion of his staff, had the leadership of the Fifth Army well in hand, stationed two regiments of the 115th Division at Romagne. Five battalions of the 236th Division arrived at Bantheville, while two regiments of field artillery were just approaching. The two regiments of the 115th Division got upon their feet to cope with a thrust launched against Cierges. We took back Cierges in short order.

In the afternoon, the enemy again attacked from the region of Nantillois. He succeeded in driving a breach into Ogons Wood[84]—halfway between Cierges and Brieulles. Parts of the 115th Division advanced against the enemy here, but did not make satisfactory progress, in view of the tanks supporting a stronger enemy. At last, in the course of the evening, a Bavarian regiment took Ogons Wood out of the hands of the enemy.

Thus, in the course of this day, we held our front as a whole. Nevertheless, it was painful to read the American Report of the Day. It stated the number of prisoners taken as now eight thousand, with a hundred guns captured.

The Americans, having sufficient effectives at their disposal, attacked in close, deeply arranged formations. The considerable number of tanks they employed created consternation, especially among our green troops. Our artillery, however, coped with them successfully. As early as September 26th, a battery at the edge of Montfaucon Wood[85] succeeded in destroying six tanks.

According to statements made by prisoners, the Americans by this time held eighteen of their divisions around Verdun. We continuously detected additional new divisional insignia. As for the west bank of the Meuse, we discovered there more than six divisions, as originally reported. That famous American crack unit, the 2nd Division, withdrew from opposite Army Unit C, and was now reported to be near Montfaucon. Between the 33rd and 4th Divisions, a brigade of the 80th Division took up a position.

There were new enemy attacks on the morning of September 29th. Although, at first, these attacks were repelled, Ogons Wood was lost once more to us. However, the enemy did not advance toward Brieulles inasmuch as our artillery, from the heights of the other bank of the Meuse, succeeded in flanking the Americans. From Ogons Wood, the opponent now pressed unsuccessfully against the near-by Cunel Wood. Finally, between 1 and 2 P. M., a fourth enemy attack, launched by a division against Ogons Wood, was repulsed with heavy losses for the Americans.

During the course of the afternoon an advance against the left wing of the 1st Division of the Guards was met with a counter attack of parts of the 37th Division of Infantry. As this operation created a gap between our wing and the Guards, four battalions of the 236th Division poured into the breach. In this way, General von der Marwitz subsequently lacked sufficient effectives to retake Ogons Wood. Renouncing this position altogether, for the time being, he also voluntarily relinquished far-advanced Cierges, ordering the West Group to establish themselves along an almost straight line from Gesnes[86] to Brieulles. The 236th Division moved in its entirety right into the front line, where it released its other units for reorganization purposes. In this way, consolidation of our lines became more perfect.

Again attacks by tanks played a big part although their shock strength was repeatedly interfered with by our artillery fire from the other bank of the Meuse. A number of prisoners were taken. They belonged to a tank battalion, newly arrived from Paris. Our infantry gradually became more adept in coping with these tanks. The brave East Prussians of the 150th Infantry Regiment put six tanks out of commission by employing hand grenades.

On the east bank of the Meuse, artillery fire and reconnoitring activity in the air grew pronounced. Some of the measures taken there had to be interpreted as pointing to an attack. That this attack, having gained ground so far, would subsequently extend to the east bank, seemed probable on account of the crooked line of our front. In addition, it seemed expedient from the enemy's standpoint to endeavour to eliminate the very disturbing flanking fire still maintained from the other bank of the river.

A captured flier was reported to have remarked to some other prisoner: "Now an attack on the other bank of the river is due, with the Briey Iron Basin as the goal. In case it is not possible to drive a wedge into the German position, we shall try to get as close to the Metz–Montmédy railroad as possible, in order to keep it under fire during the winter."

To the east of the Meuse we found leaflets addressed to the American soldiers and signed by General Pershing. In these he stressed the great importance of a general major offensive. The troops were called upon to do their very best in forcefully executing the whole enterprise. From an order by the commanding general of the Third Army Corps, A. E. F., addressed to the 1st, 3rd, 4th, 33rd, and 80th Divisions, we gathered that the 1st and 3rd Divisions had also moved from opposite the front of Army Unit C and that reënforced troops must now incessantly press against our Fifth Army. For this reason, Army Unit C, for the time being, had to be weakened still more in order to bolster up the Fifth Army.

On September 29th, I transferred my army group command from Montmédy, where it had been established for the last twenty-one months, to Longwy. On September 30th, the enemy kept comparatively quiet. Undoubtedly, the Americans also suffered heavy losses during the last fighting. They made no appreciable progress, inasmuch as they stood in need of replacements and reorganization. This respite also benefited us. We effected a restoration of our own lines during this brief period. (See map facing p. 240.)

Again, the West Group took Ogons Wood. An attack against this position, at 2 P. M., on October 1st, we contrived to throw back. Otherwise, the enemy kept quiet, utilizing this time for the relief of his forces. By then, most of his attack divisions assembled there. We estimated that the Americans now had eleven divisions to the west of the Meuse, of which at least four faced our West Group in advanced positions. It seemed improbable that the Americans would renew their attack as early as October 2nd; however, I was expecting it on the 4th of the month.

Meanwhile, the Fifth Army put in this time advantageously by placing the 28th Division of Infantry behind the left half of the West Group, while the 228th Division reënforced Group Meuse–East. We now had tolerably sufficient effectives at our disposal, although we remained still greatly inferior, numerically, to the enemy. However, this corner at the Meuse must be maintained under all conditions, especially in view of an unfavourable turn in the general situation. In Flanders and at Cambrai, we had suffered appreciable setbacks, while on the night of October 1st–2nd we abandoned St. Quentin. Once more the enemy stood along the Chemin des Dames.

Five Americans of the 32nd Division were brought in as prisoners on the morning of the 4th. They stated that their unit went out on the line as long ago as September 30th, and that the attack had been postponed because bad roads held up ammunition transport. Nevertheless, the attack was to come off soon.

Drum fire, with the suddenness of thunder, started in along the whole length of our front, to the east as well as the west of the Meuse at half-past five in the morning. The fire was heaviest against the inner wings of the Fifth and Third Armies. An infantry attack of the Third and Fifth Army Corps, A. E. F., soon engaged our West Group, and the left wing of the Third Army. In this engagement divisions, mostly fresh, flung recklessly into the battle their deeply arranged masses, supported by numerous tanks. At many points, the Americans screened their advance with heavy artificial fog.

The right wing, as well as the centre of the West Group, parried all thrusts bravely. Without wavering the least bit, our 115th Division held the ground against the 32rd American Division. On the front of the 236th Division, Ogons Wood was lost once more for some time, and once more retaken by counter attacks. Although the 80th American Division succeeded apparently in opening a breach in the front of the weak 5th Bavarian Division of Reserves assigned to the region adjacent to the Meuse, this damage was mended in the course of the afternoon by a counter attack of the Hohenzollern Fusiliers.

For some time, reports from our neighbour to the right filled us with alarm. It appeared that the two divisions of the Guards fighting there were in an unsatisfactory condition. Moreover, the 52nd Division was pressed back, as the enemy advanced to Fléville on the Aire. In support of a counter thrust, we put the 37th

Division at the disposal of the Argonne Group, and in the evening Fléville once more was ours.

Toward noon, I repaired to the battlefield of the West Group. However, I did not reach a spot sufficiently elevated to view the situation, inasmuch as the roads were covered by the low barrage fire of the enemy. Things were very lively behind the front. I talked to numerous wounded men, who all insisted that the enemy must have suffered terrific losses. They were not greatly impressed with the effect of the American artillery. The men related with pride how tank attacks had been resisted, reporting that many tanks were destroyed by artillery and machine guns. One lieutenant blew up with his guns not less than three of those monstrous tanks, if current rumours meant anything.

Our flyers, too, gave a very good account of themselves. They not only brought in important information in regard to the development of the fighting, but also succeeded in preventing the enemy from observing movements in our rear.

The favourable impression I derived from my visit to the battlefield was strengthened when I read reports received by General von Oven. In the evening, the whole Fifth Army felt in the best of humour, on account of having completely repulsed a superior opponent.

More than once before I felt the necessity of close coöperation between the West Group of the Fifth Army and Group Argonne of the Third Army. It was for this reason that the supreme command ordered Group Argonne to be attached to the Fifth Army. This group, under the command of General von Kleist, extended from our position, as far as the Argonne, over a distance of approximately 12 kilometres. The group consisted partly of the 52nd Division and the 5th and 1st Divisions of the Guards, the last only relieved by the 45th Division of the Reserves at this very moment. All the way over on the right wing, occupying the woods, lay the 2nd Division of Territorials, a unit employed there since the beginning of the war and made up of elderly, brave Swabians.

Simultaneously, at the opposite left wing of my army group, fortress as well as Group Metz were attached to Army Unit C, thus becoming subordinated to my command. In this way we achieved a more efficient unification of leadership. My army group, now reaching from Grandpré in the Argonne to Nomény, east of the Moselle, in general compared with Army Group Pershing, which aside from the First, Third, Fourth, and Fifth Army, A. E. F., also comprised some smaller French units.

Our units had already grown quite depleted. The supreme command ordered the formation of infantry regiments of only two battalions. At the same time, as was known to us, the French, too, laboured under a similar embarrassment. Only the American units were strong in effectives. According to Horsea, the English broadcasting station, not less than 311,000 Americans landed in the course of September. By now, 1,760,000 American soldiers trod European soil.

On October 5th, the opponent again attacked strongly. Aside from unimportant changes, Group Kleist as well as Group Oven maintained their ground. On the boundary between these two groups at Landres, the 41st Division of Infantry was newly stationed as reserves. On the morning of October 6th the enemy renewed his attacks. They proved especially strong.

The West Group, which had meanwhile inserted the 28th Division between the 236th Division and the Bavarians, nevertheless succeeded in repelling all these thrusts. Côbe Dame Marie, lost by the 52nd Division in the morning, was recaptured with the assistance of one regiment of the 45th Division of Reserves.

In the evening, the Americans once more launched an attack against the two groups, but after severe hand-to-hand fighting, they also were repelled. A breach driven into the lines of the 459th Infantry Regiment belonging to the 236th Division was fully remedied by concentrating the very last reserves of this regiment, under the personal leadership of the commander. Once more our artillery from beyond the Meuse had been very effective, according to unanimous statements of prisoners, who spoke of very heavy losses on their side. It was said by them that a number of their divisions had to be retired for reorganization, and that especially the 1st Division, A. E. F., suffered heavy casualties. Nevertheless, the hardy Americans stated that the attacks continue.

In the course of the night, the 2nd Division of Territorials in the Argonne, in accordance with orders received, withdrew their projecting line toward the Aire River. In this way, the village Châtel Chéhéry[87] on the Aire moved into our first line, thus forming a salient of our new front, and becoming the main centre of the enemy's thrusts launched to both sides of the river. At 10 A. M., October 7th, the Americans entered Châtel Chéhéry fighting for the so-called Châtel Hill and other elevations near by. Around noon the enemy, hardly gaining a foothold, gave up Châtel Hill, while all other attempts against other elevations were rendered abortive. Only one point, Bellevue, was occupied by the enemy and successfully held against all our counter attacks. To the west of Châtel, Swabian Territorials conducted themselves excellently.

The enemy also re-attacked Group Meuse-West. An assault along the Eclisfontaine–Romagne highway, directed against the 115th Division, broke down under our annihilating fire. Soon, fighting raged along both sides of the Nantillois–Cunel highway, where we succeeded in maintaining our positions.

Just when I went to Buzancy, to talk over matters with Group Kleist, newly attached to my command, strong artillery fire concentrated on our lost positions Châtel Hill and Bellevue. The commander of the artillery told me that his batteries, fighting uninterruptedly for twelve days, were completely exhausted. Moreover, stocks of ammunition ran short. At that very moment, one "regiment" of the 45th Division of Reserves was thrown into the fray, in order to retake Châtel Hill.

The "regiments" of these depleted divisions did not number more than 400 to 600 rifles. Of course, while on the defensive, machine guns and field pieces proved efficient, but when it came to assault operations, there was a deplorable lack of fighters in these skeleton regiments. Nevertheless, we took the hill once more.

Along the Aire, a new attack against the 37th Division was soon under way. The divisional commander told me that his East Prussian troops, although very brave, were well-nigh exhausted. Notwithstanding this fact, they succeeded in repelling the new attack near Fléville.[88] The commander of the 52nd Division informed me that his effectives were depleted. Moreover, by continually inserting reserves into the line, and through counter attacks, individual units greatly intermingled. For example, in the line of the 52nd Division, members of not less than five other divisions fought at that moment.

With the exception of Bellevue,[89] we held now all points into which the enemy so recently intruded. We noticed that the American attack suffered because it lacked unity.

Captured American flying officers declared that Wilson would treat Germany sympathetically at the peace conference, but Germany must suffer a military defeat beforehand.

As early as October 7th, very heavy traffic set in opposite our Group Meuse-East. The French 26th Division there moved in. On the morning of October 8th, drum fire seemed quite close by. All reserves at our disposal moved up closer to their respective line units.

It was at 7:30 A. M. when the American–French attack east of the Meuse was launched, partly landing against the front of Austrian 1st Division of Infantry. This division, its line already greatly widened and bent back along the Meuse, was weakened further by the detachment, temporarily, of three of its chasseur battalions. The 15th Division and the right wing of the 33rd Division also felt the American–French attack.

The French attack against these two divisions came to a standstill. The assault of the 33rd American and French 18th Divisions along the Meuse meanwhile shook the weakened line of the Austrians. The river was forced by the enemy. At the same time, he advanced to the right bank of it near Samogneux. The villages Consenvoye,[90] Brabant,[91] and Haumont, within our own lines, until then, fell into the enemy's hands. To some extent he drove beyond our main line of resistance.

It proved impossible for us to unify a counter attack of the 32nd Saxonian Division, dispatched to support the Austrians. The first units of the Saxonians, as soon as they arrived, were thrown into the battle for local assistance, as the pressing situation demanded. In this way, however, it became possible to prevent the break of a line running through Consenvoye Wood; later on, in the course of the night, the left and centre subsectors of the Austrians were taken over by the Saxonians. Behind the right wing of the Austrians, one regiment of the 228th Division was stationed.

While all this happened on the east bank of the Meuse, Group Oven on the west of the river had not been attacked with any great force to speak of. However, the Americans once more staged powerful assaults, against both sides of the Aire. There were new battles for the possession of Châtel, in the course of which the enemy succeeded in advancing his lines to Châtel Hill and the neighbouring elevations. This progress was followed by severe mass attacks against Cornay[92] which, however, were repulsed. In the evening, Côbe Dame Marie was in the possession of the Americans, but retaken by us before nocturnal fighting had ceased.

The American report of October 9th stated that three thousand prisoners were captured the day before. The enemy continued his attacks to the west and east of the Meuse.

Between the Aisne and the Aire, near and to the west of Cornay, Swabian territorials repelled all assaults; especially attacks with the so-called "Humser Hill" as the objective. From Cornay proper, to where the foe penetrated, Colonel Mayer, commanding, quickly assembled remnants of his regiment, ejected the opponent in desperate fighting from house to house, succeeding so well that 2 American officers and 164 enlisted men were taken prisoners by him. Two lieutenants of the artillery —all that was left of their unit—kept on firing the very last gun not yet destroyed, until the enemy attack definitely broke down.

East of the Aire, the enemy time and again brought new masses up to the line. Again, Côbe Dame Marie was lost with the opponent gaining ground toward Sommerance. Inasmuch as it proved impossible to eject the foe here, the 2nd Division of Territorials withdrew behind the Aire for the duration of the night.

In the line of Group Meuse–West, the 115th Division at first maintained its ground. However, after the 236th Division, in a heavy fog, succumbed to pressure and went back beyond Romagne, while, on the other side, enemy pressure also became noticeable in the direction of Sommerance,[93] the 115th Division simply retired. Adjacent to this unit, General Kreuter personally led the advance of parts of the 236th and 115th Divisions. Coöperating with a counter thrust delivered from the east, he reoccupied Romagne and stemmed the enemy's advance there.

Later, farther to the east, in the subsector of the 28th Division, the enemy fell back toward Cunel Wood, as the result of a counter attack. Our situation seemed reassured here in the course of the afternoon. However, after drum fire of the utmost severity, centre and left wing of the West Group were again attacked this very afternoon with the result that the 236th Division took refuge in the wood north of Cunel. In the course of the evening, the foe was again pushed back to the north edge of the village which we took once more during the night.

Our troops behaved extremely well in the face of the enemy's mass attacks, but reports from the Fifth Army stated that, of the two regiments of the 236th Division, only fragments survived. The resistance of the 115th Division became greatly impaired not only by enormous casualties, but also on account of increasing losses in prisoners, in the course of a stubborn resistance. Both divisions were reported to be in no shape any longer to withstand further attacks of such fury as those last. To ameliorate the situation, I ordered the 123rd Division attached to the West Group.

To the east of the Meuse, too, severe fighting went on since early in the morning, along the line from Vilosnes to Flabas. The battle opened when the Austrian 5th Regiment of Infantry, stationed adjacent to the Meuse, received the shock of an American mass attack under cover of the morning fog. It fell back after brave resistance, losing the Crown Prince Hill, a favourite observation point. A counter attack of German troops blocked further advance by the enemy.

Sivry on the Meuse was lost and retaken.

From the direction of Etraye, in order to recapture ground lost by the Austrians the day before, the 32nd Division had attacked early in the morning, making good progress at first, to halt later on when the foe resorted to counter attacks of greater strength. After renewed artillery preparation, the enemy once more attacked in the afternoon; fighting at close quarters ensued, especially in Haumont Wood. The foe gained little ground, suffering staggering losses. We, too, sustained severe casualties.

Farther to the east, the 15th Division, together with the Austrian chasseurs attached to it, again maintained their line of resistance against repeated heavy assaults. Whenever a break occurred, immediate counter attacks remedied the situation. Even after nightfall, a strong attack was repulsed.

In the evening, our line stretched from Sivry through Ormont and Haumont Woods. From the tales told by some 250 men captured by us, we could draw the conclusion that opposite Group Meuse–East not only the American 33rd and 29th Divisions, but also the French 18th and 26th Divisions, together with the French 10th Colonial Division held the enemy's line.

Activity in the air was very lively during the day. Enemy bombers, arranged in four formations of from thirty to forty aëroplanes each, advanced against our rear on the east bank of the river. In spite of the fact that all our pursuit planes went up, the opponent succeeded in advancing as far as Réville and Damvillers. Eight aëroplanes and one balloon were brought down by us. The captured American flyers, when interrogated, once more proved themselves insufficiently trained, from a military point of view, and politically uninformed.

In spite of a few setbacks, I felt that I had every reason to be satisfied with the results of the day in so far as they yielded a great number of shining examples of bravery. It had been demonstrated that, even within numerically weak units, much reliable strength was left. Nevertheless, the actual numerical losses worried me. Pointing to the importance of the Fifth Army, as the corner stone of all operations to the west and north of it, I appealed to the supreme command for additional effectives.

In the course of the evening, we were informed of President Wilson's answer to the German request for armistice preliminaries. The reply stated that there could be no negotiations before we relinquished the occupied territory. I, for my part, considered this suggestion unacceptable.

Without the enemy discovering it, the 2nd Division of Territorials retired behind the Aire. On October 10th, the enemy still shelled the deserted positions. To the east of the Aire, he cautiously groped toward the Sommerance–Romagne road, apparently drawing fresh effectives behind him.

Severe local attacks were directed by the Americans against Group Meuse–West. Some of these were executed in mass formation of greatest density, which accounted for the fact that many of them broke down as soon as they were covered by machine-gun and artillery fire. After invading a farm southwest of Romagne the opponent was ejected by a counter attack. An attack against the 236th Division, launched after a short preparatory fire, broke down before our advance. After renewed attempts to penetrate our line, the enemy toward midnight finally scored some results.

The fighting on the east bank was more severe. The Americans attacked the line Sivry–Hill 371 (known as Oak Hill), but we succeeded in holding Sivry. Part of the hill, defended for the last three days by Austrians and Saxonians, was taken in the course of the enemy's first assault, but later on reoccupied by us, thus reestablishing our old line. A new assault was repulsed in the afternoon.

The impetus developed by the enemy against the 32nd Division eventually not only succeeded in maintaining their position, but also regained Ormont Wood, lost on October 8th. The 15th Division also maintained their ground during the day, with the exception of a slight indentation. Fourteen enemy planes and two balloons were brought down. According to information obtained from prisoners, the object of the attack to the east of the Meuse was the elimination of our flanking artillery fire, which greatly interfered with progress on the west bank of the river.

New troops now arrived amounting altogether to five divisions. To be sure, two of them coming from the Third Army were utterly exhausted and expected to gain some rest here. Within the 3rd Division of the Guards, battalions did not number more than 377 men on an average.

All in all, the day had not been so bad. From the other main front, slow retreating operations were reported. Cambrai had been abandoned.

The feeling of general satisfaction with which the developments of the last few days imbued me dwindled somewhat when the Americans reported that they had taken an additional two thousand of our men prisoners. To be sure, this figure referred to the entire American front.

The enemy continued his attacks on the 11th. A local thrust, in the Argonne, to the east of St. Juvin,[94] was repelled, while we regained the Ludwig Hill by counter attacking. Enemy detachments, groping their way toward the hill to the southeast of Landres, occupied by the 41st Division, were pressed back while our assault troops reached the Sommerance–Romagne road.

Again, there were lively attacks against Group

Meuse–West. In the course of the morning, we lost the village of Cunel[95] but we took it back and held it against renewed American assaults, with our 123rd Saxonian Division of Infantry, newly arrived. Another assault, prepared by the heaviest fire of medium and large calibre guns and launched frontally against Group Meuse–West around 2 P. M., broke down with visibly heavy casualties on the part of the enemy. Nevertheless, in the course of the evening, the Americans along the Romagne–Cunel road drove before them parts of the exhausted 236th Division—just relieved by the 123rd Division. Along the western bank of the Meuse, fresh American divisions attacked, among them the 42nd and apparently, also, the 91st Division.

In front of Group Meuse–East, too, there was lively fighting; however, no unified plan seemed in execution there, with the Americans indulging merely in local thrusts at different times. The Americans that night struck out against the Austrian 1st and Saxonian 32nd Divisions, with very stubborn fighting around Oak Hill and the so-called Big Star. At different times, our infantry pursued. In the early hours of the day, Ormont Wood was lost once more. Here, Capt. Blohm, in charge of a battalion, fought his way out, although surrounded, and, reassembling the fragments of two companies, once more got the wood into our possession. Along the line of the 15th Division, not less than five attacks were repulsed.

Considerably intensified low-barrage fire by the enemy reaching our rear made itself felt disturbingly. We assumed that by now the Americans must be reenforced by French artillery. The American report of October 11th again stated that eleven hundred of our men were captured, among them a colonel and two battalion staffs.

There was less activity west of the Meuse in another day or two. Cunel, occupied by the Americans in the morning, was ours again in the evening. We held all our ground here. On the eastern bank of the river, however, the Americans brought renewed pressure to bear upon Ormont Wood and Wavrille.[96] By concentrating their artillery and recklessly sacrificing their massed infantry, the Americans tried to force a breach in our lines, in the direction of Gibercy. When, at the onset of the first thrust, the Americans effected a wedge in our lines, reserves, immediately summoned, closed the gap. All during the day, Saxonian, Prussian, Austrian, and Swabian troops fought stubbornly against Americans and French along the line of Group Meuse–East.

Captain Blohm, who had recaptured Ormont Wood the day before, defended his position all during this day. Completely surrounded, himself severely wounded, this valiant fighter, together with the last thirty of his men, made his way back to our lines when darkness fell.

The enemy's attempt to break our front turned out a failure. Our combat flyers played a very active part in the last phases of the fight. One of our units, by flying only 30 metres high, dispersed a mixed group of effectives, marching from Samogneux toward Ormont Wood.

The Austrians were now being relieved by the 228th Division. I was also informed that a number of additional divisions would be moved in, but all these troops were very much in need of rest and ordered, for the time being, to remain in the rear as reserves for the supreme command.

In the evening, we learned of Germany's reply to

President Wilson's note, which agreed to everything including the evacuation of occupied territory. The officers of my staff and I were simply thunderstruck at this news!

The Americans were quiet on the 13th, evidently because they, like ourselves, were in need of reorganization and rest. Engaged in continuous fighting for nine days, they gained but 6 or 7 kilometres along the Aire, and only 2 to 4 kilometres along the Meuse, and to the east of it. American prisoners stated unanimously that they paid for these results very dearly. In one single battalion subsector opposite Group Meuse–East we counted not less than 400 dead Americans. Prisoners, taken by Group Meuse–East, reached the number of 360 enlisted men and 6 officers. Our units utilized the quiet day to improve their positions, partly by pressing forward.

The Americans, on the following day, once again launched attacks west of the Meuse, while their allies, on the eastern bank, still rested. Late in the day, we lost St. Juvin. The enemy's main thrust, mostly carried by tanks, was directed against the left wing of the Group Argonne. Here, near St. Georges, the thrust struck the 37th Division just when the 15th Bavarian Division relieved it. As the Bavarians fell back, parts of the 37th Division again moved to the front and rushed upon the Americans with the result that we recovered St. Georges, meanwhile invaded by the opponents' tanks.

East Prussian troops of the 41st Division, fighting right near by at Landres, held out valiantly. In the course of the day, these effectives repelled not less than four massed American attacks, partly in hand-to-hand fighting, while maintaining their position. In addition, an attack launched against the village late in the evening was also repulsed.

Attacks directed against the Group Meuse–West in the course of the morning lacked unity. While the 3rd Division of the Guards, relieving the 115th Division in occupying Romagne and the terrain to the west of it, was the objective of attacks as early as 7 A. M., a thrust against the 28th Division to the east of Cunel did not come off before 9:20 A. M., and the onslaught against the 123rd Division, stationed between the two aforementioned divisions, not before 10:30 A. M., October 14th.

Early in the forenoon, the Americans opened a deep breach in the ranks of the exhausted 3rd Division of the Guards, which had been sent to me "to rest up," but had, from sheer necessity, been employed immediately. Here, also, one regiment of the relieved divisions had to go back to the front, but as it proved impossible to mend the damage, we relinquished Romagne, encircled by the Americans on both sides. We carried our line back about 800 metres north of the village. The 123rd Division bent back its wings accordingly, but otherwise held the ground around Cunel, even against a strong new onslaught which was repelled with the very able assistance of our artillery. Those enemy forces, which went through the right wing of the 28th Division, were stopped to the northeast of Cunel.

The Fifth Army reported that, of their effectives, 7 regiments of field artillery and 8 battalions of heavy artillery were utterly exhausted. An additional heavy battalion had been completely annihilated on October 4th at Haumont Wood. I was unable to replace more than about half of these exhausted units. In view of the fact that fighting grew much more intense along the east bank of the Meuse a new subsector command was formed at Beaumont between the Groups Meuse–East and Ornes, to which we attached the 1st Division of Territorials and the 15th Division of Infantry.

The lack of effectives from which we suffered now was especially striking compared with the wealth in man power at the disposal of the Americans. Regiments of their field artillery consisted of six batteries and fifteen hundred men. We were informed that during the first day of the battle, on September 26th, four relief platoons had been at the disposal of each individual battery. As far as our batteries were concerned, there were many which had no relief whatever at their disposal.

The very next day (October 15th) was enlivened by strong but not unified local attacks. The 2nd Division of Territorials prevented the Americans from forcing the Aire. The 45th Division of Reserves and the 15th Bavarian Division, launched in the morning against the rolling terrain near St. Juvin in an attempt to reoccupy this region, reached their objectives partially, but proved unable to hold their gains against the counter thrusts of a numerically superior enemy. After we had been heavily shelled by the opponent's artillery, an attack was launched against us in the late afternoon which forced us back somewhat to the north of St. Juvin. On the other hand, the 41st Division once more held their ground. The 148th Infantry Regiment advanced against the charging enemy, throwing them back after fighting at close quarters. The 152nd Regiment remained in possession of the hill southeast of Landres against all onslaughts.

Along the front of Group Meuse–West, the 3rd Division of the Guards gave way before the enemy until it got to about the middle of the wood near Bantheville.[97] By counter attacks of the 13th Division newly moved in, we succeeded in reëstablishing our line along the southern edge of the wood. The right wing of the 123rd Division, too, was invaded by the enemy. Late into the night, attacks and counter attacks were conducted here until our old lines had been regained.

Opposite Group Meuse–East, enemy pressure was exerted especially against the 32nd Division. Here fighting, mostly in wooded ground, lasted all day long, without furnishing a clear picture of the situation in general. But we managed to hold our line.

The American report of the day before again stated that an additional seven hundred and fifty men had been captured. We were also informed that since October 12th, the American army had been reorganized and that General Pershing was now the superior commander of General Hunter Liggett's First Army as well as General Robert Bullard's Second Army. It was reported that another American army, commanded by General Bell, was stationed in Flanders. We judged that the forces facing us, including the reserves at their disposal, amounted to twenty-eight American divisions, intermingled with ten French divisions. In this connection, it must not be overlooked that an American division, normally twice as strong as a German, in view of our depleted ranks, now contained at least three times as many effectives as one of our divisions. The line of the essentially stronger American First Army corresponded to that held by our Fifth Army, while positions of the American Second Army corresponded to those held by Army Unit C.

October 16th saw the continuation of the attacks.

Advancing against Group Argonne, the Americans tried to gain additional terrain on points attacked the day before. From the direction of St. Juvin and across Agron River[98] came attacks aimed at the left wing of the 2nd Division of Territorials. Champigneulle[99] and the heights on both sides of the river proved objectives of the Americans not less than four times. They eventually fought forward as far as the centre of the 15th Bavarian Division, but units that invaded Champigneulle were again ejected.

During the evening, the village was attacked once more, but without success. Again the 41st Division stemmed the onslaught, while the 152nd Infantry Regiment during the morning recaptured after severe fighting a farm and the hill southeast of Landres that had been relinquished before. By then this regiment was so exhausted that it proved unable to withstand renewed counter attacks with the result that it fell back to the north of Landres. The neighbouring wing of the 13th Division accordingly followed suit, but in general all positions as far as the Meuse were maintained.

To the east of the river, the enemy advanced around noon against the inner wing of the 228th and 32nd Divisions. Inasmuch as the wooded terrain interfered with a clear survey of the situation as a whole, the Americans pressed us back a few hundred metres. Both divisions were ordered to counter attack. However, when darkness fell the fighting let up somewhat. A surprise attack at Flabas supported by tanks was completely repulsed by territorials from Schleswig-Holstein. Not less than five tanks were found blown up in front of our lines, while the American Report of the Day mentioned that our resistance was stronger.

American fighting instructions for infantry and artillery which became known to us that day were based on principles almost analogous to those taught in our war colleges.

While the German government had apparently been ready to agree to Wilson's demand for an evacuation of the occupied territory, a resolve to resist now definitely manifested itself. I received a map for the concentration of German forces in the "Antwerp–Meuse Position." Preparatory work in this direction was to be speeded up. In accordance with this order, our front from the Meuse toward the east remained unchanged. As far as our line to the west of the river was concerned, a very difficult task faced us. Here, thirteen divisions of the Fifth Army, of which nine divisions were actually engaged in fighting at the time, were stationed. These, together with considerable artillery and other units, had to be transported across the river with the right wing of the army swinging toward the rear in the face of the enemy, while the left wing had to maintain its hold on the Meuse. In view of the great number of units which had to cross the river, the four big bridges along the Meuse down to Mouzon, and a few others which were not more than footpaths, did not suffice. It was also to be expected that the enemy, during these operations, would attempt strong advances against our pivot, in order to unhinge our new Meuse position, especially as at Consenvoye–Haumont ground had already been relinquished by us. It was absolutely necessary, in order to insure our success, to maintain this position here, and at the same time to hold sufficient forces in readiness for employment at the pivotal point.

While on October 17th, the enemy kept comparatively quiet, at 7 P. M. the inner wings of our 228th and 32nd Divisions of Infantry were employed to regain the ground lost on the day before. We fought hotly in the woods. Although we endured comparatively heavy losses, our former line was reëstablished. An American attempt to break through at 10 P. M. proved abortive.

The left wing of the Third Army lost Grandpré[100] on October 18th. There was very heavy traffic in the enemy's rear that day, indicating that the opponent intended to offer battle once more. Units of our combat flyers attacked ten tanks advancing on the Fléville–St. Juvin road and dropping bombs upon infantry units in the Aire valley. Ten enemy airplanes were shot down.

We were informed by American prisoners that their losses had been heavy; on October 16th, the 42nd Division, A. E. F., at Landres, suffered so severely from artillery and machine-gun fire, that of a company of two hundred men only fifteen survived. A first lieutenant, naïvely reconnoitring on horseback in front of the line of our 13th Division, was taken prisoner. Thus we learned that the 89th Division, A. E. F., had been moved opposite us. The French 15th Colonial Division, facing the right wing of Army Unit C, had been replaced by the 35th Division, A. E. F. We, too, concentrated troops from other fronts to replace our exhausted units.

With rain falling incessantly, there was not much action on October 19th and 20th. The American Report of the Day stated that,

> . . . since the beginning of the week, divisions from other parts of the German fronts had been concentrated to the north of Verdun. They were stubbornly defending each foot of ground against strong American attacks, to cover the retreat of the German armies, whose positions were threatened from the south and west by American advances.

An onslaught directed against the 15th Bavarian Division early on October 21st was dispersed by our fire as were advances against the 13th Division in the course of the forenoon. Around noon, there was a strong assault inaugurated by drum fire, near Cunel, against the 107th Division. Heavy fighting ensued around Hill 300, lost the day before. By the late afternoon of this day, our systematic effort to retake the hill clashed with an attack of strong reserves of the enemy. After severe fighting, we maintained the northern slope of the hill. Inasmuch as the line thus established was unfavourable, the Fifth Army resolved to withdraw the left wing of the West Group behind the Bantheville–Aincreville–Cléry[101] line. However, not before the next afternoon did the enemy occupy the deserted hill, upon which sentries merely were left. In the wood to the west of Bantheville, an attack without preparatory artillery fire advanced as far as the northern edge of the trees, forcing us to bend back our line to the north of Bantheville.

Although the enemy, during the fighting in the wooded region, suffered heavy losses in the course of these last days, he nevertheless advanced. This was due to the fact that while woods favoured the employment of masses of American infantry, they interfered greatly with tactical orders on our side and with the full exploitation of our highly developed machine gunnery.

An American attack, in the course of October 23rd, aimed against the 240th and 41st Divisions of Group Argonne, was rendered abortive under our fire.

Group Meuse–West, subjected to a drum fire of all calibres for two hours, felt no American infantry action until late in the afternoon.

Along a front of 6 kilometres' length, American infantry, in deep formations, supported by tanks, charged from Bantheville Wood, the village Bantheville proper, Rappes Wood, and the little forest southwest of Cléry-le-Grand. Under our annihilating fire, their attack, for the most part, was prevented from developing properly. As soon as the foremost tank was shot to pieces, the other tanks faced about, as did the infantry, returning to their jump-off line after suffering extreme casualties. Somehow, this whole demonstration appeared to us as if the enemy had been mistaken in regard to the location of our front line. He had charged so unconcernedly right into our machine-gun fire!

Attacks against Group Meuse–East were especially furious. Here, to all appearances, the Americans tried to break through in the general direction of Etraye–Damvillers. Ever since 6:30 A. M., a heavy drum fire reminded us of the presence of the Americans. In spite of our frustration of an attack launched by them in the forenoon, they stubbornly continued their attempts all during the day. Most of their charges halted as soon as they came under the fire of artillery and the mine throwers of the 228th Division.

After a number of attacks had broken down before the line of the 32nd Division, the latter was moved back a few hundred metres to Etraye Hill. Renewed American thrusts were repelled by counter thrusts on the top of the hill proper; an attempt to roll up our line in an easterly direction met with failure, so strong was the resistance of the 102nd Saxonian Infantry Regiment. Subsequently, fighting spread to the 1st Division of Territorials. (See map facing p. 250.)

The casualties suffered by the Americans in the course

of this day were described as very heavy. But we, too, suffered severely, especially under the American artillery fire, reaching far back to our rear. Their flyers, too, took part in the battle, with twenty-one bombers succeeding, in the course of the afternoon, in breaking through in the direction of Metz, causing damage to barracks and railroads.

The American report of October 23rd sounded quite subdued. Apparently, on account of their failure of the day before, only vanguard skirmishes and local attacks developed. An attack by the 26th Division, A. E. F., directed against the inner wing of Groups Meuse–East and Beaumont at 6 P. M. on October 24th was repulsed; a thrust farther to the east was balanced by a successful counter thrust. Air reconnoitring furnished us with the information that, around the Verdun railheads, strong contingents were assembled; not less than 16 heavy pieces, mounted on railroad cars, were counted there. During the night of October 25th, Group Meuse–East lost Chasseur Hill, but regained this position in the morning. Thrusts farther to the east came to nothing.

That the Americans had suffered heavy casualties, we deduced from the fact, that some battalions were made up of troops of the 26th and 29th Divisions. We were flattered to learn from the Horsea report that between the Argonne and the Meuse not less than fifty German divisions were employed! Considering the length of the front, fifty divisions would have been more than sufficient, but the actual number of our divisions facing the Americans was only seven. The erroneous assumption of the Americans that we had more than seven divisions in the line resulted from the fact that exhausted divisions were frequently replaced by us.

Moreover, there were always fragments left in the line of divisions that had meanwhile withdrawn. Thus, there were so many different regimental numbers represented in these seven divisions that our effectives appeared much stronger than was actually the case. American battle orders that fell into our hands on the western bank of the Meuse indicated highly detailed preparatory work in accordance with French standards. The principles underlying these orders were identical with those of our own fighting technique.

During the days from October 26th to 29th, when I was ordered to Berlin on a special mission, nothing of importance occurred. Only the flyers were very lively during this interval. Longuyon was bombed from the air and three French flyers were killed and four wounded as I got back to my command. In addition, the important railroad tunnel west of Montmédy felt the weight of heavy calibre shells.

As Austria-Hungary concluded a separate peace, all Austrian and Hungarian troops withdrew from our lines.

During the second and third weeks of October, our Fifth Army suffered the loss of 750 officers and 24,178 men. Among these were listed as "missing" 153 officers and 7,734 men. Almost one whole battalion of the 52nd Division made the acquaintance of "Edison Gas," a new combination resembling our "Yellow Cross" Gas.

The supreme command issued a number of preparatory orders for movement to the Antwerp–Meuse Position, but no definite orders for the execution of this plan came to me. We still had to hold our front line in expectation of an attack. For this, the enemy certainly prepared very thoroughly during the eight days' battle pause.

This attack finally came off on November 1st and not, as hitherto, in a series of local thrusts, but unified as to time and general plan, extending along our front from the Meuse to the Aire and reaching even to the west, as far as the Army Group of the German Crown Prince.

On our side, along a line of approximately 18 kilometres, the following units were stationed:

Group Argonne

240th Division of Infantry at Champigneulle
15th Bavarian Division west of St. Georges
—these both in active front service for a considerable time.
52nd Division of Infantry near Landres—after a short period of rest.

Group Meuse–West

88th Division of Infantry, south of Rénonville—newly moved in.
28th Division of Infantry, west of Aincreville—after short period of rest.
107th Division of Infantry, east of Aincreville
5th Bavarian Division of Reserves, near Doulcon
—both in active front service for quite some time.

Each group had only one division of reserves, the 31st and 27th Divisions, respectively. Both groups divided their reserve divisions into three parts, with one part each behind their respective front divisions. At Group Argonne, the reserves were 3 to 5 kilometres to the rear; at Group Meuse–East, 10 to 12 kilometres behind the front line. All other divisions, being greatly exhausted, had already been moved to the right bank of the Meuse.

Drum fire, extending along the entire front, started in at 4:30 A.M. Group Meuse–East, too, was kept under fire. Recognized only belatedly on account of very low visibility, the American onslaught was launched along a broad front at 7 A.M. As most of our telephone wires had been destroyed by artillery, General von der Marwitz and I received only meagre reports of developments.

The Americans succeeded in affecting a deep breach in the line of the 88th and 28th Divisions, in the direction of Andevanne Wood[102] with the adjacent wing of the 107th Divisions subsequently involved. At noon, this gap had been extended both in breadth and depth, with the Americans stationed near Imécourt,[103] Landreville, and Andevanne. The 52nd Division, too, was overrun.

I agreed with General von der Marwitz to retire his line to the Freya Position and bring back to the west bank by motor trucks the 236th Division, which had been only recently moved to the east bank of the Meuse, for a short respite.

The picture that presented itself at 5 P.M. was not rosy. The break in the centre deepened to 4 kilometres, inasmuch as the 15th Bavarian Division, too, was forced to give in, with only the two divisions on the outer wings holding their ground. The two reserve divisions, being divided into thirds and separated as to location, proved of insufficient fighting value to bring about a change in the situation.

Undoubtedly, we had suffered a defeat!

Reports coming in during the evening did not bring

any better news. The break had meanwhile extended to 8 kilometres, and the Americans were as far advanced as the Buzancy[104]–Nouart road. They had been unsuccessful in their attempt to roll up our wings by turning toward the west and east. A counter thrust of the 166th Infantry Regiment, under the personal leadership of its commander, blocked the enemy's advance toward the west, while stubborn resistance rendered by our troops, on the heights of Villers-devant-Dun,[105] held back the enemy's advance toward the east. We agreed with the superior command of Army Group German Crown Prince, which also had been furiously attacked that day, to withdraw the inner wings of the Third and Fifth Armies in the course of the night.

Horsea, broadcasting a description of our situation, proved that the opponent was very well informed. Especially our casualties, the weakness of our individual units, and the reduction of our artillery were correctly set forth. The report wound up:

> Unfavourable conditions like these serve to influence the mental state of the enemy in ever-growing measure. Nevertheless, the Germans are fighting on many points of the front with stubbornness; symptoms of a general demoralization have not yet manifested themselves.

Stressing our "resolute resistance," the American Report of the Day enumerated the villages wrested from us, giving the number of prisoners taken as 3,602 men, 151 of them being officers. Our new line remained undisturbed during the night; obviously, the enemy was unaware of the fact that it had been occupied. The line now ran from Autruche, by way of Harricourt, north of Buzancy and south of Barricourt,[106] toward Hill 343,[107] southwest of Villers-devant-Dun, thence to the Meuse.

Early on November 2nd, Longuyon once more was heavily shelled, while Montmédy came under fire from 6 to 9 A.M. The casualties here were ten dead and some wounded. In addition, six French non-combatants had been killed.

The Americans advanced, during the forenoon, against Villers only, intensifying their attacks in the course of the afternoon. Our thinned-out lines were no longer a match for the masses employed by the Americans. Hill 343, defended valiantly, was lost, and the enemy pushed on toward Tailly and Montigny. The Fifth Army, forced to embark upon the retreat across the Meuse, intended to occupy the line Sommauthe–Wiseppe in order to cover its retreat. Movement of troops grew difficult here since these effectives were greatly mixed as regarded smaller units, and in addition, the roads were very soft. The battalions of the 236th Division reached the line without their machine guns, as their motor trucks stalled in the mud. Inasmuch as the neighbour army of the Fifth Army had to cover greater distances, the latter during their rearward turn was ordered to hold their forward positions, so as not to expose the former. Accordingly, the 236th Division was brought closer to the line.

During the evening, severe fighting ensued in an effort to shake off the enemy. This was ultimately effected, in the course of the night. All this time, the enemy maintained lively artillery fire against our farthest rear, including Stenay.[108] In the course of the forenoon of November 3rd the enemy groped closer toward us, launching attacks in the afternoon. Strong masses charged against the brave 115th Division, which had been called back to relieve the 52nd Division, with the result that our weakened troops relinquished their ground in the direction of Vaux and near Belval. However, for the time being, counter attacks here reëstablished our line. While the 88th Division was severely pressed the rest of our front held out. There were local engagements on the east bank of the Meuse and on the line of Army Unit C without, however, bringing about any essential changes.

In the evening, the supreme command, in the interest of unified action, ordered that until the retreat across the Meuse all such parts of the Fifth Army as remained on the right bank of the river be subordinated to the forces associated with the Army Group German Crown Prince.

On November 4th, Groups Argonne and Meuse–West, now belonging to the Third Army, gave ground before the Americans in a northerly direction. Group Argonne was employed by the superior command of the Third Army for flank cover. Group Meuse–West, whose left wing, consisting of the 5th Bavarian Division, had already crossed over to the right bank of the Meuse and was now at Dun, resolved to stick close to the river. This unit continued to cross the Meuse during November 4th, subsequently coming once more under my command. Meanwhile, in order to prevent a gap threatening near the Meuse, when the two western groups retreated, the Fifth Army stationed two of its reserve divisions along the river, facing west; the 20th Division at Stenay and the 117th Division at Mouzay. The supreme command ordered the entire front to the west of us to retire to an intermediate position between our present position and the Antwerp–Meuse position.

At the same time, the Americans resumed pressure

against the projecting salient, on the east bank of the river, just as I had expected. Early in the morning, the Americans crossed the river from Brieulles[109] under cover of a heavy fog, and penetrated our line near Chatillon Wood.[110] We soon sent them back across the canal! In the afternoon, after heavy artillery preparation, under smokescreen, along the Meuse, and the employment of gas around the heights to the east, the Americans repeatedly tried to cross the river near Dun, Cléry-le-Petit,[111] and Brieulles. Near Dun, the enemy's attempt broke down under our fire, 100 metres west of the Meuse; at Cléry, the Americans reached the bank of the river but did not achieve the actual crossing of the Meuse. At Brieulles, however, they gained a new foothold on the other bank of the river.

Strong assaults were directed against the 228th Division, focussing on the High Oak Hill (*Hohcr Eichenberg*). From nine in the morning until late into the night, fighting was in progress there. The hill was lost and regained. In the afternoon, our line was pressed back to both sides of the road toward Réville; however, at 6 P.M., the High Oak Hill was once more ours. Here, the 35th Brandenburgian Regiment of Fusiliers proved themselves especially valiant, capturing 3 officers and 32 men of the American 316th Infantry Regiment. Between 11 and 12 P.M., the 79th Division, A. E. F., attacked once more, driving back our line slightly. Attacks directed against the neighbouring 192nd Saxonian Division of Infantry, in the course of the morning, and renewed with even stronger forces in the course of the afternoon, were completely repulsed. The 1st Division of territorials also repelled numerous attacks.

The whole front of the Fifth Army was under very

heavy fire of the Americans. Montmédy, the target of bombs and big shells, was reduced more and more to débris. When American air forces, consisting of a hundred pursuit and forty-five bombing planes, attacked Montmédy, our own flyers resolutely resisted. However, as our flyers were numerically inferior to the opponent's forces, they suffered severe losses. My old headquarters was completely demolished by an American bomb.

The Americans continued the crossing of the river and also resumed their attacks. In the forenoon of November 5th, they forced the Meuse near Liny,[112] pressing our weak forces back in the direction of the Côte St. Germain.[113] Dun and Milly fell into the hands of the Americans. Farther to the south, the Americans advanced toward Fontaines. There, the Americans were counter attacked by a regiment of Saxonian Chasseurs which meanwhile arrived with the 241st Division, and thrown back through Epinois Wood. To the south of this, other forces blocked Sartelles Wood. In the afternoon, strong enemy forces advanced from Dun toward the Côte. They suffered very severe losses when, emerging from the wood, they exposed themselves to our artillery, firing directly at them. At many points, the opponent retreated and we remained in possession of the ridge. Another onslaught, launched from Milly in the evening, we also repulsed.

In the morning, the 228th Division once more completely regained their old positions on the High Oak Hill. At 10 A.M., after a very short preparatory fire, the enemy charged in dense masses but was repelled, as were additional thrusts, between noon and 1 P.M. The enemy retained only a small advantage gained on the eastern slope of the hill. An assault directed against the 35th Regiment of Fusiliers No. 35, in the course of the afternoon, was repulsed in hand-to-hand fighting. In addition, we foiled renewed strong attacks by the 79th Division, A. E. F., against our 192nd Division.

On the morning of November 6th, an order arrived to concentrate upon the Antwerp–Meuse position. We got word also that it was desirable to execute this movement slowly.

In the meantime, the exhausted effectives of the Fifth Army had to fight on. Reënforcements arrived late and were inadequate. The Americans, meanwhile, succeeded in throwing a bridge across the Meuse south of Dun. I clearly saw that the situation could be ameliorated only by counter attacking and throwing the enemy back across the river. I lacked artillery enough for such an undertaking, to say nothing of infantry for the actual execution of such a plan. All that was left for me, under these circumstances, was to continue to hold out as long as I could.

Pushing with great strength, the Americans, in the course of the forenoon, continued their attempts to effect a breach in our lines between Dun and the High Oak Hill. After several hours under the most searching fire, and covered by a fog, they eventually took possession of St. Germain Ridge and the village of Murvaux. Counter attacking strongly, Prussian and Bavarian battalions wrested the ridge from the enemy. In the afternoon, after rushes and onslaughts to and fro, we lost the western slope of the ridge once more. In the woods between Murvaux[114] and Fontaines, I could now follow with my glasses the fighting in progress there. Continually reënforced, the enemy gained, and in the course of the day drove us through the forest. Toward evening, the Americans occupied the wooded country between Murvaux and Brandeville,[115] while we maintained the heights near Haraumont.

Although fighting for fully four weeks, the 228th Brandenburgian Division of Infantry gave a wonderful account of itself. All attacks directed against the High Oak Hill since nine-thirty in the morning were repulsed. Our combat flyer units repeatedly took part in the fighting by blocking the crossing of the river and dispersing the enemy. He was now forcing the Meuse by way of Dun.

The advance of the enemy toward Brandeville now threatened the rear of the 228th Division. We lacked means to cope with the menace by counter attacking. I left it to the discretion of the Fifth Army to concentrate on a line farther back rather than use up its effectives in weak counter attacks. Thus, the Fifth Army decided to assume the line Mouzay–West of Brandeville–East of High Oak Hill–Etraye knoll. This line was occupied during the night without interference on the part of the enemy.

I learned at this juncture that the German commission had left Berlin to get from Marshal Foch the terms of the armistice. In the evening came the disheartening news that the navy had mutinied at Kiel.

It was quiet during the forenoon of November 7th, but in the afternoon local attacks occurred. A thrust effected by the Americans between Mouzay and Brandeville was balanced by a subsequent counter thrust. Not before the evening did the enemy dispel the weak forces we left on the knoll to the northeast of the St. Germain Ridge. In Brandeville Wood, too, the enemy gradually gained. He bent the right wing of the 228th Division, and made us give up the High Oak Hill. The 192nd Division, on the other hand, defied all attacks.

The American advance toward Brandeville greatly interfered with our line, while at the same time its maintenance cost us dear on account of the great stretches of thick trees, especially the extended Woëvre Wood[116] between Mouzay and Brandeville. I therefore agreed that the Fifth Army abandon this highly unsuitable position, choosing a line farther to the rear on level ground, where our fire could secure better results. This new line reached from Stenay by way of Baâlon[117]–Louppy–Vittarville–east of Damvillers to the south of Grémilly.

The American Report of the Day revealed that on the St. Germain Ridge the Germans had defended their positions with extreme stubbornness and that possession of the ridge was gained only after strenuous fighting. It also stated that we had made desperate attempts to maintain positions along the Meuse Heights, held by us since 1914. The Americans estimated the number of our divisions, employed between the Argonne and the Meuse since November 1st, as twenty-two. How I wished that it were so!

The reorganization of the Fifth Army was hardly disturbed. On November 8th we fought merely rearguard engagements. On the other hand, traffic and reconnoitring activities of the Americans pointed at imminent battle. To our surprise, we found the level of the Meuse Canal lowered over three feet. To all appearances, the enemy had dammed the water farther up, so as to make the crossing of the river easier.

In a day or two, the enemy harried our rearguards

near Louppy and Jametz[118] and these fled back to our main line. The Americans occupied Peuvillers and Damvillers, while our 33rd and 37th Divisions repelled attacks opposite Verdun near Bezonvaux and Abaucourt. Army Unit C, too, became once more the target of thrusts conducted by forces deployed in battalion strength. From orders discovered on these occasions we learned that the Americans had orders to attack along the whole front by surprise and, without any preparatory artillery fire, to take the secondary German positions and thus ascertain how far the left wing of the Fifth Army had retreated.

When, on this day, an enemy flyer landed on the other bank of the Meuse, two of our chausseurs swam the river and returned with an unwounded officer as prisoner. This I note as one brave deed among many .

I received the terms of the armistice on November 10th. I never expected conditions so humiliating! This was not armistice but rather an unconditional surrender!

The fighting continued, with the enemy attacking all through the day. To the southeast of Stenay, the Americans beat their way to Chênois Wood, taking us by surprise. Repeating their rushes, their dashes, and their onsets, they eventually widened the gap they had made and forced us up the height north of Baâlon. Inasmuch as Stenay, together with the bridgehead held there thus far, now constituted a sharply projecting salient, the Fifth Army, abandoning Stenay proper, was to block their line from Martincourt in the direction of Juvigny. Château Louppy, for years headquarters of a group command, fell into the enemy's hands. Thrusts to both sides of the place, as well as in Woëvre Wood, proved abortive. Prisoners stated that the enemy simply obeyed orders to keep close to our heels. In repelling an extremely severe attack directed at the 228th Division, one officer and forty-three men of the 32nd Division, A. E. F., fell into our hands.

In the forenoon, the enemy smashed his way through the line of the 192nd Division, east of Peuvillers,[119] to a depth of more than a mile. Reserves, quickly assembled, collided with a new onset of strong forces. The gap in our lines deepened. Our second counter thrust, delivered with the same reserve under the personal leadership of Lieutenant Colonel von Zeschau, succeeded in pressing the enemy back to our previous ground. We took forty prisoners in this engagement.

Hot fighting followed farther to the east, but we overcame most of the attacks upon us, although Abaucourt had to be abandoned. Army Unit C captured one officer and forty-five men, of different American divisions.

During the night preceding November 11th, the enemy seized the Meuse bend, between Mouzon and Pouilly,[120] forcing the river at Villemontry and Létanne. From the bridgeheads thus established the Americans now pressed on toward the line Moulins–Inor.

News that the armistice had been signed, and that all hostilities were to cease on November 11th, at 11:55 A. M., apprised us that the cruel game had come to an end! (See map facing p. 274.)

At the front of Army Unit C, fighting ceased after a valiant counter attack by the 45th Division of the Reserves.

In the forty-six days of severe fighting, since September 26th, the left wing of the Fifth Army had been pressed back approximately 8 miles while the right, from the Argonne to the Meuse at Mouzon, had retreated about 24 miles. This withdrawal was not exclusively the result of fighting, but partly due to our resolution to retire the whole western front—a decision which, as far as the Fifth Army was concerned, amounted to a turn toward the rear.

I have frequently mentioned that we were always faced by an enemy numerically superior. I do not believe that the results of this fighting justify one side in estimating the bravery and valour of the other as less than its own.

Just a few more remarks in regard to our experience.

We were surprised by the vastness and vigour of America's military expansion. We admired the intensity with which a big army had been created, with a marvellous all-round equipment. The American army had numerically strong, well-set-up, substantial, human material, endowed with great energy. The Americans lacked military traditions, as they prevailed in the older European states, especially among the German people. Thus, the training of the common soldier, as well as of the officers, was more difficult. This training was easier to impart for defensive operations than for the offensive, so much more difficult in view of modern armament.

Lack of experience was very often paid for with great sacrifices. These were sustained with admirable equanimity. As a matter of fact, attacks were frequently launched with too little concern, and in an unsuitable manner. Subordinate leadership of the infantry and artillery, difficult in any case, appeared deficient in the course of attacks. The bravery of the American flyers amounted almost to recklessness.

The American superior command aimed at developing tactics according to the minute French pattern, but apparently it did not succeed as far as the middle and lower grades of officers were concerned. Only thus were we able to explain the frequent lack of coöperation between neighbouring units as well as those many unnecessary local attacks. Wherever operations were developed systematically, as for example on September 26th and November 1st, superior forces won.

After all, it was the astonishing display of American strength which definitely decided the war against us.

III

THE A.E.F. IN THE MEUSE-ARGONNE OFFENSIVE

By General Eugène Savatier, former Assistant Chief of the General Staff and Commander of the 34th Division, French Army

It has often been asked why General Pershing did not follow up the St. Mihiel success by penetrating farther into the enemy lines. As a matter of fact, General Pershing had at first expected a much more extended offensive. But the generalissimo of the coalition had fixed precise limits for the advance in his orders of August 30th and September 2nd. Marshal Foch had admonished the A. E. F. not to allow itself to be tempted into prolonging the battle after attaining designed objectives.

It was for this reason that on September 13th General Pétain wrote to General Pershing as follows:

> The line of resistance to be occupied by the effectives of the American Expeditionary Forces runs as follows: From Croix-des-Charmes, to the east of Fey-en-Haye, by way of Viéville-en-Haye, Jaulny, Xammes, St. Benoît-en-Woëvre, and Hattonville to the foot of the hills near Eparges.
>
> The following line of outposts has been designated as definite limit for exploitation of anticipated results: From the hills southwest of Norroy, by way of Villers-sous-Prény and this side of Rembercourt, Charey, Dampvitoux, Lachaussée, Doncourt-aux-Templiers to Wadonville-en-Woëvre and Tresauraux.
>
> From informations received at 4 P.M., it appears that to the right, exploitation objectives having been exceeded, the Americans

reached the line from Jaulny to Pagny-en-Moselle. Reports from flyers indicate that there is disorder among the enemy, in the region to the north of the Rupt-de-Mad.

If he deems it advisable, the General commanding the American troops is authorized to advance his line of resistance as far as the fortified positions of the enemy, known as Michel I, between Pagny-sur-Moselle and Jaulny.

In case such a measure is adopted, the line of outposts might also be extended, along this part of the front, to positions to be determined by the General commanding the American army.

In addition, the General commanding the American army should order all such raids as seem advantageous wherever the enemy is apparently in disorder. *Such situations may be exploited under the strict condition that the American raiding parties are to return to their base after carrying out their mission.*

The General commanding the American army will kindly keep me posted as to measures deemed necessary to carry out the above instructions.

PÈTAIN.

The above letter by General Pétain to General Pershing makes it clear that it was due to army discipline and a desire to act in accordance with the general plan of action outlined by Marshal Foch, that the American did not pursue a further offensive. Moreover, no time was to be lost at this stage of developments. September 25th had been set as the date of the attack between the Argonne and the Meuse, in which fifteen American divisions were to take part.

In connection with this enterprise, my chief, as early as September 6th, issued the following order, which clearly illustrates the part the Americans were expected to play in the ensuing developments:

September 6, 1918

Personal and Secret

Conforming to the instructions of September 3rd, an offensive will be undertaken in the direction of Mézières between the Meuse and the Suippe, in which the American First Army and the French

Fourth Army, operating jointly under the direction of the general commander-in-chief of the armies of the north and northeast, shall participate.

One operation will be conducted by the American First Army between the Meuse and the Argonne, having for its objective the capture of the Hindenburg position along the front Brieulles-sur-Meuse, Romagne-sous-Montfaucon, Grandpré, developing later in the direction of Buzancy–Stonne with the view of overflowing the enemy line Vouziers–Rethel toward the East.

Another operation will be conducted by the French Fourth Army between the Aisne and the Suippe having for its objective the successive capture of the positions along this front. This operation is to be developed in the direction of the plateaus east of the route Rethel–Signy–L'Abbaye.

The operations shall take place simultaneously toward the 25th of September. It is essential that they contain the element of surprise, and absolute secrecy must be maintained until the last moment.

FOCH.

The task of the American army in this offensive was not an easy one. It was given the nearly impossible task of breaking through the Argonne Forest, which from time immemorial has presented obstacles which have become almost legendary. I asked Marshal Foch why he delegated this sector to the most inexperienced troops.

"I did not want to do it," he said, "and I pointed out to General Pershing all the difficulties presented by the terrain.

"'But there will be troops there?' asked General Pershing.

"'Most certainly,' I replied.

"'Well, then, I ask you to let them be my own,' he said. 'I can assure you that they will overcome all difficulties.'"

General Pershing had under his orders not only the

attacking army, but also all the troops that had just been in action at St. Mihiel (the American Fourth Corps and the Second Colonial) as well as the French Seventeenth Corps, which was in the northeast and east of Verdun, and which thus linked up the two masses of American armies.

This placing of the attack troops between the Meuse and the Argonne necessitated the withdrawal of eleven French and Italian divisions and the entry into the line of American divisions reënforced by powerful artillery.

The American line of attack was arranged as follows:

To the right: The Third Corps (General Bullard), from Brabant to Malancourt. In line, 33rd, 80th, 4th. In reserve, 3rd.

In the centre: The Fifth Corps (General Cameron), from Malancourt to Vauquois. In line, 79th, 37th, 91st. In reserve, 32nd.

To the left: The First Corps (General Liggett), from Vauquois to La Harazée. In line, 35th, 28th, 77th. In reserve, 92nd.

This comprised the main attack. The facility of the advance indicated that the artillery had been well directed. A tremendous anxiety was lifted from the minds of British and French and Belgians as the bulletins began to reach headquarters. The secondary American attack was undertaken at eight o'clock by the 5th Corps of the United States army—the 1st and 3rd having gone into the main movement hours before.

From the outset, the progress of events indicated that the Americans had far more energy than the enemy—and this, as all military men know, is a sure sign of better morale. I think we French were somewhat surprised at the superior handling of the American artillery in this action. It had a marked influence upon the spirit of the infantry. We were also astonished at the failure of the enemy to check the American advance at any point. I heard some military men ask why General Pershing had not followed up so splendid a success.

"The fact is," I would explain, "General Pershing had anticipated a much deeper offensive in this direction. Perhaps some notion of a glorious entry into Metz—modelled upon that of Joan of Arc into Orleans—had turned the romantic young heads of our Americans."

Marshal Foch had fixed the limits of the offensive to General Pershing: "The objectives marked for you," the Marshal said, "are well beyond the fighting line of the enemy as it is."

General Pershing noted this detail with care, but the French commander-in-chief emphasized his admonition with these words:

"The American forces," he said, "must not be misled into prolonging the action. The line traced for you diverges as it is. Don't go farther. Don't keep the fight up when you reach your limits."

General Pershing promised obedience. Now General Pétain, having learned by this time the true nature of American nobility, also took General Pershing in hand.

"General," declared the French commander to the American, "the line you must occupy is clear. Fey-en-Haye–Viéville–Xammes–Hattonville! Remember the names. If any of your detachments are found beyond these limits, they must be brought back to the villages assigned for them in the plan of operations."

The American commander was loyal to the chief. He

knew, moreover, that before many days the forward push must be resumed in the form of an offensive between the Argonne and the Meuse. Indeed, when I reflected upon the positions to which the Americans were assigned, I was amazed at the capacity of General Pershing and his chief of staff, General Drum. They actually launched fifteen American divisions northward far beyond St. Mihiel.

The task that now confronted the American army would have tested severely the veterans of the Napoleonic campaign in Spain.

General Pershing and his men were to force their way through that Argonne Forest, which for a hundred years has been all but impassable to a military force of any size.

Now it must be pierced by twelve divisions.

The Argonne is, in fact, tortuous ground. It might well be termed impenetrable. The trees form in spots a kind of wall. A hundred years ago (and things have not much changed since then) there were four, five, or perhaps six, steep and thorny paths from west to east, affording treacherous footholds to the denizens of these recesses. These regions are known to many as the Thermopylæ of France because no foe could force them and that was the classical reference to the Argonne in the geography taught to our children at school.

Pershing and his men were, to be sure, told of some support to be derived from the army of General Gouraud, but they were well aware that a wall of dense forest growth would separate the Americans from the French as all fought their way through the labyrinth of trees.

I was glad to learn that General Bullard, keenest

champion of advance tactics in the American army, was in command of Pershing's right. General Cameron, next to him, commanding the American centre with the Fifth Corps, was well known among our colonial officers because of his Philippine campaigns. He had made a great impression through his resourcefulness in the management of the horses and the men who rode them and drove them. Nor must I forget General Liggett, whose exceptionally long experience in high command gave him prestige among the officers of the United States army.

Of all the divisions in line, only three had any artillery that was part of their organization. These three had taken part in active operations before their appearance in the Argonne. Two of the divisions had been in quiet sectors for perhaps eight weeks. One division had ten days' experience of trench warfare. Another division had enjoyed sixteen days of trench warfare. Two of the divisions had never been under fire at all.

Five of the American divisions were now for the first time in contact with their artillery.

On top of everything, a shortage of horses!

Yet General Pershing had absolute confidence in these divisions. It was useless to point to him that they were untried.

"I rely," he told Marshal Foch, "upon their morale."

It did not fail. The advance was continuous and this, as I have hinted already, is the test. The reserves of each corps protected the flanks. There were moments when the crossfire was deadly. More than one road on the maps with which we supplied these Americans had been obliterated by enemy fire. There were blockades and "jams." The food now and then failed. The filth was pervasive. Divisions with ammunition gone, with units scattered, still held on. Gassed, bombarded, cross-fired, sleepless, hungry, they held on.

All of which illustrates what Marshal Foch had taught us in the military school when we were young—morale is the thing in battle. The men who lack morale may have everything else, but they cannot go forward, and if they do not go forward, they do not win.

The most eloquent comment upon American achievement in this Meuse–Argonne offensive was the silent action of Marshal Pétain, in concert with Marshal Foch.

Marshal Foch planned a tremendous blow against the enemy in Lorraine. Even before the Americans went into the Argonne, Marshal Pétain studied the problem. The Americans were assigned a conspicuous place in the Lorraine campaign that was to open the second week of November.

The armistice alone robbed the Americans of the additional glory that was to have been theirs. When the armistice did come, they were fighting along a front that was constantly lengthening. They had lost 114,000 of their comrades.

Everywhere their splendid courage amazed us, and we applauded their successes whole-heartedly. Our affection was not based wholly upon our admiration. We were pleased to find in them our own qualities and defects, which made our mutual liking only the more lasting.

I may note at this point the insinuation that we French have formed a habit of flattering the American soldier. It is even hinted that if we know anything to his discredit, we conceal the fact.

The fact is that from the first arrival of the Americans

on our shores we studied them. If we thought they had any defects of character or of training, we made known our impressions freely. What we French say in praise of the American soldier is the sincere expression of an honest opinion. It is hinted, too, that we French are so grateful for what the American soldier did to free the soil of our country from the invader that in sheer thankfulness we say nothing of the blunders he made.

Let me remove this impression at once. We were always exact in getting reliable reports upon the condition and capacity of the troops under General Pershing. We lived in no fool's paradise where the Americans are concerned. If they made mistakes we knew all about them. If failures were serious we would say so.

I have in front of me as I write the notes of a talk I had with Commander Collignon, one of the most gifted military experts in the French army. His insight into the conditions of tactical efficiency and his close contact with the Americans gave him weight with them and with ourselves. I knew that I should get an honest opinion from him when I wished the benefit of his experience with our allies.

"Is the American really a soldier already?"

Commander Collignon echoed my query in a tone that proclaimed his enthusiasm. "He arrived a born soldier." The emphasis was marked. "The doughboy is still the same—brave, dashing, audacious even, keen at his training. All the men in the French army admire the American soldier. I think the Germans are afraid of him."

"Afraid of the American? I thought they despised him?"

The Commander laughed. "That is part of their

propaganda—to affect contempt for the American. The Germans know that the Americans do not fear them. The American has no fear of death, either."

"They fall into the hands of the Germans," I suggested.

"And they fall out. I knew a young American soldier to be captured by the Germans. He was back in half an hour. He had choked to death the German who captured him. He killed another who sought to stop him—he killed the German with a pistol he had taken from the one he choked."

Our talk turned next to the subject of the officers of the American army.

"They are not sufficiently trained," Commander Collignon admitted that frankly. "The proper instruction of an army officer," he reminded me, "requires years. I think the American officers show they are raw and unprepared. I recall the case of a company at rest in the woods when they were suddenly bombarded with gas shells. As the officer failed to give the necessary order for donning their gas masks, half of the company were gassed and a quarter of their number died. The American captain simply did not know."

I suggested that the men who were arriving in such large numbers on the eve of Foch's great offensive must show improvement.

"To be sure." Commander Collignon then mentioned an important detail. "The men are trained, but they do not show a mastery of any specialty as yet. How could they? The very material they most require to excel in, manœuvres—to say nothing of action—is not given them until they arrive in France. I have seen men in the Argonne throw away their grenades. They did not know the use of them. Not more than a mile farther on they were shelled by ambushed German guns. They were brought to a halt. They could have routed the Germans easily if they hadn't thrown away their grenades. They did not know.

"The men in the ranks are also much less disciplined than is safe for them. I do not mean that they are not ready to face fire. Quite the contrary. But they rush into the firing line because that is their temperament, because they are obeying an impulse. Hence they advance in a somewhat disorderly style."

"Discipline," I suggested, "will come with time."

"Yes," he agreed. "And the Americans are so highly individualized that it takes even longer to discipline them than to reduce the average French lad to order. The American's initiative makes it a trying task to impress subordination upon him."

"Perhaps," I ventured, "we French go to the other extreme."

"But with the Americans the density of the engaged troops is always too great. That makes the casualties too high—uselessly high. The foodstuffs do not come in at the proper time. There was one occasion when our Second Colonial Corps had to see that there were supplies of ammunition in stock sufficient to equip the American Fifth Corps on the eve of the attack. The American staff officers arrived to get the material with twenty-five big trucks for—two tons of munitions.

"They didn't know."

"That," I replied, "must have been exceptional."

"It was characteristic of the American military administration as I observed it, General. Not many days after that episode I happened to be on liaison duty. I went to the division headquarters of the troops fighting on our right. I was received by the gas officer."

"Did you ask the way to the post of the general in command?"

"Naturally. 'Right here,' said the gas officer.

"'But the General,' I said. 'Where is he?'

"'In the line.'

"'And the chief of staff?'

"'In the line.'

"'And the officers?'

"'All in the line.'

"'Then how am I to make sure of my liaison?'

"He pointed. 'Keep your eye on that board.'

"I was perplexed at such lack of coördination. 'Who,' I inquired, 'posts the information?'

"'The telephone operator.'

"He turned out to be right. And such bulletins as were posted! 'Seven o'clock—leaving for the attack.' In due time: 'Seven forty-five—the 56th Regiment is halted.' Another bulletin: 'Seven forty—the 55th Regiment has taken the village of X.' So the posting of bulletins went on.

"At eleven o'clock the General came in. He was surrounded by his staff.

"'Ah!' he cried, swinging a cane he carried, 'it was all very fine. All hands attacked with hand grenades.'

"'And Major A?' I asked.

"'Wounded.'

"'Where is Colonel B?'

"'He has a bullet in his thigh.'

"'And Captain C?'

"'Shot through the shoulder. But everything went off magnificently, gloriously!'

"That is how military administration works out in all the Americans units. The divisions just disembarked are just as casual, just as careless, just as easy-going."

"I begin to see," I mused, "why we find it so difficult to get in touch with some of the American divisions during an attack."

"During an attack? All the time, I find. General Pougin tells me that in spite of all his efforts he hasn't been able to establish any sort of connection with the neighbouring American commander."

"But the liaison——"

"Oh, the liaison—what matters a liaison to that American division commander? It does not seem to worry him if he is out of touch with his artillery, with his aviation, with his superior at corps headquarters, with his neighbours to right and to left in the line of attack. He has the American temperament. Therefore he has run along with his men to be in at the death. He does not know."

"In their own country," I ventured to plead, "the Americans adopt rough and ready methods. The most direct way to the result. That is their idea."

"The most direct way! Results! There you have it, General. The Americans have a sort of communism in the use of army tools, army wagons, army weapons. They do not observe strict rules regarding the distribution of these things. They take what they want out of the common stock wherever they find it. One day Captain B——, a liaison officer like myself, hitched his horse to a door post. He entered the house to make inquiries. He came out in five minutes. No horse! He had taken the animal into the war with him. He was much attached to it. The saddle disappeared with the horse."

"You don't know that an American was to blame?"

"The inference was natural in the light of many episodes. For example, consider what happened in a railway station. Newspapers were being distributed, and letters to French and Americans. A French messenger arrived on his motorcycle. He got off and left his machine in the waiting room. He left it where he could keep it under observation. An American came in. Seeing the wheel alone and with no apparent owner, he appropriated it. The Frenchman raised an outcry at once. The American looked around unconcernedly. 'How much?' he inquired carelessly. He was ready to buy what he could not make off with."

I record these impressions, these comparisons of notes, in order to show that we French did not fail to criticize the Americans when we thought we had provocation. There was ground for much difference of opinion. Temperaments and traits differed greatly.

I do not see that anyone was to blame, particularly.

General Pershing was most careful to see to the proper administration of the schools he set up behind the army he led. Countless efficient officers issued from these schools. All had the benefit of the soundest instruction. No less than three thousand officers came out of these schools in a single month. Their training was thorough and they brought to it the American quickness and aptitude. There was a staff school at Langres under General James McAndrew, a specialist of eminence and capacity as well as a man of charm and courage. The officers he sent out were prodigies of training. They rose through merit. But the figures involved in this training would give us French an attack of vertigo. The American army had some 9,500 officers in April, 1917.

In December, 1918, it had 183,000. Wouldn't that frighten the average instructor at a French military academy?

All these young American officers were eager and keen, loving sport, risk, and danger. They were eager for instruction. They were more positive, more affirmative than our own officers, but they regarded the war as a sort of business venture. It was what we French call *une affaire* to them.

These young Americans knew that their fathers had made war under the same easy-going conditions as they were making war now. They felt that their fathers had come well out of the struggle. If the North beat the South in the American Civil War, it was, they felt, because their fathers had been business men, trained to adapt means to ends with versatility and resourcefulness. So they thought they would change the whole face of the World War with the methods they had brought across the seas with them—Americanize the struggle.

These young Americans lost a good many of their illusions in the depths of the Argonne.

What the Americans failed to realize was the transformation that had been wrought in the tactics of warfare owing to the progress of mechanical invention. Indeed, in some respects, the science of strategy had to take account of tactical changes since the year 1914. The whole service of security was new.

The greatest tactical revolution in war was brought about by the huge effective force we were obliged to maintain at the front. The artillery for these forces was on the most gigantic scale. Food supplies were enormous but ammunition supplies had become colossal.

It might almost be said that there were no longer

infantry fights, cavalry fights, artillery duels along traditional lines. There was no room for independence and for initiative. There was a single endless line of front. There was a solitary battle from end to end, renewed fitfully under the name of an offensive.

All these things the Americans could not grasp at first. They had to master the difficulties of aviation, of gun fire, of trench warfare. They thought we were too slow, too stationary, too fatigued.

Nothing disconcerted us Frenchmen quite so much as the attitude of the white American officers toward the coloured men in the American forces.

It occurred to me that the coloured men from the United States were not culturally on a level with those troops belonging to the coloured races who make such a fine showing in the French divisions. From the time of the declaration of the rights of man, we French have striven to apply the principles of democracy to all, regardless of race or colour.

I was willing to admit that the coloured men in the American forces suffered from a handicap at home. They did not show it conspicuously in Europe. I heard the coloured men praised highly. They had come from all over the American republic, I believe.

I must say that I did not think so highly of the coloured troops from America whom I found in my sector. Nevertheless, there were American commanders who did everything possible to get a fair chance for the black men in their divisions. General Bullard had a regiment of fine coloured men in one of his divisions. He got splendid results out of them. He proved that the American coloured man has only to be understood to win respect. However, all the American officers, especially those in the lower ranks, could not adopt the attitude of General Bullard.

Perhaps I was unduly influenced in my attitude toward the coloured men by finding them in a quiet sector. They had more time to get into trouble. They had less opportunity to display the high qualities of their race. The conditions under which they found themselves were novel and difficult.

I knew, too, that the coloured man in the United States has no such position as the democratic ideal would imply. There are certain special reasons for this into which I need not enter, but for which I was prepared to make allowances.

Nevertheless, I was decidedly taken aback by the attitude of the American liaison officer, Lieutenant K——, who acted with my staff. He refused emphatically to make his appearance at the breakfast table because I had invited to it the colonel and the lieutenant colonel. This course on my part might be called obligatory. The fact that they were coloured men did not influence me against them. In fact, I have found from experience that the officers of their rank derive confidence from meeting at table their commander and his staff. There is greater intimacy which leads to more confidence, more coöperation.

The American officer was deaf to these considerations. "I like the Negroes very much," he said to me. "Every time I get back to Virginia, I kiss my old nurse. She's a good Negress. I adore her."

"But you need not kiss these officers," I urged.

"True—but I can't be on a plane of equality with them. I can't sit at the same table."

I contrived to make this worthy lieutenant see that I could draw no colour line among officers who had all alike come over the seas to aid France, my native country, in her hour of need.

"Remember," I said, "that these officers are wearing an American uniform and the American emblem."

The remark impressed him, I suspect. He saw my point of view.

Within two or three days I took advantage of an opportunity to pay a visit to Lieutenant K——'s sector. I was curious to see how things were getting on with the coloured men.

The colonel had not come to get his instructions until that morning. He could not march that evening owing to his rheumatism. Revolver shots had been fired almost in front of me at the fishes in the canal.

This was near St. Mihiel!

Such men as I could get to comprehend me had received no food for forty-eight hours!

At last I managed to shake these coloured men out of their apathy. They had horses, bicycles, telephones, and still they could not rouse themselves sufficiently to make use of these facilities for getting food to their men.

And they wore officers' stripes!

Not many days after this experience, a major on the staff of General Pershing came to ask my opinion of this coloured colonel.

"My frank opinion?"

"Nothing else. Mince no words."

I confined myself to a narration of the simple facts. The major seemed dumbfounded.

"The Negroes," I explained, "are often the merest children. They are like big boys. I have seen them in

Dahomey and Senegal. I like the black men of those regions as soldiers. I do not see in them commanders of regiments."

"This is a difficult situation," the major reminded me.

"A difficult situation," I echoed. "The war is nothing else for us all. A white colonel aided by a white staff finds it hard enough to arrive at sound decisions. I do not see that it is safe just now to entrust a body of troops, whether a battalion or a regiment, to a black man."

The major on General Pershing's staff was firm in his reply. "We've made up our minds to let this coloured colonel lead his regiment into the fight. We'll see how he acts. He's got to have his chance."

Here was a day on which the American was more liberal in his attitude toward the black man than was the Frenchman.

Humour seasoned the spirit and audacity of the more experienced American divisions; in the same way our soldiers showed "Gallic wit" in the course of the desperate struggle. Doughboy and the poilu always wore a smile. In the face of the worst bombardments and the most powerful attacks, they demonstrated a steadfastness and a tenacity which, up till then, had not been considered an attribute of armies of impetuous character.

The inexperience under fire of the young divisions reminded us of our young conscripts of 1813 "who dared not fire for fear of not being able to go through the necessary motions (then so complicated) of reloading their guns." Morale then took the place of training. We also noticed among the soldiers a certain pride which often made them refuse to put on their masks or take ordinary precautions in the face of fire. We understood that, too.

A bugler of the Zouaves was commanded by his chief to "sound the retreat."

"I don't know how," he replied. "The Zouaves never retreat."

Such behaviour is a mistake from a military point of view, but if we blame these impetuous troops, we cannot help also admiring them. And, in the same way, we admired our American brothers in arms.

We can only repeat what Marshal Pétain said when Russia was disarmed, Roumania beaten, Italy and ourselves exhausted. "Only Pershing's return call on Lafayette guarantees our victory."

APPENDIX

NOTES AND INDEXES PREPARED BY

A. PAUL MAERKER-BRANDEN

APPENDIX

NOTES AND INDEXES PREPARED BY A. PAUL MAERKER-BRANDEN

I

INTRODUCTORY NOTE

IN THE preparation of the following notes and indexes my purpose has been to arrange the references in such a way that the reader, consulting this appendix will be able quickly to find information on any part of the war treated in this volume.

The General Notes will supply the reader with additional data on engagements mentioned by the authors. The Notes on the Authors will supply him with short sketches of the military careers of the several writers and collaborators, and of the authorities quoted. The General Index covers all of the contents of this volume, regardless of source, and the Index According to Authors makes it possible to ascertain speedily what the different authorities have to say on the same, or on different subjects. Geographical Index, Index of Army Units and Index of Dates are self-explanatory. A reader seeking information on a certain engagement will find references in the General Index, in the Geographical Index, in the Index of Army Units, and in the Index of Dates. In this way, the whole range of possible questions is covered, and it is possible to trace any given engagement, place, army unit, or date.

A. PAUL MAERKER-BRANDEN.

II

BIOGRAPHICAL NOTES

On Authors and Collaborators, and on Authorities Quoted

BERDOULAT, General Pierre Emile, on July 18, 1918, was commander of the French Twentieth Army Corps, which was composed of the 1st and 2nd Divisions, A. E. F., and the French Moroccan Division. He was later Military Governor of Paris and is now a member of the reserves.

COLLIGNON, Commandant, was a member of the Liaison Service and as such, in close touch with the American Expeditionary Forces. He had many years of colonial service to his credit when, after serving against the Germans in Cameroon, he joined the French forces in Europe. He is now attached to the office of the Minister of Colonies and serving in French Indo-China.

CROCHET, Commandant, after serving with the French 407th Infantry in charge of a company, became a staff officer in March, 1918, and, as such, was detailed for liaison duty between the French staff and the American Expeditionary Forces. After the war, Commandant Crochet became a member of the faculty of the *Centre d'Études Tactiques des Montague*, previous to taking over the office of a *Chef de Bataillon* in the French 159th Infantry.

DEBENEY, General Français Eugène, was in command

when the 1st Division, A. E. F., went into action at Cantigny. To-day General Debeney is Chief of Staff in the Ministry of War.

DEGOUTTE, General Joseph, was commander of the Sixth Army during the offensive of July 18, 1918. His army was composed in part of the 3rd, 4th, 26th, 28th, 32nd, 42nd, and 77th Divisions, A. E. F. He is now a member of the Superior Council of War in Paris.

FOCH, Marshal Ferdinand, served as volunteer in the Franco-Prussian War. In 1896, he became an instructor at the War College and later on director of the Superior War College. At the outbreak of the World War, he was in command of the French Ninth Army. In 1916 he fought at the Somme, and in 1917, he became Chief of the General Staff. Appointed Generalissimo of the Allied and Associated armies in March, 1918, he was made a Marshal of France in August of the same year. He served as chairman of the Armistice Conference.

Foch is the author of two outstanding military textbooks: *Des Principes de la Guerre* (The Principles of War) and *De la Conduit de la Guerre* (On the Conduct of War).

GALLWITZ, General Max von, entered the Prussian Army in 1870 and served with the heavy artillery in the Franco-Prussian War. At the outbreak of the World War he was in charge of the Corps of the Reserves of the Prussian Guards. In July, 1915, he assumed command of the German Twelfth Army in the campaign against Russia, and later of the German Eleventh Army which invaded Serbia.

As commander of the German Second Army he fought the battle of the Somme and finally, taking over the German Fifth Army in front of Verdun, was put in charge of the *Heeresgruppe* fighting the Meuse-Argonne battles.

HELLÉ, General Joseph, during the last phases of the war was chief of staff of General Mangin. He is now a member of the Superior Council of War and staff officer of General Duport.

LEDEBUR, Major General Baron Otto von, entered the Prussian Army in 1889 and in 1903 received an appointment to the German Great General Staff. At the outbreak of the World War, von Ledebur served as Chief of Staff of the 10th Corps of the Reserves. In 1915, appointed Lieutenant Colonel, von Ledebur became the Chief of Staff of the 6th Corps of the Reserves, which fought at the Somme and at Verdun. After service on the staff of the German Fifth Army, von Ledebur was appointed Chief of General Staff of Army Unit C.

LUDENDORFF, General Erich, received his first appointment, to the German Naval Staff, in 1905. From 1906 to 1908 he was instructor at the War College and was then put in charge of a department of the Great General Staff. At the outbreak of the war Ludendorff was Quartermaster-in-Chief of the German Second Army but very soon became Chief of General Staff to Field Marshal von Hindenburg. In 1916 he was honoured with the title of First Quartermaster-General (Erster Generalquartiermeister) and as such prepared the plans for the *Friedenssturm*. Around the time of the Armistice, he went to Sweden but returned in spring, 1919, to become politically active in Munich.

MANGIN, General Charles Marie, known as "Mangin of the Black Troops," was commander of the Tenth Army during the offensive of July 18, 1918. His effectives comprised the Twentieth Army Corps composed of the 1st and 2nd Divisions, A. E. F., and the French Moroccan Division in addition to the Eleventh and Thirtieth Army Corps. General Mangin died in 1924.

REINHARDT, General Walther, entered the Württembergian Army in 1891 and was appointed to the Great General Staff in 1913. At the outbreak of the war, with the rank of major, Reinhardt acted as staff officer of the Thirteenth (Württembergian) Army Corps and later on took charge of the German 180th Infantry until he became Chief of General Staff of the German Seventh Army, which fought along the Aisne. After the revolution in November, 1918, Reinhardt was attached to the Ministry of War and ultimately became Commander of *Reichwehr* Area II at Cassel, Westphalia.

SAVATIER, General Eugène, after seeing service for fifteen years in Dahomey and Algiers, studied under Generals Pétain and Fayolle at the Superior War College. After a probationary period with the Railroad Division of the Army Staff, he was promoted to Chief of Cabinet of two generalissimos, General Tremeau and General Michel, who preceded Joffre. During the World War General Savatier commanded the French 14th Infantry and later on, during the first battle of the Marne, the 66th Brigade. In 1916 he became Chief of Staff in the Ministry of War, and in 1917 he was given command of one brigade of Light Infantry (*Chasseurs à Pied*) in Alsace. Toward the end of 1917 he commanded the 34th Division at Verdun. He is now a member of the reserves.

III
GENERAL NOTES

1. General SAVATIER's account evoked the following tribute from PAUL MALONE, Brigadier General, U. S. A.

The first soldier killed in my regiment when the Germans raided us, and on whose body you conferred the Croix de Guerre, as related in your narrative, was Private Stanley Dobiez, a man of Italian extraction, fighting in an American regiment in the defense of the soil and the rights of France. The common interests and sympathies evolved in such scenes as that pictured in your article when the body of Stanley Dobiez was laid to rest in the soil on which the sons of France had battled and died for nearly four years, will endure while memory lasts. I am grateful to have been a participant.

2. U. S. I. R. is the official French abbreviation for United States Infantry Regiment.

3. At PÉRONNE parts of the 6th Engineers, 3rd Division, A. E. F., aided the British Fifth Army with engineering work, in the beginning of February, 1918. When the German offensive opened on March 21st, the engineers, however, received instructions to retreat to the rear.

4. G. A. R. is the official French abbreviation for Group of Army Reserves.

5. D. C. is the official French abbreviation for Division of Cavalry.

6. C. C. is the official French abbreviation for Cavalry Corps.

7. A. L. is the official French abbreviation for heavy artillery (*artillerie lourde*).

8. G. A. N. is the official French abbreviation for Groups of Armies of the Nord.

9. The American 2nd Division, A. E. F., together with one brigade of Marines, was rushed to CHEMIN DES DAMES the latter part of May, 1918, as the Germans had broken through the CHEMIN DES DAMES front. The Americans arrived on June 1st and took up a position northeast, their line extending across the main CHÂTEAU THIERRY–PARIS highway which blocked the direct route to Paris. While, two miles away, the Germans were delayed by French detachments, the Americans busied themselves with defense prepara-

tions. On June 4th, the French withdrew and the Germans attacked the American line, but without success.

10. On May 28, 1918, the 1st American Division, A. E. F., captured CANTIGNY, holding the position tenaciously, despite German counter attacks. Assisted by American and French artillery, the 28th Infantry was chosen for the onslaught. The fighting, which was intense on both sides, lasted for two days and ended, finally, in another important victory for the Allies.

11. At SEICHEPREY, the Germans staged a raid against units of the 26th Division, A. E. F., on April 20, 1918. The Germans employed especially trained shock troops and subjected the Americans to an extremely heavy bombardment which led to considerable losses. In spite of the casualties suffered by the Americans, the Germans were eventually forced to withdraw.

12. On March 31, 1918, motorized machine gun units of the 3rd Division, A. E. F., assisted in preventing the Germans from crossing the MARNE. Later on, the American line was extended eastward as far as JAULGONNE, thus aiding the French in holding the south bank of the river.

13. Beginning a series of attacks on June 6, 1918, the 2nd Division, A. E. F., eventually captured strongly fortified positions at BELLEAU WOOD, BOURESCHES, and VAUX. Later on, the 2nd Division was relieved here by the 26th Division, A. E. F. BELLEAU WOOD is now known as the BOIS DE LA BRIGADE DE MARINE.

14. South of SOISSONS, the great Franco-American counter offensive started on July 18, 1918, one day after the German offensive had been definitely checked on the whole front.

15. MONT ST. PÈRE was ultimately occupied by the Americans on July 21, 1918.

16. CHARTÈVES was captured by the 3rd Division, A. E. F., on July 22, 1918. It was here on July 15 that the Germans attempted to advance from the MARNE up the valley of the SURMELIN CREEK where their advance was effectively blocked by the Americans.

17. CRÉZANCY was the jumping-off line for the American counter thrusts which stopped the German 10th Division from forcing the Marne.

18. The Forest of BARBILLON furnished the scene for the most important local repulse of the Germans when they attempted to force the MARNE. A special map, facing P. 104 illustrates the fighting at this point. It is interesting to compare General VON REINHARDT's remarks on P. 105 ff., to General HELLÉ's comments on P. 145 ff. of the same engagements. Only now certain details that

have remained a puzzle to them for years will become clear to the commanders and their staffs.

19. FOSSOY is about five kilometres from CHÂTEAU-THIERRY and was approximately the western limit of the German offensive of July 15, 1918.

20. BRETONNERIE FARM on the morning of July 5, 1918, was the objective of severe German thrusts. The Germans employed their newly developed method of "infiltration," that is, pushing forward small units of shock troops which were to attack the enemy from the rear after penetrating the line. American troops employed here belonged to the 7th and 30th Infantry regiments which were part of the 3rd Division.

21. At SOISSONS, the 1st and 2nd Divisions, A. E. F., were thrown forward at the onset of the great counter offensive which began on July 18, 1918. Both divisions entered the fight after long and arduous night marches and during a terrific downpour. The congestion of the roads and all the other obstacles which the American troops had to overcome are graphically described by General HELLÉ on P. 151 ff.

22. DOMMIERS, on the morning of July 18, 1918, constituted a part of the southern flank of the 1st Division, A. E. F., but was still within the German front line.

23. BERZY-LE-SEC was the centre of extremely bitter fighting on July 20 and 21, 1918. On the 21st, it was definitely captured by the 1st Division, A. E. F.

24. LONGPONT was in front of the jump-off line on the morning of July 18, 1918.

25. Troops of the 2nd Division, A. E. F., were employed at VAUXCASTILLE.

26. VIERZY was reached by a handful of Americans during the morning of July 18, 1918, but they were forced to retreat. However, VIERZY was ultimately captured after the main body of American forces employed here attacked the Germans from the vicinity of VAUXCASTILLE.

27. CHAUDUN was garrisoned by units of the 1st (French) Moroccan Division.

28. TIGNY was held by American forces until the night of July 19–20, 1918, when the 2nd Division, A. E. F., was relieved by a French division.

29. The southern outskirts of CIERGES were reached and definitely held by the 37th Division, A. E. F., at the end of September, 1918.

30. SERINGES was occupied by the 32nd and 42nd Divisions, A. E. F., on August 1, 1918.

31. SERGY was occupied by units of the 42nd Division, A. E. F., on July 28, 1918. Later in the day, a German counter attack forced the Americans to withdraw temporarily.

32. On July 28, 1918, the 3rd Division, A. E. F., attempted to carry the BOIS DE GRIMPETTES. The assault proved unsuccessful and during the night of July 29th, the 3rd Division, greatly exhausted after having been continuously in line since June, was relieved by the 32nd Division, A. E. F. The latter, together with the 28th Division, A. E. F., on July 30th, succeeded in occupying the Bois de Grimpettes, after fighting at close quarters.

33. Not until August 6, 1918, did the Americans definitely succeed in gaining possession of FISMES. On August 4th, despite desperate German resistance, the 32nd Division, A. E. F., gained a foothold on the southern edge of Fismes.

34. TORCY was captured by the 26th Division, A. E. F., on July 18, 1918, at the onset of the great counter offensive.

35. Around the two little villages of EPIEDS and TRUGNY the 26th Division, A. E. F., was engaged in desperate fighting, launching four attacks during July 22 and 23, 1918. These towns changed hands repeatedly until, on July 24th, the 56th Brigade of the 28th Division, coöperating with the 26th Division succeeded in seizing the objectives in question.

36. LE CHARMEL was captured by the 3rd Division, A. E. F., on July 25, 1918, after bitter fighting.

37. During the night of August 1, 1918, the Americans pushed back the Germans to a prepared position at the VESLE river but not before September 4th did the 77th Division, A. E. F., succeed in forcing the river in pursuit of the Germans.

38. On August 8, 1918, the 131st Regiment of the 33rd Division, A. E. F., coöperated at AMIENS with the British 58th Division. This was during the Franco-British offensive directed against the Amiens salient.

39. It is interesting to compare the narrative of Generel Hellé with the account of General REINHARDT regarding the BARBILLON fighting.

40. JAULGONNE was occupied by the 3rd Division, A. E. F., on July 22, 1918, after Mont St. Père had been captured the day before.

41. BEAUREPAIRE FARM, converted by the Germans into a formidable stronghold, was captured on the morning of July 18, 1918,

by the 3rd Brigade (9th and 23rd Infantry) of the 2nd Division, A. E. F., after the employment of much cold steel.

42. MISSY RAVINE was seized by troops of the 1st Division, A. E. F., on July 18, 1918. The attack began at 4:35 in the morning and ended at 8 A. M. In the course of the fighting, which was rendered difficult because of the swampy ground, many enemy flanking attacks were repulsed and eventually all German units occupying the ravine were either killed or captured.

43. PLOISY was reached on July 19, 1918, shortly before nightfall.

44. VERTEFEUILLE FARM was taken by the Marines on the morning of July 18, 1918, with the support of French tanks.

45. See Note 11.

46. XIVRAY was in the sector of the 42nd Division, A. E. F.

47. LIMEY was in the sector of the 2nd Division, A. E. F.

48. LOUPMONT RIDGE was one of the most important German points of observation.

49. FEY-EN-HAYE was close to the jump-off line of the 90th Division, A. E. F. In the course of the fighting, it was completely destroyed.

50. Tremendous stocks of war material were stored at HEUDICOURT by the Germans. The place was first attacked in the afternoon of September 12, 1918, by a small detachment of cavalry belonging to the 1st Division, A. E. F., but the attempt proved unsuccessful.

51. THIAUCOURT was captured by the 2nd Division, A. E. F.

52. BOUILLONVILLE was taken by the 89th Division, A. E. F.

53. XAMMES constituted the final objective of the American offensive.

54. PANNES was seized by the 42nd Division, A. E. F., during the first day of the offensive, September 12, 1918.

55. ST. BAUSSANT at various times prior to September 12, 1918, was held by the 1st, 26th, 82nd, and 89th Divisions, A. E. F. It had been fortified by the Germans with numerous "pill boxes."

56. REGNÉIVILLE-EN-HAYE, on September 12, 1918, was in the sector of the 5th Division, A. E. F.

57. ESSEY was seized by the 42nd Division, A. E. F.

58. BENEY was captured by the 42nd Division, A. E. F., on September 13th.

59. VIÉVILLE-EN-HAYE was reached by the 5th Division, A. E. F., on the first day of the St. Mihiel offensive.

60. MONTSEC was another important German point of obser-

vation. It is an isolated hill and was one of the objectives of the 1st Division, A. E. F., at the onset of the St. Mihiel offensive. Montsec was strongly fortified by the Germans, who evacuated it on September 13, 1918, when it was occupied by the French 39th Division.

61. Rupt de Mad, a small stream, offered great difficulties to the advance of the First Army, A. E. F. Temporary structures had to be built by engineers to replace the destroyed bridges before American tanks and other war material could move to the other side.

62. St. Benôit, after being captured by the 42nd Division A. E. F., on September 13, 1918, served as headquarters for this unit.

63. Nonsard was occupied by the 1st Division, A. E. F., on September 12, 1918.

64. Lamarche-en-Woëvre was taken by the 42nd Division, A. E. F., on September 13, 1918. It is about a mile from Nonsard. See Note 63.

65. Hattonchâtel was reached by units of the 22nd Division, A. E. F., at 2 A. M. on September 13, 1918. These troops had overrun Vigneulles during the night in order to establish connection with the 1st Division, A. E. F. The 51st Brigade of the 26th Division, A. E. F., was employed here in one of the most spectacular and successful night marches. The troops encountered great difficulties as the Germans had blocked the roads with trees, etc.

66. After heavy fighting, the formidably fortified quarries at Norroy were occupied on September 13th by the 90th Division and the 328th Infantry of the 82nd Division, A. E. F.

67. Vauquois was part of the jump-off line of the First Army, A. E. F., and was taken by the 35th Division, A. E. F.

68. Abaucourt was occupied on November 10, 1918 by the 81st Division, A. E. F.

69. Béthincourt was situated near the line from which the First Army, A. E. F., jumped off on September 26, 1918.

70. Avocourt for a protracted period was held by the 371st and 372nd Infantry, parts of the 93rd Division, A. E. F., coöperating here with the French. They were replaced, around the middle of September, 1918, by the 33rd and 79th Divisions, A. E. F., but on September 23rd, the 79th Division was taken out of line, leaving the 33rd to hold this sector.

71. Nantillois was unsuccessfully attacked by the 4th and 79th Divisions, A. E. F., on September 27, 1918, However, it was defi-

nitely occupied by the 79th Division, A. E. F., on the next day.

72. SEPTSARGES WOOD was finally taken by the 4th Division, A. E. F.

73. DANNEVOUX was held by the 80th Division, A. E. F., on September 26, 1918.

74. VARENNES was captured by the 31st Division, A. E. F., on September 26, 1918.

75. VAUQUOIS. See Note 67.

76. VÉRY HEIGHTS was occupied by the 31st Division, A. E. F.

77. MONTFAUCON, one of the chief German points of observation, lay in the sector of the 79th Division, A. E. F. It was ultimately seized by the 4th Division, A. E. F.

78. ROMAGNE, where the Germans had stored much war material, was taken by the 32nd Division, A. E. F., on the morning of October 14th.

79. EPINONVILLE was one of the important objectives of the 91st Division, A. E. F.

80. It was in the neighborhood of SIVRY-SUR-MEUSE that LA BORNE DE CORNOUILLER usually referred to as "Corn Willy Hill" was taken by the 79th Division, A. E. F., on November 4, 1918, after extremely severe fighting.

81. CONSENVOYE was in the zone of the 33rd Division, A. E. F. A bridge was built near here by American engineers which served to expel the Germans from this neighborhood on October 8, 1918.

82. At VILOSNES-SUR-MEUSE units of the 5th Division, A. E. F., supported the 15th French Colonial Division in forcing the river.

83. BRIEULLES and the wood named after this village were the scene of lively engagements on September 27, 28, and 29, 1918. The 4th Division, A. E. F., reinforced by a battalion of the 80th Division, A. E. F., eventually captured the northern edge of the Wood.

84. OGONS WOOD was not definitely occupied by the Americans until October 9, 1918, when it was taken by the 80th Division, A. E. F., which attacked for a period of four days before meeting with success. As early as September 28th, units of the 79th Division, A. E. F., had seized the wood temporarily but were thrown back by counter attacks. Renewed attempts to gain possession of the wood, with the support of the 4th Division, A. E. F., proved abortive until on October 4th, the 80th Division, A. E. F., went into action and captured the wood.

85. MONTFAUCON WOOD was attacked in the afternoon of Sep-

tember 26, 1918, by the 37th and 79th Divisions, A. E. F. Units of the 37th Division ultimately advanced as far as IVOIRY.

86. GESNES was occupied by the 91st Division, A. E. F., on September 29, 1918, but had to be abandoned. It was definitely taken on October 9th by the 32nd Division, A. E. F., after desperate street fighting.

87. CHÂTEL CHÈHÉRY was attacked on October 7, 1918, by the 82nd Division, A. E. F. On the next day, in the vicinity of this place, Sergeant Alvin C. York performed his memorable exploit.

88. FLÉVILLE was captured by the 1st Division, A. E. F., on October 10, 1918.

88. BELLEVUE SIGNAL RIDGE on September 28th fell into the hands of the 369th Infantry, A. E. F., coöperating with the French 161st Division.

90. CONSENVOYE was given up by the Germans on October 8, 1918.

91. BRABANT-SUR-MEUSE constituted the point where the 33rd Division, A. E. F., crossed the river on the morning of October 8, 1918.

92. CORNAY was the scene of spirited fighting on October 8, 1918, when it was entered by units of the 82nd Division, A. E. F. On the next day, the Germans were driven out but later on recaptured the place.

93. SOMMERANCE was reached on October 10, 1918, by the 1st Division, A. E. F.

94. ST. JUVIN was close to the jump-off line of the 80th, 77th, and 78th Divisions, A. E. F., who advanced north of this point by November 3, 1918.

95. CUNEL and the wood named after it was occupied by the 3rd Division, A. E. F., on October 10, 1918, and definitely held against strong German counter attacks.

96. WAVRILLE was captured by the 79th Division, A. E. F., on November 9, 1918.

97. The southern part of the BOIS DE BANTHEVILLE was first occupied by the 32nd Division, A. E. F., on October 19th, and definitely invested by the 89th Division, A. E. F., on October 22, 1918.

98. The AGRON RIVER was the scene of fighting by the 78th and 82nd Divisions, A. E. F.

99. CHAMPIGNEULLE was seized by the 82nd Division, A. E. F., on October 16, 1918.

100. The 78th Division, A. E. F., fought for the possession of GRANDPRÉ until October 31st, when they definitely captured it.

101. CLÉRY-LE-PETIT was reached by the 5th Division, A. E. F., on November 3, 1918.

102. The German fortifications in ANDEVANNE WOOD were part of the strongly fortified German FREYA LINE.

103. IMÉCOURT was first occupied by a battalion of the 321st Field Artillery, 80th Division, A. E. F., on November 1, 1918.

104. BUZANCY fell into the hands of the 80th Division, A. E. F., on November 2, 1918.

105. DUN-SUR-MEUSE and STENAY were the places where the Germans retreated across the Meuse, after they were attacked on November 1, 1918 by the Third and Fifth Corps, A. E. F. DUN-SUR-MEUSE was taken by the 5th Division, A. E. F., on November 5th.

106. The heights of BARRICOURT were part of the fortified German FREYA LINE.

107. HILL 43 was also part of the German FREYA LINE.

108. STENAY in the early hours of November 11, 1918, was entered by the 89th and 90th Divisions, A. E. F.

109. At BRIEULLES-SUR-MEUSE pontoon bridges were constructed in the night of November 2, 1918. Two days later, the 9th Brigade succeeded in crossing the river, in the vicinity of CLÉRY-LE-PETIT.

110. CHATILLON WOOD was taken by the 5th Division, A. E. F., on November 5, 1918.

111. CLÉRY-LE-PETIT was the point where the 9th Brigade crossed the river on November 4, 1918.

112. LINY-DEVANT-DUN was reached on November 5, 1918, by the 5th Division, A. E. F.

113. After severe fighting on November 6 and 7, 1918, CÔTE ST. GERMAIN was seized by the 5th Division, A. E. F.

114. MURVAUX was captured by the 5th Division, A. E. F., on November 6, 1918.

115. Units of the 5th Division, A. E. F., supported by a regiment of the 32nd Division, A. E. F., took BRANDEVILLE on November 8, 1918.

116. WOËVRE WOOD was wrested from the enemy by the 5th Division, A. E. F., on November 9 and 10, 1918.

117. BAÂLON was entered by the 90th Division, A. E. F., a few hours before the war ended.

118. JAMETZ was reached by the 5th Division, A. E. F., one hour before the Armistice.

119. Units of the 32nd Division, A. E. F., almost reached PEUVILLERS on November 10, 1918.

120. POUILLY on the evening of November 10th, was the place where the 2nd and 89th Divisions, A. E. F., forced the river. It fell into the hands of the Americans at daybreak of Armistice Day, November 11, 1918.

IV

INDEX ACCORDING TO AUTHORS

V

GEOGRAPHICAL INDEX

VI
INDEX OF ARMY UNITS

Divisions

Regiments

VII

INDEX OF DATES

GENERAL INDEX

THE END